DAVID MCDOWALL

BRITAIN

IN CLOSE-UP

Longman

Addison Wesley Longman Limited,
Edinburgh Gate, Harlow,
Essex CM20 2JE, England
and Associated Companies throughout the world.

First published 1993
Sixth impression 1997

British Library Cataloguing-in-Publication Data

McDowall, David
    Britain in Close-up
    I. Title
    941

Library of Congress Cataloging-in-Publication Data

McDowall, David
    Britain in close-in / David McDowall.
        p.   cm.
    Includes bibliographical references and index.
    ISBN 0-582-06461-9: £8.25
    1. Readers-Great Britain.   2. Great Britain-Civilization-
    -Problems, exercises, etc.   I. Title.
    PE1127.H75G75   1993
    428.6'4-dc20   92-18031
                                                    CIP

Set in 10/11pt Stone Informal

Produced by Longman Asia Limited, Hong Kong.
SWTC/06

ISBN 0 582 064619

Acknowledgements

We are grateful to the following for permission to
reproduce copyright material:

Cambridge Econometrics/*The Independent* for page 14;
Central Statistical Office for pages 25, 13 (top), 74 and
75 (top), 178, /Department of Transport for page 185,
/House of Commons Research Division for page 101;
Gomer Press for page 132; Health Education Authority
for page 197; Schieber & Poullier – *The Independent* for
page 201; Times Newspapers Ltd 1988 or 1990 for pages
54 and 89.

Map of Great Britain "Reproduced with the kind
permission of Brepols" on page 6.

We are unable to trace the copyright holder of the map
on page 13 (bottom) and would be grateful for any
information which would enable us to do so.

We are grateful to the following for permission to
reproduce copyright photographs:

Andes Press Agency/Carlos Reyes for page 103;
Associated Press for page 139 (top left); BBC
Photographic Library for page 28; BBC Radio for page
163; Penny Bickle for pages 16 (top), 159 and 202;
Bridgeman Art Library/D. Hockney 1967 for page 116;
British Telecommunications PLC for page 51; J Allan
Cash Photo Library for pages 19, 21, 44, 59 (top), 67,
79, 85 (bottom), 91, 105 (left), 109, 110, 111, 112 (left),
131, 171 (right), 180, 189 and 190; City of Cambridge
Department of Planning for page 77; CR Photography
for pages 94 (top right), 94 (bottom right) and 174;
© 1985 Danjaq S.A. All Rights reserved for page 144;
The Economist for page 193; D. Eppel for page 106;
Financial Times/Tony Andrews for page 141; © Granada
TV for page 164; S & R Greenhill for pages 15 (top), 16
(bottom), 22, 23, 63, 68, 83, 84 (bottom), 88, 94 (top
left), 94 (bottom left), 95, 97, 99, 149, 150, 151, 156
(left), 165, 183, 191, 192, 194 (top), 198 and 200;
Greenpeace/Midgley for page 186; N.C. Golding for page
199; House of Commons for page 32; Impact Photos/
P. Achache for page 143, /P. Arkell for pages 75
(bottom), 82, 92 (right) and 147, /J. Arthur for pages
59 (left), 100 (right), 124 (bottom) and 179, /Keith
Bernstein for page 11 (top left), /M. Black for page 66,
/C. Bluntzer for page 92 (left), /J. Calder for pages 39,
119 and 130, /P. Cavendish for pages 17, 27 and 152,
/P. Cavendish/Reflex for page 29, /S. Connors for page
71, /C. Cormack for page 115, /M. Cator for pages 135
and 162, /M. Dent for page 105 (right), /A. Donaldson
for pages 117 (right) and 134, /S. Fear for pages 84
(middle) and 96, /B. Gannon for page 196, /A. le
Garsmeur for pages 155 and 181, /D. Harden for page
86, /Brian Harris for pages 11 (top right), 11 (bottom),
12, 100 (left) and 126 (right), /P. Lowe for page 112
(right), /Mike McQueen for page 8, /J. Nicholl for pages
113, 124 (top), 125 (both) and 161 (right), /T. Picton for
page 69, /D. Reed for page 154, /B. Rybolt for pages
133 and 188 (bottom), /B. Stephens for page 18, /Homer
Sykes for pages 15 (bottom), 90 and 156 (right);
National Coal Board for page 85; Network
Photographers/Leighton for pages 176 and 188 (top),
/Sturrock for pages 20, 30, 45, 78, 173; Press Association
for pages 104, 126 (left), 128 and 172, /C. Bacon for
page 81; Q A Photo Library for page 184; Retna Pictures
for page 107; Rex Features for pages 31 (middle), 31
(bottom), 33, 34, 35, 41, 42, 43, 57, 114, 117, 139 (top
right), 142 (both), 171 and 187; Chris Ridgers for page
108; Frank Spooner Pictures/Lebrun for page 53,
/R. Tomkins for page 55; Telegraph Colour Library for
page 177; Topham Picture Source for pages 26 and 61;
Viewfinder for pages 123, 127 and 153; Zefa Picture
Library (UK) Ltd for page 175.

Front and back covers by Robert Harding Picture
Library.

Picture Research by Penni Bickle.

Illustrated by Debbie Hinks and Taurus Graphics.
Cover illustration by Tony Hannerford.
Cover design by The Design Revolution.

Contents

Author's acknowledgements

No book of this kind could possibly have been written without substantial help from the work of other writers who have written either about Britain generally, or about a particular aspect of it. My primary debt, therefore, is to them. I have listed those books which have been most useful to me and which students will find useful if they wish to read further. There are, of course, many other books which also provided invaluable help but which seemed inappropriate to include in a reading list.

I must also record my gratitude to those institutions and individuals who also helped: Lisa Blanckenhagen, John McKinlay, John Neil of the Wigtown Free Press, Jacek Opienski, Ludlow Festival Society, Dumfries and Galloway Regional Council, the City of Bradford Metropolitan Council, the Peterborough Development Agency, Liverpool City Council, the Town and Country Planning Association and the Campaign for Real Ale.

Finally, I owe a special debt to my wife, Elizabeth. She read through the text offering invaluable advice and criticism.

Sources and books for further reading:

Abercrombie, Nicholas, Warde, Alan et al. 1988 *Contemporary British Society* Polity Press

Austin, Dennis 1988 *The Commonwealth and Britain* Routledge

Budge, Ian and McKay, David 1988 *The Changing British Political System: Into the 1990s* Longman

Dahrendorf, Ralf 1982 *On Britain* BBC

Elcock, Howard 1986 *Local Government* Methuen

Finlayson, Iain 1988 *The Scots* Oxford University Press

Halsey, A H 1986 *Change in British Society* Oxford University Press

Handelman, Stephen 1988 *Uncommon Kingdom, The British in the 1980s* Collins, Ontario

Hanson, A H and Walles, Malcolm 1984 *Governing Britain: A Guidebook to Political Institutions* Fontana

Hebdige, Dick 1988 *Subculture: The Meaning of Style* Routledge

Hennessey, Peter 1990 *Whitehall* Fontana

Hewison, Robert 1987 *The Heritage Industry* Methuen

Jenkins, Peter 1987 *Mrs Thatcher's Revolution: The Ending of the Socialist Era* Jonathan Cape

Johnston, R J, Pattie, C and Allsopp, J G 1988 *A Nation Dividing? The Electoral Map of Great Britain, 1979–87* Longman

Morgan, Kenneth O 1988 *Rebirth of a Nation: Wales, 1880–1980* Oxford University Press

Nairn, Tom 1988 *The Enchanted Glass: Britain and its Monarchy*, Hutchinson Radius

Osmond, John 1988 *The Divided Kingdom* Constable

Sampson, Anthony 1982 *The Changing Anatomy of Britain* Hodder & Stoughton

Lord Scarman 1986 *The Scarman Report: The Brixton Disorders 10–12 April 1981* Penguin

Silk, Paul 1987 *How Parliament Works* Longman

Smith, David 1989 *North and South: Britain's Growing Divide* Penguin

Tugendhat, Christopher and Wallace, William 1988 *Options for British Foreign Policy in the 1990s* RIIA/ Routledge

Wiener, Martin J 1985 *English Culture and the Decline of the Industrial Spirit, 1850–1980* Penguin

Wilson, Tom 1989 *Ulster: Conflict & Consent* Blackwell

Young, Hugo 1989 *One of Us: A Biography of Margaret Thatcher*, Macmillan

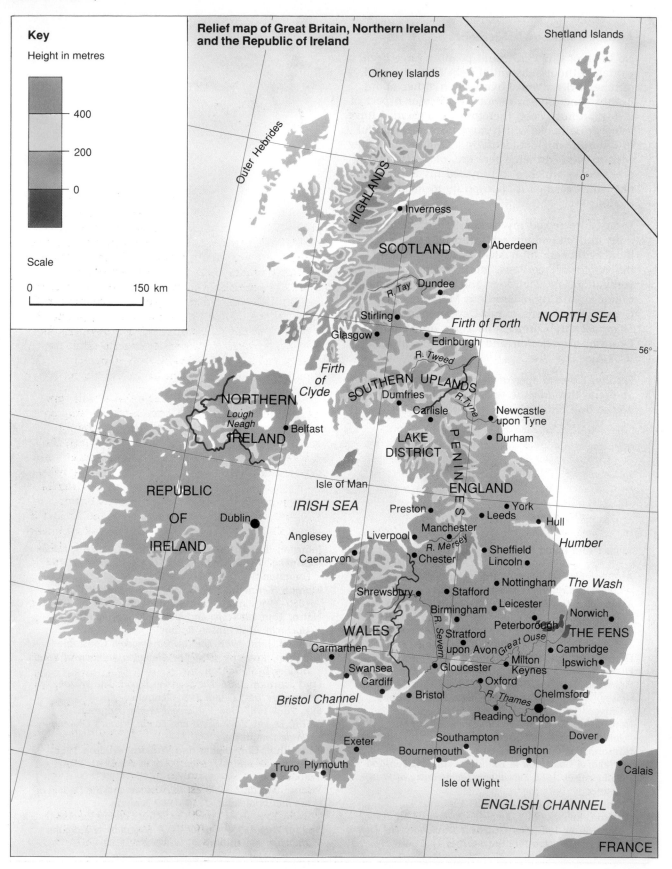

Key

Height in metres

400

200

0

Scale

0   150 km

Relief map of Great Britain, Northern Ireland and the Republic of Ireland

Shetland Islands

Orkney Islands

Outer Hebrides

0°

HIGHLANDS

• Inverness

SCOTLAND

• Aberdeen

R. Tay   • Dundee

Stirling •

Firth of Forth

NORTH SEA

Glasgow •

• Edinburgh

56°

Firth of Clyde

R. Tweed

SOUTHERN UPLANDS

NORTHERN

Lough Neagh

• Belfast

IRELAND

Dumfries •

R. Tyne

Carlisle •

Newcastle upon Tyne

• Durham

LAKE DISTRICT

P E N N I N E S

REPUBLIC

OF

IRELAND

Dublin •

Isle of Man

ENGLAND

IRISH SEA

Preston •

• York

Leeds •

• Hull

Humber

Anglesey

Liverpool •

Manchester •

Caenarvon •

R. Mersey

Chester •

• Sheffield

Lincoln •

• Nottingham

The Wash

Shrewsbury •

• Stafford

Leicester •

Birmingham •

Peterborough •

• Norwich

WALES

Stratford upon Avon •

Great Ouse

THE FENS

Carmarthen •

• Cambridge

Milton Keynes •

Ipswich •

Swansea •

Cardiff •

Gloucester •

R. Severn

Oxford •

• Chelmsford

• Bristol

R. Thames

Bristol Channel

Reading •

London •

Dover •

Southampton •

Exeter •

Bournemouth •

Brighton •

Truro •   Plymouth •

Calais •

Isle of Wight

ENGLISH CHANNEL

FRANCE

Reproduced with the kind permission of Brepols.

Introduction

The political background

This book attempts to assess the changes taking place in Britain today and to indicate the direction in which the country is travelling as it approaches the twenty-first century.

However it is impossible to do so without reviewing, in very broad outline, what has been happening to Britain in recent years. During the 1980s Britain underwent the most radical change since the economic and social measures introduced by the Labour government under Clement Attlee in the immediate post-war years, 1945–50. The architect of these changes was Margaret Thatcher, Prime Minister from 1979–90.

Attlee had established what was later called 'the post-war consensus' between the two main parties, the Conservative and Labour Parties, on fundamental economic and social matters, so that Britain could rebuild itself economically and socially following the Second World War. Margaret Thatcher destroyed belief in this consensus, radically altering the face of British government and politics.

What was the post-war consensus? Briefly, it was generally believed that from 1945–79 the two main parties, Labour and Conservative had more similarities than differences between them. Whether this consensus really existed or was only a myth, there were certainly areas of broad agreement in spite of sharp ideological differences. In the economic sphere all governments followed the principles formulated by the great pre-war economist J.M. Keynes, which stated that capitalist society could only survive if government controlled, managed and even planned much of the general shape of its economy. Both Labour and Conservatives tried to do this. The requirements of war, 1939–45, increased the belief in, and practice of, government planning.

Both parties were committed to economic reconstruction and social reform. Full employment and the maintenance of the 'welfare state' (free health and education, pensions and benefits for the old, disabled, sick or unemployed) were accepted by both parties as essential foundations of government. However, neither principle could be ensured without an expanding economy. As Prime Minister Harold Macmillan (1956–64) remarked, managing the post-war economy was like juggling four balls in the air: an expanding economy, full employment, stable prices and a strong pound. It was only in the question of full employment that post-war governments were truly successful. For twenty years, from 1955–75, unemployment remained below 4 per cent of the workforce.

Britain proved unable to juggle these balls, and its economy became characterised by a 'stop-go' cycle: periods of inflation which would be followed by crises in the balance of payments, the difference between the value of total imports and exports. Neither Labour nor Conservative governments seemed able to bring the economy out of its stop-go cycle. By its own standards Britain seemed to be doing reasonably well, but in fact it was doing only half as well as other industrialised countries. During the relatively prosperous years, 1953–73, average annual growth in Japan was 9.7 per cent, in West Germany 6 per cent, in France 5.1 per cent, but in Britain it was only 3 per cent. As a result, Britain's share of world trade fell from 13.9 per cent in 1964 to 10.8 per cent in 1970.

This poor comparative performance was reflected in the steady decline of the manufacturing industry, once Britain's proudest asset. Even after 1973, the year of worldwide oil crisis, West Germany improved its manufacturing growth by 2.5 per cent, France by 3.8 per cent, but Britain managed only a miserable 0.2 per cent. By 1980 manufacturing productivity per head in Britain was two thirds that in Italy, half that in France and less than half that in West Germany.

Throughout the period both parties had tried to achieve economic growth in cooperation with industrial managers and the trade unions. Each government tried to bring the trade unions under control. Each failed, and sought negotiated agreements with the trade union leadership to ensure agreement on pay between different unions in the same industry, 'collective bargaining' as it became known. This was partially successful, but gave the trade unions a degree of political strength they had never known before.

By 1975 there were signs that the post-war consensus was beginning to collapse. In 1974 half a million workers were unemployed, but the following year under Labour, the party most strongly committed to full employment, this figure exceeded one million, 5.3 per cent of the workforce. Between 1974 and 1978 Labour negotiated a series of contracts with unions, trading legal concessions in return for limits on wage increases. However, in the winter of 1978/79, nicknamed 'the Winter of Discontent', the trade unions refused to accept the pay increase limits, demanded by the Labour government in order to maintain its economic strategy. Largely as a result of this refusal, Labour lost the election of spring 1979, which was fought on two issues: the question of union strength and the broader question of national economic decline. While Labour proposed continuing with the economic policies it had followed through the 1970s, the victorious Conservatives, under their new leader Margaret Thatcher, offered a radical alternative which they now sought to put into practice.

Margaret Thatcher, Prime Minister 1979–90.

Margaret Thatcher and her ideas dominated British policies until she resigned in 1990. She brought an entirely new tone to government. "I am not a consensus politician . . ." Margaret Thatcher announced in one of her most famous remarks, "I am a conviction politician." In fact

she had become convinced since she took over the party leadership in 1975, that the Conservatives as well as Labour had implemented basically socialist-type policies since 1945. She was determined to destroy the position of socialism in Britain, which she blamed for the country's ills. Her targets were the Labour strongholds: council estates (homes rented by local government to people on low incomes); the trade unions; the local authorities; and the nationalised industries.

Mrs Thatcher also believed that Keynesian economics were fundamentally wrong-headed and that all controls and regulation of the economy should be removed. "You cannot buck the market," she claimed. Her philosophy, put simply, was to create a stable economic climate by low rates of inflation and taxation. This, she believed, would allow a market economy to recover. The government role in economic revival would be minimal beyond securing these stable conditions, and cutting public expenditure.

Mrs Thatcher pressed on where her predecessors had retreated. Indeed, she said at the time, "I have no time for arguments" – even with her colleagues. She arranged for the coal and steel industries to be 'slimmed down' in order to improve efficiency and meet demand but no more.

High interest rates and her refusal to assist struggling industries led to dramatic changes. By its second anniversary in 1981 the Thatcher government had presided over the greatest decline in total output in one year since the Depression of 1931, and the biggest collapse in industrial production in one year since 1921. Britain's balance of payments began to deteriorate. Its share of world trade fell by 15 per cent between 1979 and 1986, a larger fall than in any other industrialised country during that period. In 1983 the import of manufactured goods exceeded exports for the first time in 200 years. There were social consequences, too. In May 1979 there had been 1.2 million unemployed. By May 1983 this figure had risen to 3 million, over 13 per cent of the work force.

Furthermore, the stress created by Mrs Thatcher's policies began to divide the nation into areas which responded to them and ones which could not. Growth in the south of the country was three times as fast as in the rest of the country during most of the decade. The divide was not purely geographical. Mrs Thatcher's policies also led to a growing gulf between the richest and poorest all over the country.

But Mrs Thatcher was determined to break with the past and did not look back. She began to sell into private hands many publicly owned production and service companies, for example British Telecommunications, British Gas, British Airways, Jaguar Cars, Rolls Royce, even British Regional Water Authorities. She had two basic interests: to free these areas from government control and also to persuade ordinary individuals to buy a stake in these enterprises.

In both she was largely successful. Government largely gave up its traditional intervention in the economy and began to turn Britain into a 'share-owning democracy'. Between 1979 and 1992 the proportion of the population owning shares increased from 7 to 24 per cent, powerfully emphasising that the accepted philosophy of the 1980s was personal wealth rather than public ownership. Such was the attraction of this philosophy that even the Labour Party, traditionally the party of public ownership, felt compelled to accept the new realities.

Mrs Thatcher also made a strong call for 'good housekeeping', and set about controlling government spending. In central government her success was limited. It proved extremely difficult to reduce the size of the Civil Service. Some wondered if her motivation was, apart from efficiency, to reduce a system which she found obstructive.

In local government she had greater success, but the struggle was more bitter because much of local government was controlled by the Labour Party. Her government abolished the metropolitan authorities – created to coordinate the affairs of London and six other large conurbations – all of which had been Labour-controlled. She also undermined local authorities (or councils) by limiting their ability to raise money, by forcing them to allow occupants of council-owned rented accommodation to purchase their homes at attractive prices, by reducing their authority in areas like education, and by breaking up local authority bus services.

While she freed the economy from previous restraints, she also brought other areas of national life under closer central control, by stricter laws on national security, closer scrutiny of 'sensitive' material in the press or on television, and the introduction of a national curriculum for all state schools. Some people disliked the more authoritarian style of government.

Yet, by 1991, it seemed doubtful whether Mrs Thatcher's measures had actually achieved what had been claimed. Whilst trying to cut public expenditure, she faced major increases in costs: pensioners were living longer; unemployment figures stayed high; and the cost of the health service and the armed forces rose rapidly.

Fundamentally, Mrs Thatcher faced the same dilemma her predecessors had all faced since the war. The commitment to reduce government spending conflicted with the need for investment in education, training, research and development, in order to produce long-term improvements in the economy. Some felt that Britain's weakness stemmed from the failure of successive governments to plan enough, and that the real challenge was to create a powerful central planning body including both managers and trade unionists, which could evolve and implement a coordinated strategy. By 1992 government still seemed in a weak position to provide the positive intervention which economic developments indicated were necessary, and which were practised in more successful parts of the European Community.

Margaret Thatcher resigned as Prime Minister in November 1990, when she lost the confidence of over one third of her party colleagues in Parliament. Her favoured successor, John Major, took her place as Prime Minister, but his style was significantly different. His manner was softer, and it soon became clear he valued the idea of consensus more highly than Mrs Thatcher had done.

He restored Conservative popularity, but at a time when Britain was entering its worst period of recession since the 1930s. This time it was the south east that was hardest hit. By 1992 businesses were failing at a rate of 1,000 companies each week, unemployment was rising steeply, and there was a serious collapse in both domestic and commercial property markets. In April 1992, Mr Major led the Conservatives to a fourth consecutive electoral victory, albeit with a much reduced majority.

Regardless of which Party is dominant, the themes and dilemmas which marked the Thatcher years are likely to remain important well into the 1990s. For they take place within the context of a country with ancient institutions experiencing great difficulty in adjusting to the demands of the modern world. Whether this is a cause for dismay or merely curiosity, the areas both of change and stability provide ample opportunity to study the rich, varied and lively culture of an offshore island of Europe.

1 Snapshot Britain

A sense of place

The United Kingdom of Great Britain and Northern Ireland, to give it its formal title, is a highly centralised and unitary state, and its main component, England, has been so for almost a thousand years, longer than any other European country. As a political entity, however, Britain (as the United Kingdom is loosely called) is less than 300 years old, being the state which emerged from the union of the ancient kingdoms of Scotland and England in 1707.

It is widely assumed that the British are a relatively homogeneous society with a strong sense of identity, but it is an assumption that requires considerable qualification. Even after 300 years the terms 'British' and 'Britain' which are used for official purposes, can also seem very artificial. In his famous *Dictionary of Modern English Usage*, first published in 1926, Fowler wrote:

"It must be remembered that no Englishman, or perhaps no Scotsman, calls himself a Briton without a sneaking sense of the ludicrous, or hears himself referred to as a BRITISHER without squirming. How should an Englishman utter the words *Great Britain* with the glow of emotion that for him goes with *England*? His Sovereign may be Her *Britannic* Majesty to outsiders, but to him is Queen of *England*."

For centuries it has been the idea of England (or Scotland), rather than of Britain, which has been charged with patriotic emotion. The idea of England is invoked at times of national crisis, for example at the Battle of Trafalgar in 1805, when Admiral Lord Nelson's famous order to the British fleet read, "England expects that every man will do his duty." In 1939 during Parliament's emergency debate on the eve of war, one Member of Parliament (MP) called across the chamber to another who was rising to speak: "Come on, Arthur, speak for England."

One should not be surprised, either, that Fowler wrote these words under 'England'. If you look up 'Britain', 'British' and 'Briton' you will find 'See *England*.' Most people call Britain 'England', and the British 'English', as if Wales, Northern Ireland and Scotland were merely outer parts of England. Nothing, it should be said, infuriates a Scot more than ignorantly to be called English, or for all Britain to be referred to as England. Many Welsh and Northern Irish feel similarly about their identity.

While Britain is instinctively thought of by many as 'England', so also the idea of England evokes images of the Queen, Parliament, Westminster Abbey, the Tower of London and the soft landscape of the southern counties of England. This is not so surprising since almost one quarter of the British people live within 25 miles of London's Trafalgar Square. But it also reveals that England as well as Britain is dominated by the south, and particularly the south east.

Yet these symbols can be misleading. The United Kingdom is a land of great diversity, partly in its landscape, but more importantly in the human sphere. There are four territorial divisions, Scotland, England, Wales and Northern Ireland (or Ulster). They all carry a special sense of identity which is strongly affected by the tension between their own distinctive history and tradition and centralised government from London. Yet even England has local identities, which tend to be stronger the further one travels from the south east. In Cornwall, in the far south west, there is still a sense of Celtic identity, and a romantic affinity with their cousins, the Celtic people of Brittany in north-west France, persists. In the north of England, in the words of one MP, people are "warm, friendly, quick-tempered and insular". Communities such as those in the mining villages of Durham are tightly knit, with a strong sense of loyalty. The people of Yorkshire and Lancashire, too, have a strong sense of community identity that can hardly be found in the south. As one

Trafalgar Square.

The Tower of London.

Buckingham Palace.

moves closer to London, community loyalties are weaker and society is both more homogeneous and yet also more individualistic, the characteristics of a highly integrated modern society.

Each shire or 'county', the administrative division of England created over a thousand years ago, still commands its own local loyalties, still expressed in that most English of games, cricket. Even in the most homogeneous part of Britain, the 'Home Counties' (Middlesex, Hertfordshire, Essex, Kent, Surrey) around London, people can still feel strongly about their county identity. The sense of local difference may be partly a matter of history, but it is also to do with the subtle changes in landscape, architecture or even the way English is spoken, from one county to another.

England, unlike the largely mountainous countries of Wales and Scotland, is mainly lowland, except for six major hilly regions: the Pennines, called the 'backbone of England' dividing the north-west part of England from the north-east; the scenic Lake District in the north west; the Yorkshire Dales, running to the east coast of Yorkshire; the moorlands of Cornwall and Devon; and the border areas with Scotland and Wales respectively. Elsewhere the ranges of hills are relatively low, while the East Midlands and East Anglia are notably flat and featureless. In Scotland and Wales the greater part of the population is concentrated in the more lowland areas, particularly the area between Glasgow and Edinburgh, and in the east and south-east parts of Wales.

Core and periphery

There is another way of looking at the country. Throughout almost all of Britain's history, the centre of economic and political power, and therefore the largest population concentration, has been in the south of the country. The only partial exception was in the two centuries following Britain's industrial revolution, approximately 1775–1975, when the availability of water and coal led to the growth of large industrial towns and cities in the north and the north and West Midlands. But as Britain now leaves its industrial age behind, it is possible to recognise the older dominance of the south – a result of climate, agricultural wealth, and today the ease of communication with the wider world.

It is possible to draw a series of arcs outwards from London, marking an inner and outer 'core' to the country, and an inner and outer 'periphery' (opposite). The pattern may seem crude, but it roughly describes the measure of authority and prosperity radiating from London since the days of Roman Britain. The periphery, particularly Scotland, Wales, and the north of England, has always resented the power of the south and periodically has challenged it. Today, in political terms, these are the areas of Labour Party strength, a rejection of the Conservative political culture of the south.

Looking at Britain, region by region, one can see the continuing evidence of this core/periphery theory. Overall population density reveals the enduring concentration in the south east where over one third of Britain's population lives, and also in the Midlands and north as a result of the industrial age.

At the outset of the 1990s Britain's total population was just over 57 million, but although it is

The Yorkshire Dales.

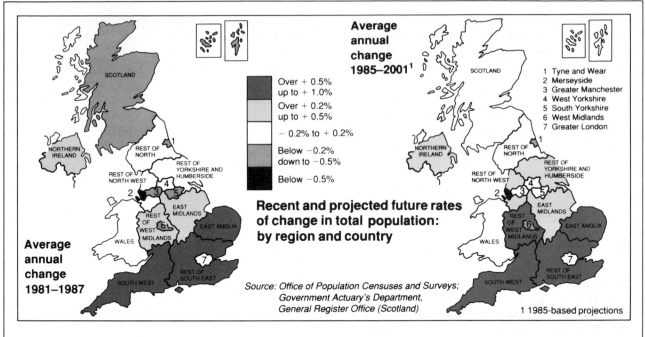

Average annual change 1981–1987

Average annual change 1985–2001[1]

1 Tyne and Wear
2 Merseyside
3 Greater Manchester
4 West Yorkshire
5 South Yorkshire
6 West Midlands
7 Greater London

Over + 0.5% up to + 1.0%

Over + 0.2% up to + 0.5%

− 0.2% to + 0.2%

Below −0.2% down to − 0.5%

Below − 0.5%

Recent and projected future rates of change in total population: by region and country

Source: Office of Population Censuses and Surveys; Government Actuary's Department, General Register Office (Scotland)

1 1985-based projections

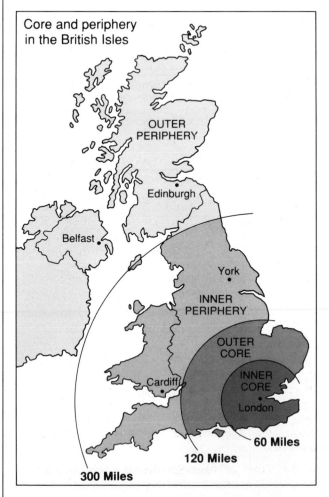

Core and periphery in the British Isles

barely increasing, the demographic pattern is changing. A continuing movement of population away from the periphery, towards the core, is evident when looking at the balance of population during the years 1981–2001 (above). There is a steady stream of young people, mainly aged between 18 and 35, who move southwards in order to improve their economic prospects. Between 1981 and 1987, Scotland, the north and north west all lost 1.3 per cent of their populations. What the map does not show is that there is a drift also from Cornwall in the far south west and from western Wales towards the core of Britain.

The north–south divide

Another way of assessing this core/periphery theory is to look at living standards and expectations in recent years. This shows very clearly that the south east, south, south west, East Anglia and the East Midlands do very much better than the peripheral areas. Over a century ago, the English novelist Mrs Gaskell wrote a book entitled North and South, about a heroine from a soft southern village forced to move to the fictitious county of Darkshire, who confessed "a detestation for all she had ever heard of the north of England, the manufacturers, the people, the wild and bleak country". Mutual prejudice between a complacent population in the south and a proud but aggrieved one in the north persists. Precisely where the dividing line between north and south runs is a matter of opinion. In the early 1980s the line was conventionally drawn from the Severn estuary (on the south Wales/England border) across to the Wash (on the north-west side of East Anglia). By 1990 the line more popularly ran from the Severn to the Humber (below).

The divide goes well beyond mere prejudice. A sharp contrast undeniably exists between the conditions of life in the north and in the south, which is likely to continue well beyond the end of the century. A survey of comparative prosperity in the 280 towns of Britain, published in 1990, shows the divide very clearly (see below). The top town, Horsham, had an unemployment rate of 2 per cent. Greenock, at the bottom, suffered 17 per cent unemployment, with the prospect that it would probably get worse in the 1990s.

The divide is noticeable in other ways, too, for example in health. In the words of one official report in 1987: "Striking disparities in health can still be observed. Death rates were highest in Scotland, followed by the north and north-west regions of England, and were lowest in the south

east of England and East Anglia." It may be added that on average people die younger in the north and the population generally is more subject to heart disease and cancer. People in the north tend to smoke and drink more heavily than in the south. The Scots, for example, spend about one third more on smoking than the national average.

Such things are symptomatic of the greater stress and harder social conditions of life in the north. This is most clearly seen in employment rates. Overall, during the period 1979–1987, there was a small, 1.5 per cent, fall in the employed labour force. The national figure, however, masks the regional variations. Employment expansion in the south east was 4.3 per cent, in the south west 7.3 per cent and in East Anglia 18.2 per cent. Everywhere else there was contraction, of which the worst were Scotland – 8 per cent, the north – 9.6 per cent, the north west – 12.1 per cent, and Wales – 12.6 per cent. As a result, during this period over 90 per cent of the job losses had been north of the Severn–Wash divide.

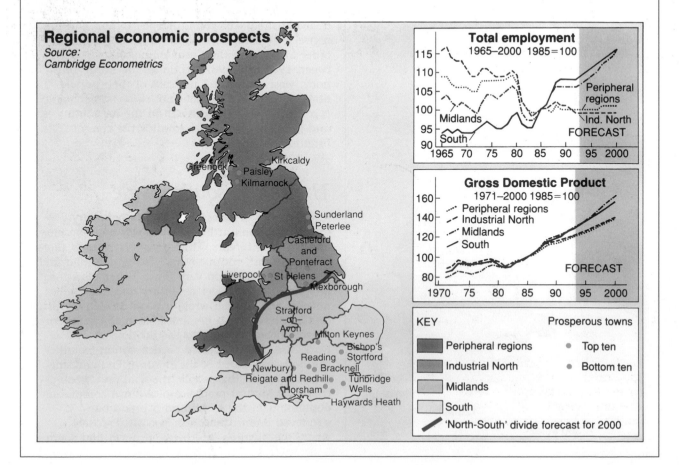

Sheffield, like many northern cities, has had to adjust to the loss of its manufacturing base.

Seeking employment at a Job Centre.

Inevitably, the existence of greater employment opportunities encouraged many in the north to follow the advice of one government minister in the early 1980s to "get on your bike" and seek work in the south. On the whole those most successful in their search were also the most employable, the best qualified. Although this may relieve short-term unemployment, it also drains depressed areas of their most talented people. Take for example Stranraer, a small town on the south-west tip of Scotland. It has no higher education facility in the locality. Those who go on to any form of further education after secondary school are unlikely to return to the Stranraer area. In other words, the whole district is annually stripped of its brightest young people. Without their talent it is difficult to see how the depressed periphery can be revived.

Single people have much greater ease in moving away in search of work than married people. This is because of the sharp difference in the price of housing. In 1990, for example, houses in the south cost on average twice as much as their equivalent in the north. This means that many married people living in the north cannot afford to move south even if they are offered a job. In any case a higher proportion of people in the north and in Scotland live in council (publicly owned) housing than elsewhere. If they move they become homeless, joining a long waiting list for council accommodation in the south. It should be noted that as the first large generation of home owners begins to die, people living in the south east are three times as likely to inherit a home as those in any other region. Thus, even in this respect, capital resources are stacked in favour of the south east.

Expensive housing in the south east.

There are plenty of exceptions to the view of prosperity in the south and of depression in the north, where there are many firms making a great success in unpromising circumstances. The largest shopping centre in Europe in 1990 was the Metrocentre in Gateshead, Newcastle, the achievement of a proud Northerner, John Hall. It is a symbol of the regional regeneration and rebirth of provincial pride that he and many other northern businessmen believe in. A world leader in the manufacture of glass, Pilkington's, resisted strong pressure in the 1980s to move south from its traditional home in St Helens, outside Liverpool. It is not only Northerners who believe in the north. Leading Japanese firms have chosen periphery areas for major investment, for example Toyota in Wales, and Nissan in Sunderland. There are also plenty of prosperous localities within an overall depressed region. Leeds, for example, boasted the fastest growing economy in England in 1989, with 50 major projects generating 12,000 jobs. The showpiece of Leeds' revival is its old shopping arcades, now revamped and renamed the Victoria Quarter.

However, there are not enough successes to reverse the overall trend. The impression of a more impoverished north persists. In the mid 1980s, for example, the north east of England

remained in the bottom twelve of the European Community's 131 regions in terms of wealth. The north west in 1983 had the highest death rate in England, the highest proportion of divorced men and the lowest proportion of 16-year-olds remaining in school, reflecting profound social and economic problems. Indeed, it is estimated that by the end of the century the north west will have lost 222,000 jobs, representing a fall in its share of national employment from 10.1 per cent to 8.8 per cent. Unemployment in the north generally is likely to remain three times higher than in the south until the end of the century. People will continue to 'vote with their feet' by moving to more prosperous areas. The government itself has estimated that during the years 1986–2001, the number of households in the south, south east, south west, East Anglia and East Midlands will increase by 15 per cent, and by only 6 per cent in the remaining areas.

The theory that businesses will relocate in the north because of cheaper labour and site costs is not borne out by experience. In practice businesses fear they will have difficulties in recruiting qualified people, a reasonable expectation if

A Japanese factory in Wales.

almost half of all 16-year-olds in the north leave school without seeking further training. There is great reluctance among most employees working in the south to move to the north. If their business relocates they are more likely to resign than move. A survey in 1988 indicated that among over 100 chief executives of companies in the south, over 90 per cent said their senior staff would resign rather than move north. Businesses prefer to seek a cheap site somewhere else in the south. Because Britain's financial sector is concentrated in London, businesses in the north find it difficult to obtain capital. Many northern businessmen would argue there is an urgent need for decentralisation, to encourage local financial centres to encourage local business. In the meantime, of those companies in the north which chose to relocate, over half have tended to move to the south.

It is questionable whether even the south really benefits from the growing regional imbalance, since in return for what may prove economic prosperity the environment is degraded by very high population concentrations, heavy air and road traffic, and urban development. It is doubtful whether this imbalance will change unless government returns to the policy generally applied up to 1979 of providing incentives to economic growth in the under-developed areas, and discouragements to the continued concentration in the south.

City and market town

Eighty per cent of the British people live in towns or cities of 100,000 inhabitants or more. Yet most of these town dwellers would prefer to live in the countryside if it were possible. This has a lot to do with a national state of mind, discussed in Chapter 8. Nevertheless, people are moving out of larger cities, some going to the countryside (discussed below), and others to smaller towns. In the 1960s London had a population of 8.5 million. By 1981 it had fallen by 20 per cent to only 6.7 million. Liverpool, in the north west, has suffered urban decline compounded by its location. In 1937 its population was 867,000. It was still 745,000 in 1961, but since then has fallen to 469,000, and will have only half its 1937 population by 2001. Several impoverished inner city areas, including Liverpool, experienced major riots during the 1980s.

Inner city Liverpool.

In fact there has been a flight from the great cities ever since the middle of the nineteenth century, when industrialisation made them such unpleasant places to live and when the invention of the railway made it possible to commute to the city from more pleasant areas. Take London, for example. Until the First World War most of the middle classes and a smaller 'service' class moved to London's new suburbs which reached into the countryside enclosing a large number of villages within a 25-mile radius.

During the middle years of the twentieth century, the 1920s to the 1970s, mainly professional middle-class people started to move out beyond 'suburbia' into the towns and villages of the Home Counties. They could either afford a motor car or the rail fares, and so could live in what were still quiet country towns. Places like Tunbridge Wells, Sevenoaks, Reigate and Redhill, Guildford and Dorking all acquired a new population of professional people who commuted daily to work in the City. Much of the countryside between these towns and Greater London was designated a protected 'Green Belt'. Many other cities did the same, in order to protect their hinterland from uncontrolled urban sprawl.

In the late 1970s and 1980s the pressure to move out of London and its suburbs intensified. There were two main reasons for this. The most important was the steep rise in house prices in the London area. The other reason for moving was to escape a marked decline in the quality of life in Britain's larger cities. In London, for example, traffic congestion and pollution made life in the 1980s much less attractive than it had been in the London of the 1960s. Since house prices in the Home Counties had risen to virtually the same level as those in London itself, people began to look further afield. For those prepared to spend up to two hours travelling to work by rail each day, it was possible to buy a larger house perhaps 160 miles or more from London, in areas around Brighton, Salisbury, Bristol, Oxford, Northampton, Cambridge, Peterborough and Norwich. Similar, though less pronounced, effects have become evident around other large cities, particularly the more depressed ones. Finally there was another smaller but growing category of people who, thanks to the new information technology, no longer needed to work in central offices. Two London boroughs, for example, 'outposted' their computer and finance departments in 1990, one to Sheffield, where rents were much lower, and another to Barnstaple, a market town in the

picturesque county of Devon. An increasing number of people were even able to work from home, linked by computer and fax facilities to their employer. Possibly up to half the people working in London will be working from home by the end of the century. If this comes about, it must be expected that more people will leave London.

Commuters on their way to work in London.

The danger for Britain's large cities is that they will have impoverished inner areas, in which only the poorest live, while everyone who is able to will try to live on the edge of the city or outside it, shopping by car at the new large shopping centres sited on city ring roads. The growth of such large shopping centres spells danger for the old-fashioned high streets of city suburbs. If people find it more attractive to shop by car, they will find that high street shops will close and local economic decline will set in, just as it has already done in some inner city areas. Thus, unplanned free-market growth may strike at the roots of that local community coherence which still strongly exists in many city suburbs, particularly those based on old villages long since swallowed up by city growth.

An out of town supermarket that threatens the traditional high street.

The attraction of the new 'boom' towns, usually with populations under 150,000, is the higher quality of life, good transport links and diversified economy. Most of them are in the southern half of England, for example Banbury, Bury St Edmunds, Cambridge, Colchester, Huntingdon, Milton Keynes, Reading, Swindon, Warwick and Worcester. Exeter represents the most western of these boom towns. One or two are significantly further north, for example Warrington and Harrogate, and Wrexham in north Wales. Wrexham's fortunes changed when two large Japanese electronics companies, Sharp and Brother, both established factories there, attracted by low labour costs and improved road access to Manchester. It is hard to exaggerate the psychological effect of Japanese investment on local prosperity, for their confidence draws in British investors who would otherwise have had little confidence in a small market town in a low income area. Warrington suffered heavily in the early 1980s with the loss of jobs in steel and aluminium production giving it a high unemployment rate. By 1990 unemployment was below the national average thanks mainly to diversification into non-manual or 'white-collar' jobs, and a shrinkage in the proportion of manual, or 'blue-collar' jobs, and most important of all, new confidence resulting from local successes.

Yet, it is still within the south east that the greatest small town growth is taking place. The population of Milton Keynes grew by 41 per cent between 1981 and 1988. In terms of economic growth Horsham, in West Sussex, overtook nearby Crawley in 1990 as one of the fastest growing towns in the country. Access to London by road and rail is easy, and Gatwick airport is nearby. Traditionally a quiet market town, Horsham has become a busy and prosperous shopping centre for the area, with a large commuter population but also with a high level of business in the town itself. Its largest employer is a large insurance company. As happens in most growing towns, the emphasis is on service industry rather than manufacturing and the job vacancies are for those with skills and educational qualifications. Few unskilled workers are wanted in these boom towns.

'Sunset' and 'sunrise' areas

The pattern of prosperity, or lack of it, is evident in the areas of development and stagnation in the country. The sunset areas are broadly those where traditional industries have collapsed during the past twenty-five years, for example cotton goods in Lancashire, car production in the West Midlands, coal and steel production in south Wales, Tyne and Wear, Durham and parts of Yorkshire, and shipbuilding in Tyne and Wear, Clydeside and Belfast. Yet the north has its sunrise areas, those areas where significant new economic activity is occurring, for example between Manchester and Leeds, but unlike the large areas in the south, prosperous parts are far more patchy in the north.

The most sensational sunrise areas are in the outer core (and the outer edge of the inner core areas) of Britain. Of these, the most notable is the 'M4 Corridor', the band of once lovely countryside stretching westwards from London to Swindon and beyond. Easy access to London's Heathrow airport, and to the M25 (London orbital), M3 and M4 motorways has made the towns west of London highly attractive to the new high technology industries which grew rapidly during the 1980s. As a result, development and employment growth has been intensive. The town of Bracknell is a good example. It was a small town of barely 40,000 inhabitants when it was designated a new town in the early 1960s. By 1971 its population had grown to 65,000, by 1990 to 96,000, and it is expected to reach 110,000 in the mid 1990s. Bracknell is not alone. Reading, Newbury, Hungerford, Basingstoke and Swindon all grew rapidly during the 1980s. However, as each becomes densely populated, with high house prices, some companies and employees move further afield to avoid the overdevelopment to which they have contributed.

Another major area of development is across Cambridge and East Anglia. Access to London, to the excellent scientific and technical resources of Cambridge, and to low-cost industrial areas and housing has made this area particularly attractive to high technology and service industries. As a result East Anglia, the most sparsely populated part of England, but with excellent seafreight facilities for Europe, had remarkable population growth during the 1980s, at a rate of 1 per cent per annum.

A sunset area: industrial dereliction.

Town and country

It is obvious that, especially in the south and south east, the pressure created by the growth of towns along the M4 Corridor and other development areas, and by the increasing departure of people from the cities, has been particularly felt in the countryside. In fact, it would be true to say that almost all of rural England has been affected. Large numbers of mainly middle-class families have bought cottages in the country, either to live in or to use as holiday homes.

This migration into the countryside has changed the nature of village life. Many villages today have a substantial proportion of commuters, people whose home is in the village but who earn their living elsewhere. This is in complete contrast with only half a century ago, when villages were much smaller and were populated by those who made their living out of the country, primarily farmers and farm labourers. In Hampshire, for example, there is not a single village left which is not almost entirely commuter-based, its inhabitants travelling to work anywhere from the Solent to the south, to Avon (Bath–Bristol) to the west, or the M4 Corridor towns or London to the north and north east.

This migration has transformed occupancy. Pretty old cottages have been bought at higher prices than most local people can afford. The local poor have been steadily squeezed out, particularly during the past twenty years, into low-cost or publicly owned rented housing on the edge of the village.

Village geography has also changed. The pressure for housing has led to intensive infilling and expansion onto open land in and around villages. The county of Berkshire, for example, has doubled its housing stock since 1960. Reading, Wokingham and Bracknell have all expanded so that they almost form one single conurbation. Pressure has been particularly acute around London, with successive governments trying to infringe the 1947 Town and Country Planning Act which protects the Green Belt. According to government estimates, 700,000 new homes are needed in the south east during the 1990s, of which 570,000

Low cost public housing on the outskirts of a village.

homes will be outside London. The pressure to expand onto 'green-field' sites, in other words the countryside, will be very great. So far the pressures have been largely resisted. Between 1954 and 1981 the built-on area of the south east rose from 11.9 per cent to 15.7 per cent. It may reach 17 per cent by the end of the century. In 1990 there were at least sixty new towns and villages proposed in different parts of rural England.

The pressure on rural housing is an area of tension between long-established country people and middle-class newcomers. Local people often resent the way they have been displaced into cheap housing on the edge of the village. It is the newly arrived commuting middle classes who are generally more anxious to protect their picturesque village from further housing development. Most villages threatened with nearby new housing developments quickly organise campaigns to oppose their implementation. However, truly local people sometimes regard commuters as hypocritical, since they do not have to earn a livelihood locally.

The pressure of people is also felt through tourism, in areas which receive heavy use during the summer. Two notable areas in danger are the Lake District, first made famous in the nineteenth century by the great romantic poet William Wordsworth, and the Peak District in the Pennine Hills, running between Lancashire and Yorkshire. National parks in Britain are already significantly different from those in most of Europe, because they are already man-modified landscapes. Many of the landscapes now run the risk of development as leisure facilities. By 1990 there were a dozen major leisure complexes in the Lake District. The more people use or interfere with these national parks the more they will be degraded. Britain faces a major crisis in tourist damage both in its cities and countryside. The sheer numbers of people wishing to visit Westminster Abbey or to walk the Pennine Way are literally wearing these facilities away.

The countryside probably also faces more systematic exploitation than in any other country in Western Europe. The English countryside has

Hikers on the Pennine Way.

changed more in the past 40 years than in the previous 400 years. The main threat comes from farming. The pressure to improve yields, a feature of government policy since the food shortages of the Second World War, has had a damaging effect on the countryside and the structure of farming. This pressure has led to increased capitalisation and mechanisation, and this in turn has led to the disappearance of smaller, less profitable farms in favour of much larger enterprises. The concentration of farmland in a few wealthy hands is a particularly British phenomenon. The average farm in Britain is much larger than in any other West European country.

Intensive large-scale farming has changed the traditional landscape in many parts of England. In order to make maximum use of mechanisation many farmers have torn up thousands of the hedgerows that characterised the English landscape. Well over 100,000 miles of hedges – enough to encircle the world four times – have been removed since 1947. Some East Anglian fields are now 500 acres in size. Half the country's ancient lowland woods have been cleared for farmland since 1945. In addition the intensive use of chemical fertilisers has led to substantial pollution of rivers, and the destruction of fish and other wildlife. In the late 1980s there was growing concern at the degradation of the countryside. A vigorous nature conservation lobby, rivalled possibly only by that in Holland, may be able to halt the progressive degradation of the rural environment.

Modern agricultural methods have also led to a sharp decline in the farming population. In 1946 there were 739,000 full-time agricultural workers. Over 600,000 of these have disappeared since then. One Cambridgeshire farmer, for example, today employs only six people where his father employed eighty-five people, yet manages to produce twice as much. In the mid 1980s overproduction became a problem, and farmers are now encouraged to produce less food per acre. However, it is unlikely that farmers will return to previous methods, either by restoring hedgerows or by reducing the use of chemical fertilisers.

Rich and poor

What happened to over half a million farm labourers? Many sought other unskilled or semi-skilled work, some in nearby towns. Because of their very low income many found it almost impossible to move to town. Others have found it impossible to find work. The countryside remains an area of high unemployment, and one quarter of all rural households live in comparative poverty. The desire of the rural poor for better economic prospects, even at the cost of new housing estates in the village, contrasts sharply with the views of newly arrived middle-class people who do not want picturesque villages spoilt.

However, rural poverty is often forgotten because it is overshadowed by the far larger problem of

A homeless person sleeping rough in a London park.

urban poverty. Although there is a higher proportion of both rural and urban poor on the periphery, particularly in the depressed areas of the north, the most casual tourist in London can easily find signs of desperate poverty among the homeless who sleep rough in the centre of the city. Most of Britain's poor live in the run-down areas which exist in almost every large town or city. The most notorious of these are in London, Liverpool, Birmingham and Bristol, but only because it was in these cities that the anger of poverty exploded in riots during the 1980s.

During the 1980s the gap between the richest and poorest in Britain grew significantly after over thirty years of relative stability. This was a direct result of economic policy and of changes to the tax system which intentionally rewarded the richest most, on the assumption that the highest income earners were the most productive members of society. In 1989 it was estimated that the richest 200 people in Britain owned assets equivalent to 8 per cent of the gross national product, including 7 per cent of the land.

In contrast, during the period from 1979 to 1987 the number of people living on less than half the national average income doubled, from roughly one tenth to one fifth of the whole population. In fact poverty seems to have increased during the 1980s more rapidly than elsewhere in the European Community. However, while the number of poor people undoubtedly increased during the 1980s, it is also true that the remaining 80 per cent of the population were probably somewhat better off than they had been in 1979. The real difficulty was that the gap between rich and poor grew. The richer a family was, the more they tended to benefit during the 1980s, and the poorer they were, the less they benefited. This trend seemed set to continue into the 1990s.

Britain's diversity is, therefore, a good deal more complex than merely the variety of its landscape, or quaint cultures like Scottish bagpipes, Welsh harps and northern brass bands. During the closing years of the twentieth century the physical landscape is changing rapidly as a result of economic and social change. Although these have been discussed in contrasting terms, north and south, town and country, rich and poor and so forth, it will be clear that these themes interact. It is not possible to look at the comparative prosperity of the south without considering its implications for the countryside, or for the decaying cores of its cities. Nor is it possible to consider, for example, the unfortunate impact of modern farming without seeing it in the context of a highly integrated modern society. In many respects the British people find themselves caught between their idealised view of Britain and its institutions and the less comfortable realities at the approach of the twenty-first century.

Questions

Section analysis

1 A sense of place: What is the difference in usage between the words 'British' and 'English'?

2 Core and periphery: Which is the 'core' area of Britain, and which is the 'periphery'? Give reasons why the core continues to be dominant.

3 The north–south divide: Which of these two images, core–periphery or north–south divide, do you think best describes the socio-economic differences in Britain? Explain your choice.

4 City and market town: Why have cities de-clined in population while towns and villages outside cities have increased? Is there a similar development in your country?

5 Sunrise and sunset areas: What does the author mean by sunrise and sunset areas? Find examples of each from the text.

6 Town and country: There is in Britain a popular desire to move into the countryside. What social and environmental problems does this movement cause?

7 Rich and poor: What happened to the gap between rich and poor during the 1980s, and what were the main causes?

Chapter analysis and discussion

1 Which of the following statements is the best summary of Chapter 1?

a Britain is a highly homogeneous country in which suggestions of a north–south divide, or of great disparity between rich and poor are exaggerated.

b Britain is a sharply divided society in which one is conscious of huge differences in culture and wealth.

c The idea that British society is homogeneous must be qualified by cultural, social and economic variations.

d Britain is a dynamic country with picturesque and charming regional variations.

2 List the ways in which the regions of Britain differ most clearly.

3 Find evidence in the text to support the follow-ing statements:

a During the 1980s there was an increasing proportion of the population that could be described as poor.

b The English countryside is suffering serious degradation.

c The economic boom in the 1980s took place mainly in the southern half of Britain.

d Business is very unwilling to relocate in the north.

4 Are there marked regional differences in your country? If so, are they similar to those in Britain? Are there other kinds of divisions in your country which do not apply in Britain?

Visual interpretation

Consider the following map indicating regional average weekly household disposable income in 1989. What does the map indicate? Does it confirm or qualify ideas such as the north–south divide, and core–periphery?

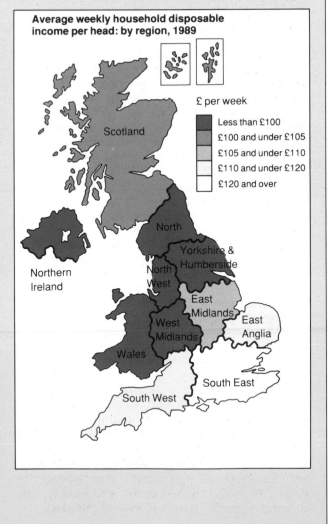

Average weekly household disposable income per head: by region, 1989

£ per week

Less than £100
£100 and under £105
£105 and under £110
£110 and under £120
£120 and over

Scotland

Northern Ireland

North

Yorkshire & Humberside

North West

East Midlands

East Anglia

West Midlands

Wales

South East

South West

2 The system of government

Britain is a democracy, yet its people are not, as one might expect in a democracy, constitutionally in control of the state. The constitutional situation is an apparently contradictory one. As a result of an historical process the people of Britain are subjects of the Crown, accepting the Queen as the head of the state. Yet even the Queen is not sovereign in any substantial sense since she receives her authority from Parliament, and is subject to its direction in almost all matters. In short, she 'reigns' but does not rule. Technically, if confusingly, British sovereignty collectively resides in the three elements of Parliament: the Crown, and Parliament's two chambers, the House of Lords and the House of Commons.

This curious situation came about as a result of a long struggle for power between the Crown and Parliament during the sixteenth and seventeenth centuries. In 1689 Parliament won that struggle, because it controlled most of the national wealth. It agreed to allow the Crown to continue to function within certain limits, and subject to Parliament's control. No constitution was written down either then or since, and the relationship between Crown, government, Parliament and people – and their respective constitutional powers – has been one of gradual development. The state – itself sometimes called the Crown – operates on precedent, custom and conventions, and on unwritten rules and assumptions.

The Crown

The reigning monarch is not only head of state but symbol of the unity of the nation. The monarchy is Britain's oldest secular institution, its continuity for over a thousand years broken only once by a republic that lasted a mere eleven years (1649–60). The monarchy is hereditary, the succession passing automatically to the oldest male child, or in the absence of males, to the oldest female offspring of the monarch. By Act (or law) of Parliament, the monarch must be a Protestant. Succession is automatic on the death of the monarch, confirmed later by a formal coronation ceremony. The coronation of Queen Elizabeth II in 1953, for example, took place over a year after she became queen.

The coronation of Queen Elizabeth II.

In law the monarch is head of the executive and of the judiciary, head of the Church of England, and commander-in-chief of the armed forces. However, since 1689, the monarch's sovereign powers have been formally limited by the idea that national sovereignty resides in 'the Crown in Parliament' – the idea that the Crown is only sovereign by the will of Parliament.

The remaining powers of the monarch are basically to summon, prorogue (or suspend until the next session) and dissolve Parliament; to give royal assent to legislation passed by Parliament; to appoint government ministers, judges, officers of the armed forces, governors, diplomats and bishops of the Church; to confer honours, such as peerages and knighthoods; to remit sentences passed on convicted criminals; and finally to declare war on or make peace with an enemy power. In practice, of course, with the exception of a few honours she is free to decide herself, the monarch discharges all these functions on the direction of the government. In most matters of state, the refusal of the Queen to exercise her power according to the direction of her Prime Minister would risk a serious constitutional crisis.

Nevertheless, the function of the monarch is politically important. For as someone who reigns but does not rule, the sovereign separates the 'magic' of sovereignty, publicly visible in many ceremonies, from the power of the executive head of state. This contrasts with executive presidential systems of government. Away from the public gaze, the monarch plays a more practical role. The Queen is visited regularly by her Prime Minister to receive an account of Cabinet decisions and to be consulted on matters of national life. Since 1952 the Queen has given audience, as it is called, to ten Prime Ministers and her thirty years' experience gives importance to these meetings.

Whitehall – the seat of government

'Her Majesty's Government' governs in the name of the Queen, and its hub, Downing Street, lies in Whitehall, a short walk from Parliament. Following a general election, the Queen invites the leader of the majority (or largest, in the absence of an overall majority) party represented in the Commons, to form a government on her behalf.

Government ministers are almost invariably members of the House of Commons, but infrequently members of the House of Lords are appointed. These are at a disadvantage since it is in the Commons that the government is expected to explain its conduct of affairs. All government ministers, even the Prime Minister, who are members of the Commons, continue to represent the parliamentary 'constituencies' which elected them. Unless the government is a coalition – the last of these was formed during the war years 1939–45 – governments today are drawn solely from one political party. But this has not always been so. During the nineteenth century leading politicians were far freer to follow their own convictions or ambitions rather than party discipline.

Most governments consist of about one hundred ministers, but the essential core is the Cabinet, the twenty or so most senior ministers invited by the Prime Minister to belong to it. Cabinet government demands collective responsibility and confidentiality. Within the Cabinet the Prime

John and Norma Major outside 10 Downing Street.

Minister is first among equals. In theory this encourages balance and prudence in both policy and action. In practice the Cabinet principle can give rise to tension. While a Prime Minister must give strong leadership, he or she must allow for each minister to exercise responsibility within their field and should encourage collective decision-making on controversial issues, particularly ones beyond the responsibility of one ministry.

The potential for tension was dramatically revealed in 1989 when the Chancellor of the Exchequer (responsible for finance) suddenly resigned after persistent rumours over some years about the Prime Minister's overbearing manner in Cabinet. In explaining his resignation, he gave a classic definition of the Cabinet principle: "For our system of Cabinet government to work effectively, the Prime Minister of the day must appoint ministers that he or she trusts and then leave them to carry out the policy. When differences of view emerge, as they are bound to do from time to time, they should be resolved privately and, wherever appropriate, collectively." The ex-Chancellor made this statement to the House of Commons, for all ministers are accountable to it. Although not the case on this occasion, once the confidence of a majority of his or her colleagues has been lost, a Cabinet minister has no choice but to resign.

Because of the enormous increase in government business, all senior government ministers – most of whom have the title of Secretary of State – have junior ministers (Ministers of State or Parliamentary Under-Secretaries) to help with the workload. They are all subject to the rules of collective responsibility and must not disagree publicly with government policy.

Although government is essentially political, it depends upon a permanent body of officials, the Civil Service, to administer the decisions of ministers, and to keep the wheels of government – in its broadest sense – turning. The Civil Service, employing almost 600,000 people, is expected to discharge its responsibilities in a politically impartial way. Civil servants must be as loyal to an incoming government as to the outgoing one, however much as private individuals they may be pleased or dismayed at the change of government. Those civil servants wishing to stand for Parliament must first resign from the Civil Service.

The heart of the Civil Service is the Cabinet Office, whose Secretary is the senior civil servant at any given time. The responsibilities are considerable, including the proper and smooth running of the whole Civil Service as well as serving ministers collectively in the conduct of Cabinet business and ensuring the coordination of policy at the highest level. In each ministry or department the senior official, or Permanent Secretary and his or her immediate subordinates, Under-Secretaries and Assistant Secretaries, remain responsible for assisting their minister in the implementation of government policy. In practice this is a two-way process – cleverly portrayed in the 1980s in two famous satirical television series, *Yes, Minister* and *Yes, Prime Minister* – in which alongside genuine cooperation there is also a permanent trial of strength between the political will of the minister and the concern of civil servants to minimise departures from known and trusted methods of government.

The Prime Minister, Cabinet Secretary and Principal Private Secretary, as portrayed in the television series, Yes, Prime Minister.

Both sides are tempted to view the other as a potential obstacle to good government, but both also moderate the dangers implicit in one or other party enjoying unchallenged powers. Innovative governments, both Conservative and Labour, have at times suspected the Civil Service of political hostility. In the words of one ex-minister, the Civil Service is "a beautifully designed and effective braking mechanism. It produces a hundred well-argued answers against initiative and change."

In fact the record since the nineteenth century demonstrates a strong tradition of loyalty on the part of civil servants towards their ministers. Furthermore, in practice, a minister and his or her senior civil servants will be the strongest of allies in fighting for the interests of their department, or ministry, against competing ones, particularly in allocation of the financial budget.

Westminster – the seat of Parliament

Her Majesty's Government, in spite of its name, derives its authority and power from its party representation in Parliament. While the government machinery is frequently referred to as 'Whitehall', Parliament is known as 'Westminster', since it is housed in the Palace of Westminster, once a home of the monarchy. Like the monarchy, Parliament is an ancient institution, dating from the middle of the thirteenth century.

Parliament is the seat of British democracy, but it is perhaps valuable to remember that while the House of Lords was created in order to provide a council of the nobility for the king, the Commons were summoned originally in order to provide the king with money. The more money a king demanded the more the Commons questioned its use. Because of its financial power, its ability to raise or withhold money, the House of Commons eventually – from the seventeenth century onwards – gained power not only in matters of finance but also of legislation over both the monarch and also the Lords.

Parliament is the supreme legislative body of the state. Free from the constraints of a written constitution it may make any laws it pleases. It could even prolong its own life without consulting the electorate, if it chose to do so. Thus Parliament, rather than the will of the people, is clearly

The Houses of Parliament.

the real sovereign power in the state. The only guarantee against parliamentary tyranny is the sense of tradition and reasonableness of its members.

Furthermore, in practice it is not Parliament as a whole which is sovereign, but the government of the day and its supporters, since they almost invariably form a majority in the Commons. For the duration of its normal term, five years, the government of the day may enact or implement its policies, so long as it can ensure party support in the Commons. In the words of one distinguished and long-serving parliamentarian who has sat in both the Commons and the Lords, Britain's parliamentary system is in practice a form of "elective dictatorship", an important qualification on the idea of Britain as a democracy.

Parliament's functions today are to pass laws, to raise enough money through taxation to enable the government to function, to examine government policy and administration, particularly its financial programme, and to debate or discuss important political issues.

The life of a Parliament is not fixed, and the government of the day may call for a general election at any time during its five-year term. Each Parliament is divided into annual sessions, running normally from October to October with breaks for public holidays and for a long summer 'recess' (usually late July until October).

The electoral and party systems

For electoral purposes the United Kingdom is divided into constituencies, each one of which elects a Member of Parliament to sit in the House of Commons. To ensure equitable representation four permanent Boundary Commissions (for England, Wales, Scotland and Northern Ireland), make periodic reviews to adjust electoral boundaries and redistribute seats. Today there are 650 seats in the Commons, one seat on average for every 66,000 electors.

All British citizens (including citizens of the Irish Republic resident in the UK) may vote, provided they are aged eighteen or over, are registered, and are not disqualified by insanity, membership of the House of Lords or by being sentenced prisoners. Voting is not compulsory, and a general election normally attracts about 75 per cent of the electorate, a decline in participation of about 8 per cent since 1945. The candidate in a constituency who gains most votes is returned as Member to the Commons. In this 'first-past-the-post' system, other candidates, even if they come close to the winner, will not get a seat in Parliament.

If a Member of Parliament (MP) resigns, dies or is made a peer during the lifetime of a Parliament, a by-election must be held in his or her old constituency to elect a new member. No candidate requires the backing of a political party in order to stand for election, but today no independent candidates succeed in being elected. MPs are normally chosen by the constituency branch of the party, from a list of suitable candidates issued by the party headquarters. Where the winning party of an election only just gains the greatest proportion of the national vote, this can lead to a substantial distortion of democratic will in actual representation in the Commons. The 1987 election results clearly reveal the problem:

Party	% of vote	% of MPs
Conservative	42.2	57.7
Labour	30.8	35.2
Alliance (Liberal/SDP)	22.6	3.4

The political party system has evolved since the eighteenth century, and since the first half of the nineteenth century has been essentially a two-party system. Today, this two-party contest is between the Conservative Party (still known by their previous nickname, the 'Tories') and the Labour Party, which emerged at the end of the nineteenth century as a result of the introduction of universal male suffrage and the decline of the Liberal Party.

The Conservative Party is the party of the Right, identified with the idea of economic freedom and until 1979 with the idea of resistance to change. It has successfully portrayed itself as the party of patriotism. As in the nineteenth century, it appeals to a 'property-owning democracy', and as a result its support tends to lie with the wealthier classes, receiving much money from major business and financial institutions. It gives emphasis to the importance of law and order, and the maintenance of strong armed forces to protect British interests. It is highly disciplined, and accepts the direction of the Prime Minister. Conservatives tend to be reluctant to express dissent from the leadership publicly.

A Conservative Party conference.

The Labour Party is less disciplined but possibly more democratic, with more open disagreements between the leadership and other party members. Labour is preeminently the party of social justice, though its emphasis is less on equality than on the achievement of wellbeing and opportunity for all members of society. It tends to put the collective wellbeing of society above individual freedom, in the economic sphere at any rate. Traditionally it has been committed to public ownership of major industries, and to economic planning. The trade union movement, which founded the Labour Party, remains influential in the evolution of party policy. Each union executive is able to cast the vote of its entire membership, with the result that some party resolutions are to some extent a contest between the larger unions.

John Smith became leader of the Labour Party in July 1992.

The Liberal Democrats' conference – the Party leader, Paddy Ashdown, is seated to the right of the speaker.

The Liberal Party, which traces its origins to the eighteenth century 'Whigs', merged with the new Social Democratic Party in 1988 to become the Liberal Democrats, after fighting the 1987 election unsuccessfully as an alliance of both parties. It seeks to attract the votes of the middle ground between Labour and the Conservatives, but has also tended to attract opponents of the Conservatives, dominant in the south of England, and opponents of the Labour Party, dominant in the north.

Since 1945 the Conservatives have formed seven governments and Labour six, although in practice during the period 1945–90 the Conservatives have governed for twenty-eight years and Labour for only seventeen. Since 1979 the domination of the Commons by the Conservatives reveals the strength and weakness of the first-past-the-post electoral system. They have enjoyed a large majority in the Commons although at the elections of 1979, 1983 and 1987 more people voted against the Conservative Party than for it.

The House of Commons

The dynamic power of Parliament lies in the House of Commons. Of its 650 Members, 523 represent constituencies in England, 38 in Wales, 72 in Scotland and 17 in Northern Ireland. There are only seats in the Commons debating chamber for 370 members, but except on matters of great interest, it is unusual for all members to be present at any one time. Many MPs find themselves in other rooms of the Commons, participating in a variety of committees and meetings necessary for an effective parliamentary process.

The shape of the Commons debating chamber makes an important comment on the political process in Britain. Unlike many European chambers which are semicircular, thus reflecting the spectrum of political opinion in their seating plan, the Commons is rectangular, with the Speaker's (the Presiding MP) chair at one end, and either side of it five rows of benches running the length of the chamber. On one side, to the Speaker's right, sits Her Majesty's Government and its supporters, and on the other Her Majesty's Opposition, composed of all Members who oppose the government. The front benches on either side are reserved for members of the Cabinet and other Ministers, and Opposition spokesmen, known as the 'Shadow Cabinet', respectively.

Behind them sit MPs from their own party, known as 'backbenchers'. The layout implies two features of British political life: that it has traditionally been a two-party system and that the process is essentially adversarial (indeed, a red line on the floor in front of each front bench still marks the limit – a little more than two swords' lengths – beyond which a Member may not approach the opposite benches).

The Speaker is chosen by a vote of the entire House, although in practice the party leaders consult their supporters in order to achieve informal agreement beforehand. The Speaker is responsible for the orderly conduct of business, and is required to act with scrupulous impartiality between Members in the House. In the words of the Speaker in 1988, "It's not my duty as Speaker to bend arguments in any way, but to ensure that everything that happens here is seen clearly by those who put us here. We are, after all, the servants of those who put us here: the electorate." The Speaker is assisted by three deputy speakers.

The former Speaker of the House of Commons.

Unlike peers, who can only claim expenses, MPs are paid salaries, approximately twice the average national wage, but substantially less than most MPs could earn outside the Commons.

The House of Lords

The upper chamber of Parliament, the House of Lords, is not democratic in any sense at all. It consists of four categories of peer. The majority are hereditary peers, a total of almost 800, but of whom only about half take an active interest in the affairs of state. A smaller number, between 350 and 400, are 'life' peers – an idea introduced in 1958 to elevate to the peerage certain people who have rendered political or public service to the nation. The purpose was not merely to honour but also to enhance the quality of business done in the Lords. Only one quarter of these life peers are women. All life peers are created on the recommendation of the Prime Minister of the day, with nominations also sought from opposition parties. Nine of the most senior judges, the Lords of Appeal in Ordinary, are also entitled to sit in the Lords. Finally, alongside these secular peers, the Lords Temporal, are the twenty-six most senior bishops and archbishops of the Church of England, the Lords Spiritual. The lords of appeal – known as the Law Lords – and the Lords Spiritual are the ancient non-hereditary component of the Lords.

Until 1911 the Lords were able to reject bills passed in the Commons, and thus frustrate not only the government of the day, but also the will of the Commons. Since then the Lords have been unable to challenge financial legislation, and have only been able to delay other legislation (since 1949 for no more than one session) but not prevent it. Their only other surviving discretionary power is to veto an attempt by the Commons to prolong its own life beyond its five-year term. The role of the Lords, therefore, is now more to warn than to frustrate over-zealous governments, and they have done this more by the proposition of amendments to legislation which causes them unease, than by direct opposition.

Although there are over a thousand peers entitled to sit in the House of Lords, average daily attendance is only about 300 and most of these are life peers, who retain a strong interest in the affairs of state. The House is presided over by the Lord Chancellor, the senior law officer of the state. The position is not like that of the Speaker, for the Lord Chancellor is not impartial, but a government officer and besides, the Lords are expected to conduct their business in a far more orderly fashion than the Commons. He is responsible for the administration of justice and he is also an automatic member of the Cabinet.

The House of Lords in session.

A larger number of peers support the Conservative Party than either Labour or the Liberal Democrats, who collectively with independent peers (who, unlike the Commons, have 'cross-benches' across the back of the chamber to sit upon), can marshall almost the same number of active peers as the Conservatives. In 1988 there were 446 Conservative peers, 117 Labour peers, 61 Liberal Democrats, 25 Social Democrats and 226 crossbenchers. This preponderance in favour of the Conservatives arises partly because the majority of hereditary peers sympathise more with the Conservative Party than its opponents, but also because Labour declined to nominate candidates for life peerages for a period during the 1980s since its party policy included abolition of the Lords, on the grounds that it was an undemocratic anachronism. Despite this preponderance, however, no Conservative government can be absolutely sure of a majority, if its proposals are controversial. Peers, of whatever party loyalty, are far freer to vote according to their own convictions rather than party policy than are members of the Commons.

Parliamentary procedure

Each parliamentary session begins with the 'State Opening of Parliament', a ceremonial occasion in which the Queen proceeds from Buckingham Palace to the Palace of Westminster where she delivers the Queen's Speech from her throne in the House of Lords. Her speech is drafted by her government, and describes what the government intends to implement during the forthcoming session. Leading members of the Commons may hear the speech from the far end of the chamber, but are not allowed to enter the House of Lords. During the next five or so days, the government and Opposition debate aspects of the Queen's Speech in the Commons and vote on the amendments which the Opposition proposes. Since the speech is a statement of policy, defeat on any such vote would oblige the government to resign.

For most of the year the Commons adopts a routine of meeting each weekday afternoon, and 'sitting' until about 10.30 p.m. although it sometimes sits beyond midnight. On Fridays the

Commons sits from 9.30 a.m. through to 3 p.m., rising early in order to allow MPs to return to their constituencies for the weekend, where they must make themselves available and accessible for local matters, complaints and attendance at formal functions. The proceedings of Parliament are public, and space is available for a small number of people, especially the press, to listen. Since 1803 the proceedings of Parliament have been published the following day as *Hansard*, named after the man who first began to publish the record. Proceedings of both Houses are also now televised, the Lords since 1984 and the Commons since 1989.

The manner in which business is conducted is the result of custom and precedent, from which have emerged 'standing orders' which govern the details of practice in each House.

Each day begins, after brief opening formalities, with Question Time, lasting approximately an hour. MPs are able to ask ministers or other MPs questions on any point they may choose. Questions must be handed in 48 hours ahead, to allow ministers and their departmental staff time to prepare an answer. Naturally, both the Opposition and the party of government seek to use this period in order to reveal the weakness of their opponents. Once a minister's formal answer has been given, supplementary questions may be asked which the minister is expected to answer. Ministers and their civil servants are expected to have anticipated what further questions may be asked. Supplementary questions are used by the Opposition to outmaneouvre a minister and reveal a weakness in government policy, or perhaps by an MP anxious to persuade the

The State Opening of Parliament.

Prime Minister's Question Time in the Commons.

Parliament's most important function is to create law. A draft law takes the form of a parliamentary bill. Most of these are public bills, implementing government policy. A bill is normally only drafted after exhaustive consultation with concerned professional, voluntary and other agencies. Proposals sometimes take the form of 'white papers', stating government policy, which can be debated before a bill is introduced. 'Green papers' are published when the government wants a full public discussion before it formulates its own proposals.

The process of passing a public (or government) bill is similar in both Houses. Its publication in printed form is announced in the chamber, and this announcement is called its 'first reading'. Its 'second reading', usually a few weeks later, is the occasion for a full debate in the House, unless there is general assent that a debate is unnecessary. If necessary the bill is passed to a committee which considers whether amendments would be desirable in the light of MPs' criticisms or concerns. At the 'third reading' the revised bill is considered in its final form, and a vote taken if necessary. The bill then passes through the Lords in a similar fashion. Once a bill has completed its parliamentary procedures, it is sent to the Queen for royal assent (the third formal element of Parliament), by which it passes into law as an Act of Parliament. Royal assent has not been refused since 1707.

government to modify its course of action. On two afternoons each week the Prime Minister will answer questions on general policy matters. These occasions are usually the most lively.

After Question Time, the main debate of the day takes place. Time is given on twenty-four days during a session for individual MPs representing neither government nor Opposition to introduce debates or 'private Members' bills'. But most of the time available in any parliamentary session is devoted to scrutiny of government spending, and debating new bills the government wishes to introduce. The system of debate is much the same in both chambers. It originates in a 'motion' (a proposal) 'moved' (proposed) by a minister or Member of the House. The Speaker then proposes the question as a subject of debate.

This is not quite as spontaneous as it may seem. The Leader of the House (appointed by the government) agrees with the Prime Minister the general business, including debates, which they want. Twenty opposition days each session allow the Opposition to choose the subjects for debate. At the end of a debate the Speaker asks MPs if they accept the motion. If there is disagreement, there is a division as MPs enter either the 'Aye' (yes) or 'No' lobbies, corridors running either side of the Commons chamber. A bell rings throughout the House six minutes before the lobby doors close to enable MPs, wherever they may be in the House, to vote. Party 'whips' (or managers) stand outside the door of the lobby into which they expect their party's Members to pass. Unless it is a free vote, Members who ignore party policy risk the strong displeasure of the party leadership.

Parliamentary committees

It is natural that both the Commons and the Lords should form committees to consider specific matters or bills passing through Parliament. The Commons have a number of 'standing committees' which examine bills during the procedural stages until they become law. Scotland, Wales and Northern Ireland are all represented by permanent standing committees. In addition standing committees are appointed to consider specific bills. Between 16 and 50 MPs are normally appointed to a standing committee, usually reflecting the balance of party representation in Parliament.

In 1979 a new and important 'select committee' system was created to examine and monitor government departments and policies, and the manner in which ministers discharge their responsibilities. One reason for doing this was the difficulty individual MPs had in scrutinising government activity adequately. Another was the increase in party discipline which made it difficult for MPs to act independently of party policy. Members of the governing party tended to support government policy and action; those of the opposing party tended to criticise it. There had already been one or two select committees for particular matters, but this was the first time a comprehensive scrutinising of government departments had been attempted.

The select committee system consists of fourteen individual committees 'shadowing' the expenditure, administration and policy of the main government departments. Each committee has a more or less permanent cross-party membership, all of whom have acquired considerable expertise in their respective fields since 1979. They give an opportunity for MPs to act more independently of their party than they are able to do in the debating chamber. During the period of Conservative government in the 1980s, for example, a number of select committees, including their Conservative members, were strongly critical of the government.

This, briefly, is the constitutional and political system of Britain. As will be seen in the following chapter, the system as currently operated gives rise to considerable controversy. Some people are dissatisfied with its fundamental principles, and others with what they believe are the dangers of the way the system actually operates.

Questions

Section analysis

1 The Crown: What are the powers of the monarch?

2 Whitehall: What does 'cabinet government' mean? What are its strengths and weaknesses?

3 Westminster: Why did the Commons become more important than the Lords? How was the Commons strong enough to defeat the Crown in the seventeenth century?

4 The electoral and party systems: Explain the main differences between the Conservative and Labour parties.

5 The House of Commons: Draw a diagram showing the shape and layout of the House of Commons debating chamber. Give reasons why you think this arrangement is better or worse than the more common semi-circular debating chamber.

6 The House of Lords: Do you think the Lords is a democratic institution? Give reasons for your opinion.

7 Parliamentary procedure: Do you think the 'parliamentary day' is the most useful way to deal with matters of public policy and the enactment of law? Compare it with the practice of the parliamentary chamber in your own country.

8 Parliamentary committees: Why are parliamentary select committees valuable?

Chapter analysis and discussion

1 Find evidence in the text to support or contradict these statements:

a Britain is a completely democratic country.

b There is a balance in government between partisan politicians and an impartial Civil Service.

c The House of Lords is of little constitutional or political value.

d The first-past-the-post electoral system does not necessarily serve the electorate well.

2 Britain is a democracy, yet its people are not, as one might expect in a democracy, constitutionally in control of the state. Does this surprise you? If so, why?

3 Who rules Britain: the Crown, the Commons, the Lords, the Prime Minister, the Cabinet, the Civil Service? Where does the greatest power lie in your country?

4 If you were British, which political party would you support, and why?

Visual interpretation

Here is a diagramatic representation of the theoretical political hierarchy. Do you think it reflects reality? (Refer to "Westminster – the seat of Parliament".) If not, draw your own diagram.

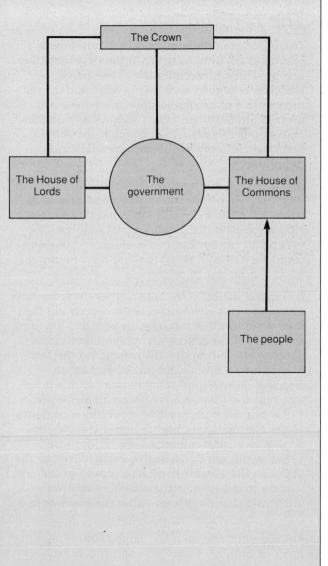

3 Government and politics: debate and change

The constitution

The previous chapter gives a brief and broad outline of the way in which Britain's constitution and government actually work. The practice, however, is a good deal more complex than the theory. This is inevitable since the system has evolved gradually and been shaped by tradition and precedent rather than through the definition of a coherent and logical constitutional framework.

In the eighteenth century, as a result of the 1688 political settlement, Britain was more democratic than any other European state and maintained its reputation as a democratic model well into the twentieth century. But is it a leader of European democracy today? Except among the complacent, there can be less certainty.

Increasing doubts have been voiced since the later 1970s and throughout the 1980s concerning the state of Britain's democracy. In part this has been the result of an apparently more authoritarian government during the 1980s fulfilling the fears of many that Britain did indeed endure an "elective dictatorship". One reason for this belief was that the Conservative governments of the 1980s had all been voted to power by a minority of the electorate, yet had reshaped the country according to that minority view. In the early 1980s, while the Conservative Party moved to the Right, so the Labour Party also moved to the Left, leading to a fear that the country might suffer unrestrained control from either the Right or Left.

However, underlying such fears was a more fundamental one, that the haphazard development of Britain's unwritten constitution was no longer a sufficient safeguard of democratic and individual rights. For critics of the present arrangement, the idea of the Crown in Parliament enshrined in the 1688 settlement no longer works since neither the Queen nor the Lords can effectively oppose a government which commands a majority in the Commons. In fact there is no constitutional protection at all either for the nation as a whole or for individuals against a political party commanding a majority in the Commons. By law even the courts cannot challenge the legislation of Parliament. In the words of Lord Scarman, one of Britain's most able lawyers, "An elected government untrammelled by constitutional limits or constraints, is a menace to our liberties whether it be a dictatorship of Right or Left, of a majority or a minority."

In 1988 a group of distinguished politicians, lawyers, academics, writers and journalists, including Lord Scarman, began to campaign under the title *Charter 88* (harking back to the charter of 1688) for wide-ranging reforms. They called for a Bill of Rights, to protect individual liberties, and for a written constitution to define and limit the powers of Parliament. Undoubtedly this call was partly explained by a belief that government during the 1980s had curtailed personal liberties more than any previous post-war government, particularly on the grounds of national security. Whether or not that belief was justified, it was undeniable that the British government during the decade had been found guilty of infringing the European Convention on Human Rights more often than any other member of the European Community. In 1990 the European Court of Justice made an historic decision, that British courts must suspend any Act of Parliament which imperils the rights of citizens guaranteed by European Community law. Parliamentary sovereignty is, therefore, being infringed. But the real clash between the English doctrine of parliamentary sovereignty and European law may have to await the occurrence of a case which Parliament chooses to fight.

Charter 88 also called for the reform of the House of Lords, to make it a democratic and non-hereditary chamber, and for the introduction of proportional representation (PR) to replace the current and distorting first-past-the-post electoral system. The latter demand was not new, since it had been called for by some politicians of the Right uneasy about Labour's dominance during the 1970s. And in the case of the House of Lords, there had been various proposals to abolish it since the nineteenth century.

A reform of the House of Lords is likely to be a major topic of debate in the 1990s, since Labour is pledged to reform it, making it an elected body. Because of the government's majority in the Commons since 1979, the Lords have emerged as the principal forum where changes have been made to government legislation. But a second *elected* chamber might threaten the present constitutional powers of the Commons. It is one thing for the Commons to reject legislative amendments by an unelected House of Lords, since they do not represent the people. It would be quite another matter for the Commons to

reject the amendments of an elected chamber. An elected upper chamber would have to be established with careful attention to the constitutional implications for the Commons, and the balance between the two chambers of Parliament.

With regard to proportional representation, the call for its introduction has become increasingly insistent since the 1980s. In part this has been a response to the duration throughout the decade of a government supported by only a minority of the electorate but enjoying an overwhelming majority in the Commons. But it also reflects the frustration of a large number of people who cast their vote for a negative reason, to keep one or other of the two major parties out of power. Such voters reflect a popular distrust of any party that strays far from the centre ground of British politics. They also reflect the fear that government can be controlled by a minority of the electorate.

These people believe that proportional representation would temper the power of any one party in the Commons and lead to more moderate government. The call for proportional representation was specifically advanced during the 1980s by the

Trooping the Colour, part of the ritual of royalty (see over).

alliance between the old Liberal Party and the new Social Democratic Party, which then merged to become the Liberal Democrats. Those advocating proportional representation increased in number during the 1980s. By the end of the decade a growing number, but still a minority, of Labour MPs supported the introduction of PR. A party decision on PR is likely to depend on the long-term electoral prospects of the Labour Party (see page 50).

There is a strong counter-argument in favour of the present first-past-the-post system, most keenly supported by members of the two main parties. These see defects in almost every proportional representation system practised in Europe, most importantly the danger of successive weak coalition governments. The distortion of the present system is, they claim, a virtue rather than a defect, since it ensures strong government. In a sense, therefore, the debate is about the balance between, and respective virtues of, strong government and strong democracy.

Such calls for constitutional reform are unlikely to disappear, and may become more insistent. The problem, of course, is that no government once elected will wish to restrict its powers. The idea of constitutional restrictions on Parliament's sovereignty is strongly opposed by leading members of the Labour Party. As Labour's deputy leader, Roy Hattersley, remarked in the mid 1980s, "British democracy is – for better or worse – based on absolute sovereignty of Parliament. . . . What Parliament has given away, Parliament can take back." This is precisely the point that reformers fear. A Bill of Rights without a written constitution which limited Parliament's sovereignty might prove worthless. It may be that only a constitutional crisis will persuade the electorate whether or not a written constitution is necessary.

The emergence of a strong but shortlived third force in British politics led to the natural fear of the election of a 'hung' Parliament, in 1983 and again in 1987. This did not happen but if it had, it might have triggered a grave constitutional crisis. If no party had been able to form a government, nor conclude a coalition agreement with another party, the Queen would have been in the difficult position of deciding how to resolve a constitutional deadlock. Indeed, it would have forced her to exercise powers which have long lain dormant. Even without a hung Parliament the monarch, through the phrase 'the Crown in Parliament' masks the effective sovereignty of the Prime Minister of the time. Without a written constitution what would happen if either the monarch or the Prime Minister decided the other was acting unconstitutionally? Such possibilities raise the whole question of the function of the monarchy in Britain at the end of the twentieth century.

The monarchy

The apparent solidity and permanence of custom and tradition are, of course, strong characteristics of British culture. But they are highly deceptive, for the institutions which appear to embody the permanence of these traditions are not static. The monarchy is a good example, since although it had already been limited by the constitutional revolution of 1688, its function began to change radically in the nineteenth century and has been changing ever since. In the nineteenth century, Queen Victoria's German husband, Albert, recognised more readily than his wife the fundamental changes taking place in society. If the monarchy had a future, it should no longer seek support from the rapidly declining old aristocracy (which had been important politically in the eighteenth century), but concentrate on the increasingly powerful urban classes created by the Industrial Revolution. Albert and Victoria began that process by making royalty more public, and consciously offering to the nation a model of family life. The middle and working classes of Britain's growing towns and cities loved it.

The government and old ruling élite, too, saw the monarchy as a useful means for stability in an age of rapid social and economic change. With Queen Victoria's Golden Jubilee in 1887, the government consciously remodelled the monarchy, laying emphasis on its ancient rituals as somehow embodying the soul of the nation. Most of the formalised ritual was invented at this time, giving the public a new sense of national identity after the massive upheavals of the Industrial Revolution. In short, the monarchy gave the public a romantic link with a largely imaginary past.

Had the First World War been lost, Britain, like Russia, Austria and Germany, might well have lost its monarchy. In fact, the monarchy emerged from this trial strengthened as the anchor of the nation. George V attended the first football Cup Final at Wembley and made skilful use of radio to become a truly popular monarch. George VI made the monarchy yet more popular by his refusal to leave London during air attacks on the capital during the Second World War. By remaining in Buckingham Palace after it was itself hit, and by tours of the most badly bombed parts of London, George VI and his consort, Elizabeth (the Queen Mother), became the most loved people of Britain.

Since then the monarchy has gone from strength to strength. Never before has the Royal Family been the subject of such national and international interest. Despite the obvious contradiction between democracy and monarchy, the Royal Family has remained immensely popular. There is a widely-held but contradictory attitude towards the monarchy, that on the one hand it is important because it embodies national identity, but on the other hand that it is merely a harmless but colourful part of our heritage.

Almost 80 per cent of the population are strongly in favour of the monarchy, and probably fewer than 10 per cent are opposed to it. Indeed the monarchy has penetrated so deeply into national consciousness, that many British, according to one book on the subject up to one third of the nation, at some stage in their lives dream about the Royal Family – for example, that the Queen is their mother, or that she comes to tea, or that the dreamer rescues some member of the Royal Family from some danger and enjoys the latter's undying gratitude. Comic as this may be, it reveals a popular state of mind, a fascination with royalty that hardly existed in previous centuries. In a country that prides itself on championing democracy, it can only be described as irrational.

This is what one spectator at the Queen's Coronation in 1953 had to say:

"I had a sudden feeling, craning at my glimpse of the bare-headed Queen at her anointing, sitting motionless with lowered eyes under her gold canopy, a sensation that was like something spoken aloud: 'There is a secret here.' . . . What was that secret, I could not say. No doubt it was a primitive and magical feeling which ancient and beautiful ceremonials still evoke, in no matter how rational a breast."
(Margaret Lane, The Queen is crowned. *New Statesman Coronation Issue* June 1953)

But perhaps most nations require some element of mystery or 'magic' in their sense of identity. For the British the monarchy effectively separates this element from executive power. There is a reverential, almost religious attitude to the sovereign. As Karl Marx's friend, Frederick Engels, remarked a century ago, "Nowhere is a non-ruling person more revered than in England."

Popular fascination means not only that approximately twenty books are published in Britain each year on the Royal Family, but popular magazines all over Europe feature British royalty frequently. Fascination and reverence go further. Even ordinary items used by the Queen, for example cutlery used on a royal visit somewhere, acquires sanctity and may be put on view for people to see. This reverential attitude is partly to do with that "magical feeling" but it is also to do with a British love of hierarchy.

The British expect both the sovereign and heir apparent to marry someone worthy of the honour, a member of foreign royalty or of the British nobility – another curious contradiction with the idea of democracy. The sanctity of the sovereign is such that she will shake hands but it is *she* who shakes the hand. Otherwise she may not be touched – since it implies disrespect to the royal personage. Prime Minister Margaret Thatcher and US President Reagan were on such good terms that they embraced when they met. The idea of the Queen embracing anyone apart from blood relatives or other royalty is unthinkable, however friendly she might be.

Popular deference during a royal visit.

Engels' remark was accurate in another sense, for although the Queen does embody the unity of the United Kingdom, she is very much England's Queen. There is a (slight) weakening in the sense of loyalty to the monarchy the further one travels away from the south east of England, either geographically into Wales and Scotland, or economically, among the unemployed of the north of England. In short, those on the outer edge of prosperous Britain identify less easily with the monarch.

The Royal Family find the adulation of the nation a major and constant challenge. Their position remains dependent on being seen, and on being seen to be a worthy symbol of the nation. They must therefore seek press attention, for without press coverage the Royal Family would lose most of their importance. Yet in doing so, the Royal Family run the constant risk of becoming a real-life version of a soap opera, a larger-than-life family drama with its heroes and villains. Soap operas are about glamour and tend to be undignified stories. The Royal Family, for all the coverage and all the gossip, must maintain a sense of dignity or they fail in their purpose. Those members who allow themselves to appear most like soap opera characters are the ones who also fall most easily into disrepute.

Royal dignity is expressed formally through the ceremonies invented at the end of the last century, but at a day-to-day level even clothing is chosen to ensure dignity. The Queen wears colourful clothes which meet the need to be visible in public (at home she almost always wears quiet colours), but otherwise her clothes are staid, a reminder that she stands for stability and continuity. She even wears a hat in public, a substitute crown. Prince Charles and his father, Prince Philip, always dress correctly for the occasion, another expression of stability increasingly out of tune with changes in popular fashion. But their style goes with the view Prince Charles expressed in 1981: "Monarchy is, I do believe, the system mankind has so far evolved which comes nearest to ensuring stable government." It is a message about the preservation of the existing order of things and about the powerful influence royalty must have on national life. The clothes Prince Charles wears must be seen to affirm this view of royalty. It is rumoured that Prince Charles owns a pair of jeans, but it is unlikely he will be seen wearing them. Even Princess Diana, the most fashion-conscious of royalty, does not merely follow fashion but leads it, her relative height and slender figure reinforcing the ideal, and becoming a fashion symbol for the nation.

Image for royalty is vital. In 1987 the press accused Princess Diana of a frivolity unsuitable for a future queen. Since then her image-makers have made sure that the serious and caring sides

Princess Anne visiting a Save the Children Fund project in the Sudan.

to her character have been noticed – sitting with AIDS victims in hospital, or shaking hands with lepers during an overseas tour. In this she follows the example set by Anne, the Princess Royal, whose work for the Save the Children Fund has earned her the respect of the nation.

Authority, even without power, is also essential for the British monarchy, but some wonder whether this is desirable. In practice, for example, the Queen is above the law, partly because judges are 'Her Majesty's Judges' and it is her law they exercise, but also because it is unthinkable that she or anyone in her immediate family should appear in court as a defendant. Their authority derives from many sources apart from constitutional ones, for example from their clothes and also from their speech. When Margaret Thatcher began to dress, as it was thought, like the Queen, and talked of 'We' (as royalty traditionally do) rather than 'I', many people resented her regal manner. Their style of education and their sporting image (horse riding, polo, and skiing) lend weight to their authority. It would be difficult, for example, for a state school-educated, football-playing, prince with a regional dialect to command the same respect.

Royal authority is expressed in other ways, ones which are careful to avoid the accusation of interference in political life, yet undoubtedly are. Every week the Queen receives the Prime Minister to discuss the matters of state, as she has been doing since 1952. This experience gives her immense authority. It is impossible that the Queen should always be in sympathy with her Prime Minister. During the miners' strike, 1984–5, for example, the Queen let it be known she wanted the government to make more effort to settle it. In November 1988, more controversies came to the surface. The Queen's concern over the growing gap between rich and poor in Britain – a result of government policy – filtered out into the press. A few days later it was rumoured that the Prime Minister had advised her not to accept any forthcoming invitation to visit the Soviet Union. It was considered improper advice, and Palace sources let it be known that the Prime Minister had been obliged to apologise. In two other areas of foreign policy the Queen let it be understood that she sharply differed from her Prime Minister, on British policy towards South Africa and also on relations with the rest of the Commonwealth. Such examples, and the considerable press coverage they receive, indicate the Queen's ability to support or undermine her Prime Minister.

Prince Charles has attracted even more comment for his interventions. He is in a difficult – indeed a unique – position. No Prince of Wales before him has been under such pressure to make a successful career of being Prince of Wales, with the reasonable expectation that he may not become king until he is over sixty. In spite of a view sometimes expressed in the right wing press, that intelligence is a drawback in royalty, Prince Charles has energetically made himself very well informed and active on a number of issues: homelessness and housing, inner city decay, small business enterprise among the unemployed, and most noticeably, architecture.

Such activities seem thoroughly worthy of a future king, and it is admirable that he has made it his business to be familiar with the social and economic ills of the nation. He is, in the words of one newspaper, "a more caring, knowledgeable and assiduous Prince of Wales than any previous occupant of the post". But it is impossible to be active without causing disagreement. His book *A Vision of Britain* (1989), which expressed his largely Post-Modern views on architecture, was received with approval by the general public which strongly favoured his 'human scale' views and hated much Modernist architecture. But many architects were angered by what they considered his ill-informed and conservative approach to their profession, and they resented the potentially damaging influence he could wield on account of his position. The problem for members of the Royal Family who take an active role in national life, is that while it may be thought desirable for the nation's wellbeing, it is hardly democratic.

There is great danger for the Royal Family in descending into potentially controversial areas of national life. Walter Bagehot, whose book *The English Constitution*, published in 1862, quickly became the classic analysis of the way in which Britain is governed, wrote of the Crown: "Its mystery is its life. We must not let in daylight upon magic. We must not bring the Queen into the combat of politics, or she will cease to be reverenced by all combatants; she will become one combatant among many."

Because this reverence still persists, relentless criticism of members of the Royal Family may be understood, in the words of one *Times* editorial, as an attack upon the very idea of Britain. Emotional feelings about the Royal Family are probably deeper than, for example, in any other European monarchy.

Prince Charles launching his book, A Vision of Britain.

Should the nation pay for an undemocratic institution? The Queen is reputed to be the wealthiest person in Britain. No one outside the Palace knows for sure the size of the Royal Family's private fortunes, but some press estimates put it at about £5 billion in 1988. The Palace will not disclose what it considers a private matter. The Queen's wealth is free of all taxes, which means that she is not subject to any of the taxes used to limit wealth acquisition among the richest people in the country.

Yet the Queen and other members of the Royal Family also receive a large sum from the taxpayer, known as the 'Civil List'. This, too, is free of tax, and is provided specifically to cover the expenses of the Royal Family in the discharge of its public duties. It is not a salary, and is provided for a ten-year period on an assumed rate of inflation for the period. As a result, at the beginning of the decade, in 1991, the Queen was allocated an annual income of £7.9 million, even though her predicted expenditure for 1991 was only £5.9 million. Although the intention is for the surplus at the beginning to offset a predicted shortfall towards the end of the decade, the government has guaranteed that it will make up any overall shortfall with an extra grant. On the other hand, if the actual rate of inflation is less than that predicted, there is no mechanism for the Queen to return to government the savings

that have been made. These savings become the Queen's own property.

The government has agreed on this ten-yearly payment because it agreed with the Palace that an annual request from the Queen for funds was undignified. But a government funding one of its own ministries in this way would be considered financially reckless.

In addition there are some conspicuously expensive items which are payed for by the taxpayer, for example the Royal Yacht *Britannia*, which by 1991 was costing the taxpayer £9.2 million yearly. The yacht has been justified through its dual role as a hospital ship, but it has never been used in this role in spite of the wars in the Falklands (1982) and the Gulf (1991). In 1990 the Royal Train cost £2.3 million to maintain and was also paid for by the taxpayer. One irritated journalist wrote in 1988, "Have a royal family if you must. But have a quiet one away from the tabloid headlines, have a frugal one . . . have a democratic one to whom *nobody* curtsies. And have one which pays for itself."

The debate about the role and cost of the monarchy will continue, but it is doubtful whether much will change before the end of the century. The monarchy, whether it is a rational institution for late twentieth-century Britain or not, is too popular.

The Royal Yacht, Britannia.

Government

During the early post-war period, up to the 1960s, the two-party system seemed to ensure good government. The combination of Cabinet government and party discipline in the Commons seemed to provide a balance between efficient government and public accountability. By the mid 1960s growing economic difficulties began to raise questions about the effectiveness of this kind of government. Many felt that greater long-term economic planning was required, and that this could only be achieved by reducing the major changes in policy following each change in government. By the early 1980s the growing centrist movement, characterised by the Social Democratic Party, aimed to "break the mould of the two-party system".

British governments have always been weak in securing the cooperation of the leadership of unions – the Trades Union Congress (TUC) – and of industry – the Confederation of British Industry (CBI). On the one hand governments tended to tell unions and management what they must do, rather than agree goals by discussion, and on the other, both the CBI and the TUC were unable to ensure the cooperation of their memberships. The CBI was unable to hold down the price of products, and the TUC was equally unable to hold down the level of wage claims. An effective government economic policy requires genuine cooperative planning between the three elements, government, industry and the unions. During the 1980s government went in the opposite direction, allowing industry to follow the market, and excluding the unions from any participation. Many question whether this approach has been any more successful, and it is probable that future governments in the 1990s will try to achieve a greater degree of economic consensus and planning.

Does government assemble the right talents to achieve such objectives? One criticism that has been made repeatedly since the 1980s is that Westminster provides too small a pool from which to draw sufficiently talented government ministers. According to one senior government adviser during the early 1980s the talent pool from which ministers were drawn would be wholly inadequate for any multinational corporation. For the civil servants of each department, however, there is the fear not only of ministers who fail to grasp the complexities of forging coherent policies but also of ministers who have strong ideas but ones

A trade union demonstration for better pay.

which the permanent departmental staff are convinced are fundamentally wrong. The criticism is not confined solely to ministers. There is also unease about the way in which all the senior Civil Service posts are filled by career civil servants. As with ministerial posts (which are confined to parliamentarians) there have been a number of experts calling for more open recruitment of top Civil Service posts from outside the more narrowly experienced Civil Service cadre.

There has also been a serious problem of overload, with ministers and civil servants trying to handle an increasing demand upon their time. This problem, of course, is not new, and the first attempt to assess and remedy it was made in the mid 1950s. Apart from the increased use of junior ministers, nothing very much happened. Almost forty years later the problem is worse than ever. One recommendation made then, but ignored, was to create regional bodies which could relieve central government of some of its burden. Although this has not yet happened, regional devolution is likely to be a governmental theme in the 1990s.

In fact, during the 1980s there was a move in the opposite direction, towards stronger, more authoritarian, central government. Edward Heath, for example, a previous Conservative Prime Minister, accused the government of authoritarian behaviour when he said, "I find it unparliamentary that the government not only takes no notice of amendments or proposals, but often fails to answer any questions that are put to it in debate."

Government secrecy also became a widely discussed issue in the 1980s. Despite discussion in the Commons, much of government in Britain has always gone on in secret. The Cabinet's tradition of secrecy conceals a much wider network hidden from public view. In constitutional theory power should reside in the Commons, yet there are probably about 200 formal committees working on different aspects of government policy under Cabinet direction. Yet with the exception of four – defence and overseas, economic strategy, home and social affairs, and legislation – which in 1979 the Prime Minister admitted existed, the remainder are secret. Officially they do not exist. All those who participate in these committees, both ministers and civil servants, may not disclose any discussion in these committees, nor even admit their existence. Yet these committees are the 'engine room' of government. According to constitutional theory, power should rest where the public can see it, but in practice Britain is governed by a largely hidden system.

While in opposition, Conservative and Labour Prime Ministers have called for more open government but almost without exception they have all maintained secrecy once in power. As one senior Cabinet minister remarked in the mid 1980s, "Margaret [Thatcher] doesn't even believe in open government for the Cabinet."

Yet governments also deliberately put information into the public arena on an unaccountable basis, sometimes to undermine the position of an uncooperative minister, as happened on several occasions during the 1980s (see 'Lobby' briefing, page 167). Such action invites similar behaviour from upset government servants, as also happened during the 1980s (see the Ponting affair, Chapter 10). As Prime Minister James Callaghan once joked, "You know the difference between leaking and briefing: leaking is what you do, briefing is what I do."

The Civil Service

Britain prides itself on a politically impartial Civil Service. This, in theory, is because the Civil Service Commissioners responsible for selecting civil servants are answerable to the Queen, and not to the Prime Minister. In 1984 there was a crisis when the government appointed a man outside the Civil Service to a senior post without first referring his name to the Commissioners. One Commissioner threatened to resign and said he would only agree to the government appointment if the government made a public apology and promised never to do the same again. He got his way.

The ethical quality of the Civil Service has been generally outstanding, higher than that expected in business or industry. For Peter Hennessy, the leading commentator on Britain's bureaucracy, its qualities are:

---

1) probity – there is no 'hand in the till'; 2) care with evidence and respect for reason; 3) a willingness to speak truth to those in power (i.e. ministers) but a readiness to carry out ministerial instructions to the contrary, if overruled; 4) an appreciation of the wider public interest when there is danger that the policy of central government is made without due care; 5) equity and fairness in treatment of the public; 6) a careful concern for the law; 7) a constant concern for Parliament, its needs and procedures – i.e. no lying and no misleading; 8) a constant concern for democracy.

These are incredibly high standards – achieved mainly through the maintenance of a tradition of exacting standards over the past century. It cannot be said that the Civil Service does not from time to time fall short of these standards. The highly popular television series, *Yes, Minister*, demonstrated how such high standards need not necessarily prevent devious cunning. One Cabinet Secretary in the 1980s became more famous for his admission that he had been "economical with the truth" than for anything else. Nevertheless, the standards remain, and are the qualities of which any Civil Service would rightly be proud.

However valuable such qualities might be, they do not guarantee an effective Civil Service. During the 1980s there was a growing debate concerning the ability of the Civil Service to respond to the demands of effective government. Peter Hennessy has suggested that the demands on central government in the twenty-first century might well be: short-term crisis management; medium-term planning for programmes proposed by a political party and adopted in Parliament; strategic thinking on central issues of the state, defence, energy, foreign policy, the welfare state and so forth; the management of tax gathering and social security; managing major services such as national health and education.

The problems of the Civil Service as these challenges approach, and as it nears the end of the century, are basically twofold: to cope more effectively and efficiently with the same overload which is felt by ministers and parliamentarians, and to divest itself of the 'institutional mentality' which can so easily determine policy.

At the end of the 1980s there was a growing recognition that the Civil Service is not a truly centralised body under a single professional head, but is more of a federation of departments, comparable with a multinational company, with a small headquarters (the Cabinet Office and Treasury) to which divisions and companies are answerable for their overall stewardship. In the past there had been an assumption that the head of each government department, the Permanent Secretary, was responsible for everything that happened in that department.

In 1989 an entirely new policy, entitled *The Next Steps*, was introduced under the direction of Margaret Thatcher herself. The only efficient answer to management problems, *The Next Steps* argued, was to evolve a new structure whereby many management decisions, previously referred to the Permanent Secretaries, could be delegated to a new body of managers. This would leave Permanent Secretaries and their colleagues free to concentrate primarily on policy matters.

As a result of *The Next Steps*, large monolithic departments are now being broken down into executive agencies. In 1989 management of the National Health Service was detached from its parent ministry, the Department of Health, and the Department of Social Services began to be divided into a number of executive agencies, each responsible for providing a measurably more efficient service to the public. Almost thirty such agencies in different government departments were in operation by the end of 1990.

Breaking up large ministries into such executive agencies is extremely complex. Further delegation of financial and managerial powers is planned, freeing senior civil servants from responsibility for the smaller details of departmental spending and

for developing management skills at lower levels. By the end of the century three quarters of the Civil Service are expected to be in executive agencies. Major doubts, however, surround this major reform. In the past, the Civil Service was able to attract some of the best brains in the country, and these were applied to both policy and management of government services. Will the executive agencies be able to attract the same quality as the residual, but clearly more attractive policy departments? It may well take time for such doubts to be clarified.

The other fundamental problem is the paralysing effects all institutions suffer from when tradition, or institutional mentality, determines the conduct of affairs. This danger is particularly great in an organisation which recruits its managers direct from university, in effect earmarking its top managers thirty years before they assume the top posts. Can this be right?

The present system largely excludes non-Civil Service entry into Whitehall's higher ranks. It is natural that the Civil Service, despite its high quality, should in part acquire its own institutional view of the world, one that tends to be resistant to ideas from outside. The idea of a self-perpetuating 'caste' or cadre is perhaps most strongly seen in the diplomatic service. In 1988, out of 667 in the top cadre of diplomats, 484 had studied either at Oxford or Cambridge University. Out of the top 800 not one had attended polytechnic rather than university, only one in ten was female, only one of the 800 was black. But even in the rest of the Civil Service one need only look at the background of its top people to recognise there is strong uniformity of background. Of the 32 Permanent Secretaries in 1988, thirteen had studied at Oxford and eight at Cambridge, three at the London School of Economics. Barely any Permanent Secretaries had entered the Civil Service in mid-life from outside the system. The overwhelming proportion had entered direct from university. It had been widely assumed that the pattern was becoming more varied. But research in 1990 showed that the proportion of Permanent Secretaries who were university graduates increased from 83 per cent in the years 1945–64, to 93 per cent in the years 1965–86. Furthermore, only 13.7 per cent of Permanent Secretaries, during the years 1965–86, had joined the Civil Service after gaining another kind of professional experience, compared with 48 per cent at the beginning of the century, 1900–19.

If fewer candidates were recruited direct from university to fill the top cadre, and if more were recruited direct from the private sector – business, industry and the professions – for the three highest grades, it might make for a more effective, efficient and responsive government machine. It might also make sense to open more posts in specialised areas to scientists and professionals from outside.

Parliament: in need of reform?

Is Parliament really sovereign, or is it merely a 'rubber stamp' for government, as many critics say? Because any government, by definition, enjoys a majority in the House, in practice Parliament's main function is hardly to pass legislation. That is done by the government and its supporters. As one parliamentary report in 1978 noted, "The balance of advantage between Parliament and Government in the day-to-day working of the Constitution is now weighted in favour of the Government to a degree which arouses widespread anxiety. . . ."

It was for this reason that over fifty Commons Select Committees were established soon after. Although these were not given the power to compel evidence from ministers, both ministers and officials have increasingly, and voluntarily, testified to them. Since 1980 these committees have had the power to act not only as policy investigators but as legislative committees as well. Commons Select Committees have undoubtedly strengthened Parliament's power against deaf government.

The real function of the Commons is as a forum in which to examine and criticise government administration. As Bernard Weatherill, Speaker of the House in the late 1980s, remarked, "Government has to come to the House of Commons every day and go on trial." Its other important function is to prepare young politicians for holding office in government.

Yet there is wide unease concerning the functioning of Parliament as a check on government. Margaret Thatcher, for example, increasingly abandoned parliamentary debate in favour of more easily managed public performance. She compared badly with previous Prime Ministers. On average she made a speech every 49 parliamentary days, compared with the average of every 24 days for other Prime Ministers since 1945. She intervened in debates every 110 parliamentary days, compared with every 14 days in the case of her post-war predecessors. She became a far harder target for the Opposition to attack, since she was less frequently exposed to the dangers of parliamentary debate. It remains to be seen whether future Prime Ministers will also avoid the perils of the Commons as much as possible.

Some older MPs also regret that the Commons is no longer as disorderly as it used to be, with real outbursts of passion by members on both sides of the House. As one senior Conservative MP remarked in 1989, "The present Tory backbenchers don't even begin to compare with those of, say, the 1930s. Then there was a more consistent threat of independence." The decline of independence results from the steady increase in party discipline and the knowledge among many backbench MPs that if they hope for government office one day, they must avoid any public challenge of party policy. As Labour has discovered to its cost, allowing members greater freedom to express personal views easily creates an impression of division and disagreement over fundamental policy, and it was easy for the Conservatives, with stronger party discipline in the 1980s, to present Labour to the electorate as unfit to govern while it remained incapable of internal agreement. Somehow parliamentary government must find a balance between the increasingly authoritarian presentation of party policy and the disorderly or disobedient behaviour of party members which have shown Parliament at its best, as the national forum for passion and principle.

The quality of Parliament also depends upon the importance given it. British MPs are among the worst paid and worst equipped legislators. As a result of this low level of pay, 72 per cent of MPs have some kind of outside employment. One in three MPs act as paid parliamentary consultant for some outside organisation or company, with duties ranging from speaking in the House to advice on parliamentary tactics. By the end of the 1980s a growing number were working for public relations companies specialising in lobbying. Some research assistants to MPs were in reality full-time employees of lobbying companies.

Not only are the MPs among the worst paid, but the Commons also sits for twice as many hours as most Western legislatures. An average backbencher spends sixty-seven hours per week on parliamentary business while Parliament is sitting, and forty-eight hours while it is in recess. Much of this heavy load, incidentally, results from European Community-inspired business.

How should the burden be lightened? In 1957, the Liberal leader, Clement Davies, wrote to Prime Minister Harold Macmillan:

"Not only are ministers overworked but MPs are overworked. In both cases their energies are to a very considerable extent devoted to matters with which they should not be directly and personally concerned. The Parliament of Westminster should be concerned with general policy, both at home and abroad, and it should be relieved of duties which could be undertaken and better performed by regional sub-Parliaments or councils."

In 1989 Professor Crick, an expert on the workings of Parliament, remarked that Britain needed "federation for the United Kingdom . . . which would not be like any other kind of federation. . . . Obviously a British federation would be a relationship between the centre and different nations with very different needs, not a uniform thing." By coincidence, within hours of this statement, the Labour Party pledged a future Labour government to the establishment of a Scottish Assembly. It is likely that this would be followed by calls for a Welsh Assembly, and possibly for English regional ones as well. In 1979 a referendum in Scotland had failed to attract sufficient support for a national assembly, while the Welsh actually voted against an assembly of their own. Since the governing party, the Conservatives, won only 14 per cent of the Scottish seats and 21 per cent of Welsh ones in the 1987 election, the resurgence of regionalism – and greater freedom from the consequences of the English vote – is likely to be a theme during the 1990s.

On 21st November 1989 the House of Commons was televised in debate for the first time. The most remarkable aspect of this innovation was that it had been resisted for thirty years, since it had been first proposed in 1959. Many MPs feared that the public would not react favourably to what they saw and that this might lead to pressure for reform. There is a distinct difference between what viewers might see live from the Commons, and the carefully arranged public appearances of senior politicians. During the 1980s the art of political presentation had been strongly influenced by professional advertisers, themselves influenced by what happens in politics in the United States. Indeed, during the 1980s

government spending on advertising and publicity increased fivefold. It was not surprising therefore that the government was particularly reluctant to allow the public to see the 'unmanaged' debates in the Commons.

As a result strict rules were applied, much stricter than in the Lords, which had been televised since 1984. These were designed to prevent the public seeing undignified aspects of Commons life, like outbreaks of anger or uproar, or even the Speaker obtaining advice on procedure. Critics felt that if Parliament genuinely embodied the dignity of real liberty, nothing could be more undignified than censoring what happened in Parliament in this way. Even the BBC regretted the rules as denying viewers "a full, impartial and meaningful impression of events". Yet, even with such restrictions, the measure has probably increased confidence and interest in the political process of the Commons, a condition vital to the effectiveness of British democracy.

People and political parties

It is, perhaps, inevitable that with a growing debate about the kind of government Britain should have, and about its unwritten constitution, there has also been increasing discussion of the need for electoral reform.

However, before considering the introduction of proportional representation, the idea dominating all discussion of reform, it would be useful to consider the changing pattern within the current electoral system. Any examination of the electoral results in the period 1979–87 shows a growing north–south divide in the way people vote. There has always been a preponderance of Conservative voters in England, and particularly the south, while Labour's strongholds have tended to be in the industrial centres of the Midlands and the north.

This pattern has grown stronger, as Labour's declining hold on the south east indicates. Until 1979 Labour had won many seats in the south and east of Britain, particularly in London. Even in its defeat in 1979, it still could win thirty-six out of eighty-four parliamentary seats in Greater London and fifteen other seats in the south and east. But by 1987 it could win only twenty-three seats in Greater London and two in the rest of the south. Seen from Scotland or Wales, both strongly Labour, the Conservative Party now dominates England's politics, and the most strongly Conservative region, the south, dominates the rest of the country.

Another change which happened during the 1979–89 decade was the polarisation of the general geographical voting pattern. Conservative constituencies became more Conservative, Labour ones became more strongly Labour. This has led to fewer 'marginal' parliamentary seats and more predictably 'safe' ones, hardly helping a lively democratic system.

Labour could expect to go on winning overwhelmingly in Wales and Scotland and in the north of England. But the majority of constituencies are in the south of England, where the population is most dense, and the population of the south is growing while in many of the Labour areas of the country the population is either static or shrinking. This is not merely a north–south divide, but also a city–county one too. Labour's strongholds have always been the great cities, particularly the six metropolitan areas. However, since the last constituency boundary changes in 1976, there has been a population movement away from these metropolitan areas into the suburbs, smaller towns and commuter villages of the Conservative dominated shires. In 1993 the next boundary changes will be made, and based on these demographic shifts, they will almost certainly lead to an increase of about twenty seats in Conservative areas, and a corresponding loss in traditional Labour ones.

Consequently, in order to prevent continued Conservative victories during the 1990s, Labour (with or without the assistance of a third party) has to increase its support very substantially among all classes in order to win some of the safe Conservative seats in the south. In the past a swing from one party to the other of 3 or 4 per cent would assure it of election victory. For Labour this is no longer so. At the outset of the 1990s it needed a swing of more than 10 per cent overall, but with the prospect that if the demographic shift continued, it would have to increase this swing progressively through the 1990s to be assured of winning subsequent general elections. Otherwise, Labour's future is one of progressive electoral weakness.

While the geographical divide has increased, the class divide has diminished and is likely to continue doing so. In the past Labour could count on the solid support of manual and most skilled workers throughout the country. The working class, 47 per cent of the electorate in 1964, was only 34 per cent by 1983, while the middle class – managers, professionals, supervisors and white-collar workers – increased from 36 to 51 per cent in the same period.

In addition there was a great change in outlook during the period of Thatcher government. This was partly a result of the changing mood of the 1980s, with an emphasis on individualism encouraged by government. But it was also the specific result of the Thatcher policies of encouraging the electorate to buy shares in the newly privatised industries, and of encouraging council tenants to purchase their homes from the local authority. As a result, among those who bought the new shares, many of whom were traditional Labour supporters and had never bought shares before, 54 per cent voted Conservative in 1987. The Conservatives also won a larger share (36 per cent) of the vote of manual workers in 1987 than ever before. This swing was highest in the south of England. Conservative encroachment among skilled workers, also part of the traditional Labour vote, was even greater. In 1979 Labour won 45 per cent of the skilled-worker vote. By 1987 this had fallen to 34 per cent.

If Labour lost much of its solid blue-collar, or manual worker, support – by both shrinkage and desertion – during the 1980s, the Conservatives also found that support from the middle classes fell slightly in each election. In 1987 they obtained only 55 per cent of the middle-class vote, the lowest since 1974. Among university graduates the Conservatives suffered a 9 per cent drop in support during the period 1979–87.

It is possible to say that while class – blue-collar or white-collar – was still the main determinant of the way people voted in the 1970s, by 1990 tenure was increasingly important: whether voters owned their own home, or owned shares. Class identities, particularly in the south, have been in decline, but the pattern of change is uneven. For example, in 1987 barely half London's electorate voted according to class identity, but more than three quarters of Glasgow's did.

The decline in voting loyalty by class has also resulted in a decline in overall loyalty for the two major parties. In 1951 97 per cent of the vote went to one or other major party, but by 1987 this had fallen to 73 per cent. In the 1980s both main parties received their lowest share of the national vote since the 1920s, a worrying development for both of them. In fact, by the end of the 1980s much voting was negative: to keep a

Don't forget to register by Monday 18th November.

Phone 0272 272 272. You could buy a bit of BT.

The privatisation of British Telecom: advertising the chance to buy shares.

disliked party out of power. About half the whole electorate is reckoned to have switched its voting preference at some stage.

Given the overall trends described above, the situation is more serious for Labour than the Conservatives. But can Labour reverse the process? The long-term trend shows a persistent decline in support. As a leading Labour politician foresaw in 1959, "The Labour Party will probably decline . . . by about 2 per cent at each successive general election." Taking into account variations from one election to another, this prophecy has been reasonably accurate. By 1992 it could expect only 35 per cent of the national vote, based on traditional voting patterns. In order to change this trend, Labour must widen its appeal in the 1990s to capture the centre ground, but without losing the old, if shrinking, working-class loyalty it enjoys.

If Labour's long-term prospects (even if it wins an election in the 1990s) are discouraging, should it consider supporting the introduction of proportional representation? This way it would have a better chance of defeating the Conservatives, but it would probably necessitate forming a coalition with the centre party, the Liberal Democrats. This is likely to become a growing debate in Labour ranks during the 1990s. By 1990 probably almost half of Labour's MPs favoured some kind of electoral reform.

However, a majority of both main parties are critical of PR as operated by other members of the European Community. They do not wish to lose the present constituency system, and fear that PR would result in government paralysis as the price of fairness. The Conservative Party is likely to remain strongly hostile to PR, since the present constituency system increasingly works in the Conservatives' favour. The present system offers a greater assurance of strong government, which Conservatives particularly favour. Centre party support for PR, on the other hand, is grounded in bitter experience. In 1983 centre parties attracted 22.6 per cent of the national vote, but gained only 3.4 per cent of seats in the Commons. But the Liberal Democrats have little chance of achieving the introduction of PR unless it is also adopted by Labour.

It is only once it is in power that Labour will be able to introduce such a major electoral reform. Yet once it is in power it has less incentive to do so, unless it looks to its own long-term future.

Proportional representation remains an attractive option for many, possibly a majority of voters. The more the two-party system becomes predictable both in its overall and in its local results, the less reason people have to participate. Already there has been a decline in voting in Scotland and in rural Wales, reflecting frustration and alienation. The greater the sense of deprivation and distance from London, the greater the proportion of the electorate that does not bother to vote. If people on the outer periphery of national life, either geographically or economically, continue to abstain in elections, there is a growing argument in favour of a system that, because their vote has significance, draws them back into electoral participation.

The challenge to the political parties

The changing character of the electorate obviously has long-term implications for Britain's political parties. It was the political centre which first recognised the basic changes taking place. By the end of the 1980s, an analysis of surveys carried out over more than ten years showed class loyalties slowly giving way to a new system of values.

According to this analysis, there are three broad categories of voter, although it is admitted that few voters fitted these characteristics exactly. First, there are those concerned with survival and security, who value the virtues of loyalty and solidarity. They are generally people on lower incomes who vote Labour. They are about 30 per cent of the population and are in decline. Second, there are those ambitious for success, wealth or power, for whom outward appearances are important. They are 'self-made', natural Conservative voters. By 1990 these were reckoned to be 34 per cent of the population, but also in decline. Third, there are those concerned with personal development and individual freedom, with a tendency towards strong moral motivation, for example concern about world ecology, nuclear power or weapons, or civil liberties. Such people constitute 36 per cent of the population and are increasing.

The Liberal Democrats were the first to make political use of this survey, to demonstrate that their own political views most closely reflect the growing third category. Although this is undeniable, it is less clear whether they can attract voters to vote for them. At the end of the 1980s the Liberal Democrats were still without an issue with which the electorate could easily identify, except for the introduction of PR. Yet until PR is introduced, the Liberal Democrats can only hope for electoral progress based upon negative voting – the hostility of some voters to the dominant party – in the south, the Conservatives and in the north, Labour. From their viewpoint it is a frustrating position.

With its own traditional vote shrinking, Labour will try to capture as much of this third category as possible. As long as the electoral system remains unchanged, and as long as Labour remains the only realistic alternative to the Conservatives, it is likely to win the larger share. After 1979 Labour had fallen apart, to the point where its future was in serious question. It was widely seen by the electorate to have fallen under the control of the extreme Left. During the second half of the 1980s the Labour leadership slowly regained its authority and began to present a more attractive policy to the electorate. By 1990 its policies had moved towards the centre so that in many areas they were hardly different from those of the Liberal Democrats.

In the process Labour has thrown off some of its less popular traditional characteristics. Although it has never been truly socialist, it has tried to dispel the idea that it intends to return to the nationalisation of major industries, or that it intends central economic planning. It has now accepted, in a way it did not up to the mid 1980s, more use of market forces and less central control. But, in the words of one senior Labour politician, it believes that "a socialist willingness to intervene in the national interest in order to make good the deficiencies of the market is a necessary ticket to our industrial future". In practice this means encouraging diversity, individual enterprise, decentralised economic organisation and more consumer choice. In addition, although traditionally suspicious of Britain's membership of the European Community, from 1987 Labour openly supported full participation as essential to the country's political and economic future.

By 1990 Labour also openly accepted that the trade unions had wielded too much power in the past and had also been too undemocratic. It still faced the challenge of finding how the trade unions could continue to play a role in the party without dominating it. The power of the unions is still expressed through the 'block vote'. Each union affiliated to the Labour Party can cast its membership's votes for or against policies proposed at the annual Labour Party conference. Out of a party electorate of just over 6 million, 5.7 million votes belong to the unions, overwhelmingly to sixteen large ones. When unions were much smaller, and each with its own view, this process made some sense, but in the 1980s several large unions to a great extent controlled Labour's policies. Yet Labour no longer represents the unions as strongly as it once did. In the 1964 election 73 per cent of trade unionists voted Labour. By 1987 this had fallen to 43 per cent. What voting power should the unions therefore have?

For Labour the difficulty is that it is almost entirely dependent on the unions for its funding. In 1986 6.9 million trade union members were contributing to party funds. Under the 1984 Act, every ten years each union must ballot its members to see if they wish to continue contributing to party funds. Labour must find an acceptable balance between representing union concerns sufficiently to maintain its financial base, and appealing to the wider public which is deeply suspicious of union power. Making this adjustment is likely to be an important theme for Labour in the 1990s.

Just as Labour depends financially on the unions, so the Conservative Party depends upon big financial and industrial companies for support. A survey in 1989 showed that 333 companies gave £4.5 million to the Conservative Party (or close associates) during 1988. Another £9 million was received from undisclosed sources, probably from both companies and private individuals. Thus the Conservatives, as much as Labour, remain financially identified with their traditional support base.

Like Labour, too, the Conservatives may need to change the basis of their appeal during the 1990s. 'Thatcherism', a rightist interpretation of Conservatism, which believed in a wholly free market economy and wanted to reduce the role of the welfare state, was increasingly unpopular by the end of the 1980s. After ten years of 'Thatcherite revolution' opinion polls suggested that more people wanted a planned economy than uncontrolled capitalism, and almost four out of five considered the creation of wealth less important than the creation of a more caring society. More than half those questioned also said they were willing to pay higher taxes in order to obtain better public services.

With the succession of John Major as Prime Minister in 1990, the Conservative Party began quietly to retreat from the Thatcherite emphasis of the 1980s in order to attract the growing third category of voters sought also by Labour and the Liberal Democrats. Within a year of Mrs Thatcher's departure, Conservative resistance to closer integration into the European Community had moderated considerably; hostility to a modicum of economic planning to modify the bad effects of the free market abated; and it seemed probable that some of the local government powers removed by Mrs Thatcher, and believed by many Party members to be dangerously undemocratic, might be restored.

In the early 1990s the policies of the Labour, Conservative and Liberal Democrat Parties were coming closer again. Indeed, it could be said that the differences between the right of Labour through the Liberal Democrats to the left of the Conservatives, were less than the differences *within* either the Labour or Conservative Parties. All this will continue to make the ability to maintain party discipline a basic test of fitness to govern. Yet it is the possibility of a decline in party discipline and an increase in loyalty to specific issues by individual members which will give the role of Parliament a new lease of life.

Questions

Section analysis

1 The constitution: If Britain has managed perfectly well since 1688 without a written constitution, why should it need one now? Give your own opinion.

2 The monarchy: Do you think the Royal Family is of benefit to Britain? Give reasons for your answer.

3 Government: Questions are being raised about the effectiveness of the British system of government. What are they? What changes would you propose?

4 The Civil Service: What two basic challenges, according to the author, face the British Civil Service today? Which of these two challenges is being tackled and which, apparently, is not?

5 Parliament: In what ways can Parliament act as a check on the power of the government? Do you think Parliament's powers should be greater?

6 People and political parties: Why has the Labour Party become progressively weaker, whatever its ideology?

7 Find evidence in the text to support or contradict these statements:

a People still vote according to class loyalties.

b Labour has moved away from its less popular, traditional policies.

c Conservative policies are Thatcherite policies.

Chapter analysis and discussion

1 There are varying levels of demand for the following reforms to Britain's political system:

a Protection of individual liberties

b The introduction of a written constitution

c Reform of the House of Lords

d The introduction of proportional representation

e Changes in financing the monarchy

f Greater openness in government

g Reorganising the Civil Service

List those reforms which you think are necessary in order of importance, and give your reasons.

2 A famous novelist, John Buchan, wrote in the 1930s: "The essence of the British Monarchy is that the king, while lifted far above the nation, should also be the nation itself in its most characteristic form."

Is this desirable? Do you think this is true of the Queen?

Visual interpretation

Consider the opinion poll below.

1 Imagine you are British and respond to the questions. What are the points on which you a) agree and b) disagree with majority British views most?

2 What points made in the chapter are confirmed, in your view, by this opinion poll?

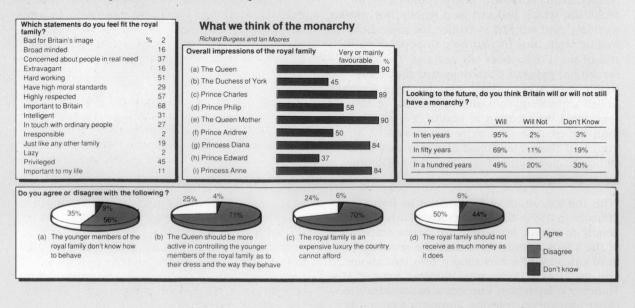

Which statements do you feel fit the royal family?

	%
Bad for Britain's image	2
Broad minded	16
Concerned about people in real need	37
Extravagant	16
Hard working	51
Have high moral standards	29
Highly respected	57
Important to Britain	68
Intelligent	31
In touch with ordinary people	27
Irresponsible	2
Just like any other family	19
Lazy	2
Privileged	45
Important to my life	11

What we think of the monarchy

Richard Burgess and Ian Moores

Overall impressions of the royal family — Very or mainly favourable %

	%
(a) The Queen	90
(b) The Duchess of York	45
(c) Prince Charles	89
(d) Prince Philip	58
(e) The Queen Mother	90
(f) Prince Andrew	50
(g) Princess Diana	84
(h) Prince Edward	37
(i) Princess Anne	84

Looking to the future, do you think Britain will or will not still have a monarchy?

?	Will	Will Not	Don't Know
In ten years	95%	2%	3%
In fifty years	69%	11%	19%
In a hundred years	49%	20%	30%

Do you agree or disagree with the following?

(a) The younger members of the royal family don't know how to behave — 35% / 9% / 56%

(b) The Queen should be more active in controlling the younger members of the royal family as to their dress and the way they behave — 25% / 4% / 71%

(c) The royal family is an expensive luxury the country cannot afford — 24% / 6% / 70%

(d) The royal family should not receive as much money as it does — 6% / 50% / 44%

Agree / Disagree / Don't know

4 The forces of law and order

In 1989 four Irishmen, known as the 'Guildford Four', were released after fifteen years' imprisonment, when it was revealed that the police interrogation on which they had been convicted in 1974 had not been properly conducted. The four had been imprisoned for planting a bomb in a Guildford pub which had killed a number of people. At the time there had been great popular outrage and a determination to bring those responsible to justice. But the wrong men were imprisoned.

One of the Guildford Four on their release.

The release of the Guildford Four came at the end of many years' campaigning led by prominent figures in British life, the Catholic Archbishop of Westminster and two Law Lords, Lord Scarman and Lord Devlin. Their release caused the government, the judiciary and the police considerable embarrassment for three main reasons: the police had obtained confessions by improper methods of interrogation; certain vital facts which would have established the innocence of the accused did not emerge in court although these facts were known to the police; and finally, previous appeals had been unsuccessful, indicating how hard it was to persuade the judiciary that a mistake might have been made, and to overturn a previous decision.

The release of the Guildford Four occurred at a time when the way the legal system in England and Wales worked was being questioned by a new reforming Lord Chancellor, Lord Mackay, whose experience had been within the Scottish legal system.

The legal system of England and Wales

The law is one of the most traditional areas of national life and the legal profession has jealously protected its position against outside attack. Its main virtue is its independence from the system of government and as such, a safeguard of civil liberties. Its main vice lies in its resistance to reform, and the maintenance of its own privileges which may be contrary to public interest.

The legal system for England and Wales (there are separate ones for Scotland and Northern Ireland) does not have a criminal or civil code, but is founded upon two basic elements: Acts of Parliament or statute law, and common law which is the outcome of past decisions and practices based upon custom and reason. Common law has slowly built up since Anglo-Saxon times one thousand years ago, while Parliament has been enacting statutes since the thirteenth century. Generally speaking, almost all criminal law is now set out in Acts of Parliament, while the greater part of civil law still depends upon common law, the weight and guidance of previous similar decisions.

A Crown Court in session may not be photographed.

Dealing with crime

The initial decision to bring a criminal charge normally lies with the police, but since 1986 a Crown Prosecution Service (CPS) has examined the evidence on which the police have charged a suspect to decide whether the case should go to court. Generally it brings to court only those cases which it believes will be successful, a measure to avoid the expense and waste of time in bringing unsound cases to court.

There are two main types of court, magistrates' courts (or courts of first instance), which deal with about 95 per cent of criminal cases, and Crown Courts for more serious offences. All criminal cases above the level of magistrates' courts are held before a jury.

There are about 700 magistrates' courts in England and Wales, served by approximately 28,000 unpaid or 'lay' magistrates or Justices

of the Peace (JPs), who have been dealing with minor crimes for over 600 years. JPs are ordinary citizens chosen from the community. In the past there has been a tendency for these to be white, male and middle class. In recent years, however, women and members of ethnic minority communities have been recruited to give a more representational balance.

A court normally consists of three lay magistrates who are advised on points of law by a legally qualified clerk. They may not impose a sentence of more than six months imprisonment or a fine of more than £2,000, and may refer cases requiring a heavier penalty to the Crown Court.

A Crown Court is presided over by a judge, but the verdict is reached by a jury of twelve citizens, randomly selected from the local electoral rolls. The judge must make sure that the trial is properly conducted, that the 'counsels' (barristers) for the prosecution and defence comply with the rules regarding the evidence that they produce and the examination of witnesses, and that the jury are helped to reach their decision by the judge's summary of the evidence in a way which indicates the relevant points of law and the critical issues on which they must decide in order to reach a verdict. Underlying the whole process lies the assumption that the person charged with an offence is presumed to be innocent unless the prosecution can prove guilt "beyond all reasonable doubt".

Like Parliament, Crown Courts are adversarial, contests between two opposing parties. Neither the prosecution nor defence counsel is concerned to establish the *whole* truth about the accused person. Both may well wish to avoid aspects which weaken their case that the accused person is either guilty beyond reasonable doubt or that sufficient reasonable doubt exists for that person to be declared "not guilty". Had, for example, the whole *known* truth been revealed in court in the case of the Guildford Four, they would almost certainly have been acquitted.

A person convicted in a magistrates' court may appeal against its decision to the Crown Court. An appeal against a decision of the Crown Court may be taken to the Court of Appeal (Criminal Division), but it is seldom successful. The Court of Criminal Appeal dislikes overturning a Crown Court decision unless the evidence is overwhelming or there has been some error of legal procedure. The highest court in the land is the House of Lords, which will consider a case referred from the Court of Appeal where a point of general public importance seems to be at stake. In practice the Lords are represented by five or more of the nine Law Lords.

The treatment of offenders

The sentence passed on an offender is decided by the judge or magistrate, within the limits for the offence set down by Act of Parliament. Punishment may take the form of a fine, imprisonment, or probation under the supervision of a professional probation officer. The death penalty was suspended in 1965 and abolished in 1969. Had it still been in force six years later, the Guildford Four would almost certainly have been hanged. Their release in 1989 probably spells an end to efforts by some MPs, supported by over half of the electorate, to reintroduce hanging. The wrongful

conviction of innocent people discredits the finality of hanging.

Imprisonment is used significantly more in Britain than elsewhere in Europe: at the end of the 1980s for 18 per cent of those who came before the courts. In 1989 Britain had a detention rate of 97.4 per 100,000 of the population, ahead of Turkey, with 95.6 per 100,000 of the population. In the words of the director of a rehabilitation organisation in 1988, "Not only do we use prison significantly more than neighbouring European countries with similar crime rates, we have also sharply increased our readiness to imprison offenders over the last decade."

Since the beginning of the 1980s the state of prisons has been a controversial subject, partly because of the government belief that many offenders are not being properly punished and partly as a result of repeated disorders in British prisons.

The main causes of such riots have been the very overcrowded conditions in which most prisoners serve their sentences, and the decaying and primitive conditions of many prisons. A nineteenth-century prison in Leeds, for example, was designed to accommodate 642 prisoners, but in 1988 was actually holding 1,345. Wandsworth Prison in London was described by its board of visitors as "disgusting and degrading", lacking adequate lavatory facilities. As a result of such poor conditions and overcrowding the prison staff, as well as the prisoners, suffer from low morale.

Inside a nineteenth-century prison.

In 1990 a major riot at a nineteenth-century prison, Strangeways, in Manchester, ended only after a siege lasting almost a month, during which two men died, and millions of pounds' worth of damage had been done to the buildings. Although it is generally recognised that far too many offenders are imprisoned, the prison population in England and Wales alone increased from 42,000 in 1978 to 47,000 in 1986, and is expected to reach about 56,000 by 1994. The level for all Britain had reached 56,000 by 1989. Yet government only began to encourage judges to reduce the number of prison sentences, or the length of sentence at the end of the 1980s decade.

An unhappy aspect of the system is the imprisonment of some of those awaiting trial. At one remand centre, Risley, this led to ten suicides during the 1980s, creating public outcry. Several were young adults, aged between seventeen and twenty. Risley already had a poor record. It had been built in 1964 and by 1969 there had already been twelve suicides there. As one newspaper remarked, "It is a poor reflection on British attitudes to offenders of any sort that a remand centre could be custom-built in the 1960s without internal lavatories." The Chief Inspector of Prisons described Risley as barbarous and squalid. The average time spent in Risley awaiting trial is eight weeks, but some spend as much as a year there. Furthermore, 5 per cent are acquitted, and another 35 per cent are then given non-prison sentences. Time spent in remand centres like Risley is unlikely to reconcile offenders to society. Yet during the period 1978–89 the number detained on remand almost doubled, from 5,500 to 10,500.

Young offenders

The age of criminal responsibility is ten (except in Scotland where it is eight). Children between the ages of ten and seventeen usually appear before a juvenile court, where it is decided whether the child should continue to live within the family, subject to supervision, or whether he or she should be taken into local authority care (with foster parents or in a community home). Such offenders normally attend special schools. Some are required to attend special centres on Saturdays, for leisure activities and skills training. Some are required to do community service. All arrangements must be reviewed every six months. Such arrangements may seem responsible, but are

they adequate? Britain has a serious problem with young offenders. The peak age for committing crime is fifteen. One in four criminal offences is committed by teenagers under sixteen. By that time crime is for many already a lifestyle.

Hardly surprisingly, concern has grown in recent years at the high number of re-offenders among those under seventeen taken into care or put into detention centres. One alternative, the 'supervision-in-the-community' scheme started in 1987, was able to show that the re-offence rate among those it had helped was half that of similar offenders who had been sent to prison. This new approach is being encouraged by the government.

As a result of serious incidents, such as occurred at Strangeways and Risley, there will probably be pressure for reform of the penal system in the 1990s. In 1987 a government-appointed commission made two recommendations: first, the creation of humane conditions and a sense of purpose for prisoners during their time inside prisons; second, a major reduction in the length of prison sentences and in the number sent to prison, with alternative arrangements like supervised housing, probation hostels, community service schemes and other kinds of supervised work projects. Neither of these recommendations was new, but Britain has remained reluctant to put them into practice.

The legal profession and the courts

Traditionally the legal profession has been divided into two distinct practices, each with entrenched rights: only solicitors may deal directly with the public, and only barristers (professional advocates) may fight a case in the higher courts (Crown Courts and the High Court). Both have maintained their own self-regulating bodies, the Law Society for solicitors and the Bar for barristers. A member of the public dissatisfied with the services of a solicitor may complain to the Law Society, but this does not often take action against its own members except in the case of some gross offence or negligence. The Law Society has often infuriated members of the public by advising them to take their complaint to another solicitor.

There are only about 5,000 barristers, and they are the senior branch of the legal profession. Traditionally, only they have been able to reach the top of the profession, a High Court judgeship. In order to become a barrister, a candidate must obtain entrance to one of the four Inns of Court, law colleges which date from the middle ages, complete the legal training and pass the Bar examination. The Inns of Court have maintained their autonomy and privileges, and been more resistant to attempts at reform than almost any other British institution. A newly qualified barrister will enter the 'chambers' of an established one, and slowly build up experience and a reputation as an effective advocate in the higher courts. In due course, a successful barrister may be appointed a Queen's Counsel, or QC, known within the profession as 'taking silk'.

difficult cases around the country, and about thirty other judges, all of whom belong to one of the divisions of the High Court of Justice.

Briefly, the High Court has: the Chancery Division, dealing with company law, bankruptcy and the administration of estates of those who have died; the Family Division, concerned with family law, divorce, custody of children, etc.; and the Queen's Bench Division, headed by the senior judge below the Lord Chancellor, the Lord Chief Justice. The Lord Chief Justice can decide which judge should hear a case, and his advice will be given careful consideration by the government. The Queen's Bench Division, to which all High Court judges belong, divides its time between civil work in London, the Central Criminal Court (usually known as the Old Bailey) where many of the most famous criminal cases have been heard, and work in the provincial Crown Courts.

Barristers coming out of court.

The Old Bailey.

There is no judicial profession in England. All judges are appointed by the Lord Chancellor from among experienced barristers. Some become circuit judges, of whom there are about 300, assigned to 300 or so 'county courts' throughout the country. Above these are about fifty High Court judges, who deal with more important or

The Lord Chancellor combines three distinct functions. As head of the legal hierarchy, he selects judges, QCs and magistrates and may preside over the Law Lords if he so wishes. He is Speaker (presiding officer) of the Lords, theoretically responsible for discipline in the House. Finally, as a political appointee, he is a member of the Cabinet and the government's chief legal adviser. In theory, therefore, the authority of the legislature and executive of Britain are not separated. However, it is a firmly understood tradition, that while judges may not declare an Act of Parliament void, their independence from government is a fundamental duty.

England has fewer professional judges than most countries, eight per million compared with thirty-four per million in the United States and even more in some countries. In the words of one retired Lord Chancellor, "We have an extraordinarily small legal profession and I regard this as thoroughly beneficial to society. I'd rather have too few lawyers than too many as in the United States. Lawyers are indispensable to any civilised society, but they have limitations and weaknesses." Ralf Dahrendorf, one of Britain's foremost academics, who grew up as a German, puts it another way: "Britain is neither a litigious society in which individuals and groups fight out their battles by calling on the courts, nor is it a state society in which the courts are used as instruments of explicit domination. . . . Where there is liberty, the law is always the second best instrument for defending it."

However, the way in which judges are selected remains a matter of controversy. The Lord Chancellor's freedom to appoint judges allows successive products of the Bar to reinforce what Anthony Sampson, a leading analyst of British institutions, calls "the most extreme British example of a closed and self-regulating community". They tend to be detached from the broad sweep of society, almost entirely male and belonging to the professional middle class. A survey in 1978 showed that three quarters of senior judges were educated at public (i.e. independent) schools, and that their work experience was limited largely to the Bar. Critics argue the need for a broader class intake, including far more women and members of ethnic minorities, and this is beginning to happen. The appointment of a new Lord Chancellor, Lord Mackay, in 1987, was remarkable for two reasons. He was the son of a railwayman, educated within the state education system and, as a Scottish advocate, his whole professional career had been outside the English Bar. His appointment caused a considerable stir. In 1991 the first black female ever was appointed Queen's Counsel.

The Scottish system

The Scottish system is similar to the English one, but is more influenced by Roman law, as in Europe. Its main civil courts are the Sheriffs' courts (like Crown Courts) and the Court of Session. The Court of Session is divided into an Outer House (a court of first instance) and the Inner House (a court of appeal). The Inner House has two divisions of four judges respectively, one under the direction of the Lord President, and the other under the Lord Justice Clerk.

Less serious criminal cases are tried in the Sheriffs' courts, but more serious ones go to the High Court of Justiciary. Juries in Scotland are made up of fifteen rather than twelve citizens. Minor offences are dealt with in district courts (the equivalent of magistrates' courts). The senior law officer in the High Court of Justiciary and in all Scotland is the Lord Justice General, and the Lord Justice Clerk is second in rank.

Unlike in England, where the Crown Prosecution Service is a recent innovation, Scotland's Lord Advocate is responsible for all prosecutions. The work is carried out on his behalf by his deputy, the Solicitor General for Scotland, and by local officials, known as 'procurators fiscal'. The Secretary of State for Scotland, always a Scottish MP but usually also one who is a lawyer by profession, is responsible for the appointment of most judges.

Reforming the law

Lord Mackay soon showed his determination to reform England's legal system. In 1988 he proposed certain changes: to permit solicitors as well as barristers to act as counsel in the higher courts; to allow people wishing to take legal action to enter into a 'no win, no fee' agreement with lawyers; and to allow building societies and banks to provide conveyancing services (the legal work involved in the purchase and sale of property). Under these measures the Bar will lose its monopoly in the higher courts, and solicitors will lose their monopoly on conveyancing, which provides the major part of their income. The no win, no fee scheme will allow many more people who believe they have a strong case but cannot afford the enormous legal costs of going to court to make an agreement with a lawyer willing to take the risk. All these measures are designed to make access to the law easier for the consumer.

The one major fear is that without an income from conveyancing, many ordinary 'high street' solicitors' firms may go out of business.

More fundamentally, there is criticism of the adversarial system in criminal courts. Research indicates that up to 300 prisoners are wrongfully convicted each year. Partly as a result of the case of the Guildford Four, two Law Lords called in 1989 for the introduction of an inquisitorial system of justice that would take the questioning of suspects away from the police, and give it to a special body of professional and non-partisan interrogators. They claim that fewer guilty people would go free, and fewer innocents would be wrongfully convicted.

The police

In early 1990 a major feature article in one of Britain's leading papers was entitled, "What's gone wrong with the Police?" It referred to the frequency of scandals during the 1980s involving the police. These scandals concerned the excessive use of violence to maintain public order (Brixton riots 1981, the miners' strike 1984–85, the Wapping strike 1986, the anti-poll tax riots 1990); violence in the questioning of suspects (particularly, but not exclusively, in connection with Northern Ireland); the fabrication of evidence and the extortion of forced confessions (the Guildford

Riot police at an anti-poll tax riot.

Four and the 'Birmingham Six' (see page 128)); and corrupt practices, for example the falsification of records concerning the successful solution to crimes. It also commented on the severe loss of morale among the police, and the high number of police who resign from the force on account of stress.

Twenty-five years ago, the British police force was a source of great pride. Unlike police in almost every other country, the British policeman enjoyed a trusted, respected and friendly relationship with the public. The 'bobby on the beat' made it his business to learn his neighbourhood. In return, the public placed a high level of trust in his integrity. This is probably a rosy and idealised view of the past. But it was a source of pride that almost alone in the police world, the British bobby was unarmed. As Ralf Dahrendorf says, "It is hard to exaggerate the significance of the fact that the British police did not, and very largely do not, carry weapons." The British police are probably still among the finest in the world, but clearly there are serious and growing problems. A survey commissioned by three authoritative police associations at the end of the 1980s reported that one in five people believe that the police use unnecessary force on arrest, falsify statements, plant evidence and use violence in police stations. It also reported that only 43 per cent of white people interviewed and only 29 per cent of blacks believed the police treated all people fairly.

In such circumstances there is clearly a critical need to rebuild public confidence. But what should be done? The problem is partly structural. In 1990 there were still fifty-two separate police forces operating in different parts of the country. Each force is answerable to a local police authority, composed of magistrates and local councillors. In the case of London's Metropolitan Police (the 'Met'), the authority is the Home Secretary himself. But police authorities have very limited powers. They can appoint the chief officer (the Chief Constable), subject to Home Office approval, and they may ask questions and advise concerning police work.

In practice, however, each Chief Constable is responsible for all operational and administrative decisions. The police authority cannot give direct instructions on such matters, nor can the Home Secretary (except in the cases of London and Northern Ireland). In 1966 a judge ruled that a Chief Constable, like any police officer, cannot be told which particular laws to enforce or refrain

from enforcing. Traditionally Chief Constables have disliked attempts at local control even more than those of central government. The result is that except in the case of police violation of the law, or a case of gross negligence, it is extremely difficult for elected representatives at the local level to exercise direct control. In the 1984–85 miners' strike, for example, the local police authorities were powerless to moderate the aggressive tactics adopted by the police to defeat the miners.

In addition, until 1987 the police investigated alleged police malpractice themselves. Although a Police Complaints Authority now exists, it is not fully independent. It must rely on officers from one police force to investigate the malpractice of another. It is widely believed that police loyalty still prevents effective and impartial internal police investigation. Following the Brixton riots, Lord Scarman recommended that the police should not be allowed to investigate allegations of police misconduct. This recommendation awaits full implementation.

Because of such limitations, democratic control of the police in practice does not properly exist. Concern at the political use of the police increased during the 1980s with the frequent political use of police to maintain public order in controversial situations, for example strikes and demonstrations against government policy.

There has also been growing concern about the other police function: the control of crime. Until 1984 no British citizen had any formal protection against police intimidation except customary ones, the right to silence and the right to see a solicitor. The right to silence in Northern Ireland was removed in 1988. Since 1984 there have been statutory codes of practice to be followed in the arrest and questioning of suspects, including the requirement to tape-record (for court use) all interrogations. This should improve things but it needs to be remembered, in the words of one ex-policeman, that "cells and detention rooms are known as places where officers can free themselves from legal and formal organisational rules".

Until 1986 the English police were responsible not only for the detection of crime but also for prosecution. They often prosecuted in cases where the evidence was not strong enough to obtain a conviction. In 1978, for example, half of all those pleading not guilty to criminal charges were acquitted in court. Many, perhaps around 45,000 cases yearly, were prosecuted where a 'formal caution' would have had a deterrent effect. Since 1986 an independent Crown Prosecution Service for England and Wales has followed Scotland's longstanding practice of choosing when to prosecute. This has led to fewer prosecutions, but a higher rate of conviction.

An improved code of conduct, and changes in the administration of criminal law, help the police improve their performance. However, in an age of increasing popular violence and disrespect for law and order, the great challenge for the police is to recapture the respect of the public. Frustrating as this may be for the police, the challenge is to show greater restraint rather than aggression under provocation. It is also to shift the emphasis back from the more exciting image of armed or armoured law enforcement to a softer image of policing in the form of the friendly but firm neighbourhood bobby. In the longer run, the way the public feel about the police is of fundamental importance to police ability to control crime and maintain public order. Unfortunately, neighbourhood policing has far lower status than crime control.

As the challenges of modern society become more complex, the response of the police has been to seek more manpower and more money. In 1962 the ratio of police to public was 1:602. By 1982 this had increased to 1:394. This has neither prevented an increase in crime nor in public disorder. More brainpower rather than manpower would probably improve police efficiency. Police officers have traditionally worked themselves up

Women police tend to be assigned to community work, and miss out on promotion.

the career ladder from the lowest rank, of constable. It is possible that a new cadre of commissioned officers will be formed in the 1990s to attract more highly educated entrants into the force. It can be argued, too, that the current prejudice against the recruitment or promotion of women and ethnic minorities needs to be overcome. The more the police force reflects the different elements of society, the better will be its ability to police by consent rather than by coercion.

However, there has also been a gulf between senior police officers, sensitive to the wider implications of police work, and the lowest ranks who can easily feel frustrated, hostile and prejudiced towards particular categories of the public, for example, the ethnic minorities. The danger of creating a separate officer cadre is that the damaging gulf within the force, between senior (commissioned) officers and lower ranks, may grow.

There is also a strong case for reducing the present fifty-two forces down to, say, ten, and for creating one central criminal investigation body, which can direct its resources more efficiently than the present serious crime squads in each force. The case against such reorganisation is that it will reduce local accountability even further. In a perfect world improved organisational structure would be accompanied by closer consultation with each local community, and closer scrutiny by Parliament.

Whatever balance is struck during the 1990s between police powers and accountability, it is unlikely ever to be perfect. It is vital to an effective democracy that this balance remains one for periodic popular debate and review.

Questions

Section analysis

1 The legal system: What are the two basic sources of English law?

2 Dealing with crime: There are two main types of court in England and Wales, Crown courts and magistrates' courts. What are the differences between them?

3 The treatment of offenders: How does the British way of treating offenders differ from treatment in your country?

4 Young offenders: Young offenders may be put into detention centres or supervised in the community. Which system is more effective?

5 The legal profession: Do you think that a relatively small legal profession, as in Britain, is desirable? Give your reasons.

6 The Scottish system: There are two distinct legal systems in Britain, the Scottish and the English. Which is more similar to that in your country?

7 Reforming the law: What are the key legal reforms currently being introduced?

8 The police: What has gone wrong with the police? Based upon the information given, list the basic concerns the average citizen might have.

Chapter analysis and discussion

Which of the following statements are correct, and which are incorrect? Find textual evidence for your decision:

1 Partly as a result of the wrongful imprisonment of the Guildford Four and the Birmingham Six

a the legal system of England and Wales was questioned by Lord Mackay.

b the Law Lords wanted to remove the power of the police to question suspects.

c the public have less confidence in the police.

2 The legal system of England and Wales

a is based on a written legal code.

b assumes that a person is innocent unless he or she has been proved guilty.

c has more professional judges that most other countries.

3

a The highest court in the land is the House of Lords.

b Magistrates' courts are presided over by Justices of the Peace who have a legal training and receive a salary.

c A jury of twelve citizens makes the decisions in a Crown court.

4 The police in Britain

a make the initial decision to bring a criminal charge against someone.

b do not generally carry guns.

c are generally respected by the public as much today as they were twenty-five years ago.

Textual interpretation

1 "We expect him [the average police officer] to be human and yet at the same time para-human. We welcome official protection, yet resent official interference. We employ him to administer the law, and yet will ask him to waive it. We resent him when he enforces a law in our own case, yet demand his dismissal when he does not elsewhere . . . . We expect him to be a member of society, yet not share its prejudices and values."
(From the 1987 report by the Commissioner of the Metropolitan Police.)

Do you consider this an adequate defence for police conduct in the 1980s? Give reasons and evidence for your point of view.

2 Anthony Sampson has written: "Their [High Court judges'] attitude to the political and social problems of our time is shaped and determined by their class, their upbringing and their professional life . . . . Their attitude is strongly conservative, respectful of property rights and highly authoritarian."

Do you think Anthony Sampson's view is important? Give your reasons.

5 Local government

The system

England (with the exception of Greater London) and Wales are divided into fifty-three counties, within which there are 369 districts. Forty-seven of these counties, which are 'non-metropolitan', and all districts, have independent and locally elected councils. In Greater London itself the local government authorities are the councils of thirty-two London boroughs and the Corporation of the City of London (see page 78), while the six metropolitan counties (Greater Manchester, Merseyside, Tyne and Wear, West Midlands, West Yorkshire and South Yorkshire) are divided into thirty-six district councils. In mainland Scotland there are nine regions, divided into fifty-three districts, and there are three all-purpose authorities for the island groups, Orkney, Shetland and the Western Isles. In Northern Ireland much is administered by area boards, but local services are provided by twenty-six district councils.

These county (or regional), district and borough councils provide the range of services – health, education, waste disposal, police and fire services – necessary for everyday life. The county councils usually look after the wider and larger responsibilities like planning, transport, highways, traffic regulation, health, education, and fire services. In principle, the local authorities have control over the local police, but in practice their control is extremely limited since the police may argue that they are directly answerable to the Crown (see page 62).

District councils are usually responsible for environmental health, housing, and refuse collection. Each county or borough department negotiates with its appropriate central government ministry concerning its affairs, for example in education, or highways and transport. The introduction of local regulations, 'by-laws', may only be done with government approval. Scotland, Wales and Northern Ireland each have a minister who is responsible not only for that country, but also for tailoring the function of government, thus coming between other government ministries and the local authorities of these three countries.

It is the basic principle of local government that local people can devise a better system for the local context than can central government. As a result there is no standard system, since in each county the local authorities have the freedom to organise and administer services as they think will best suit the area. Closely related to this efficiency principle is the democratic one – the right of people to organise community affairs as they think best.

A borough waste disposal service.

Each authority is composed of elected councillors, who form the governing body, and permanent local government officers, the local equivalent of the Civil Service. Elected councillors, unlike MPs, remain unpaid, although they can receive a financial loss allowance for performing council business and also allowances for necessary expenses. Most of those who stand for election, predominantly men, are local business or professional people. Some of them work for purely idealistic reasons while others may be politically ambitious or believe that their position as councillor will help advance their own business or professional standing.

Each council elects a chairman, or in boroughs a 'mayor', and in Scotland a 'provost', almost invariably from the majority party represented on the council. Councillors are elected for four years. All councils, except at parish level, delegate committees, usually composed of certain councillors and some appropriate officers employed by the council, to consider policy, problems and expenditure in particular areas of council activity, for example education. Generally, the public may attend any council or committee meetings.

Local government employs almost three million salaried officers, one tenth of Britain's entire workforce. Nearly half of them are in the education service. All senior local government officers are appointed only with approval from the appropriate government ministry. Authorities differ in the number of services they put out to private contract rather than handle themselves.

Expenditure by local authorities is about one quarter of total public expenditure, and one third of this local government expenditure is on education (see page 148). Just over 50 per cent of local government expenditure is financed from central government. The rest is raised locally, by local taxation and by the collection of rents, fees and payments on property or services provided by the council. The system of both central and local finance for local government is highly complicated and controversial, and is discussed more fully below.

Central government normally seeks to supply the extra funds necessary to provide services adequately, and to offset the differences in wealth and in service requirements between different areas. These differences are naturally particularly great between, for example, a densely populated but wealthy area in the south east of England,

The Mayor of Stratford upon Avon meeting two old soldiers of Chelsea Hospital.

and a remote thinly populated part of highland Scotland.

The tension between central government and local democracy

There has always been a tension between local and central government, between civic freedoms expressed locally and the intervention by central government in the national interest. This tension, which has been growing particularly since 1945, raises important questions about local freedoms and the power of central government. Hardly surprisingly there has been a tendency for the political party in power to insist on the importance of central government intervention, and of the opposition party strongly to defend the right to local democracy. In 1976, for example, a Labour government told all local authorities to arrange secondary education on non-selective lines, forcing them to combine the traditionally separate schools for children of higher and lower ability. In 1980 the Conservative government applied penalties – by cutting central government grants – to local authorities which spent more than it thought was reasonable. In 1983 it set limits on local authority subsidies for local transport services.

Technically, Parliament is sovereign and may grant or limit the powers of the local authorities which administer Britain at the local level. Nevertheless, in many cases, local government is much older than Parliament itself. The division of the country into shires, or counties, occurred over a thousand years ago and until 1974 remained largely unchanged. During the middle ages, many cities and towns, or 'boroughs', were granted charters by the king, permitting them to govern their own affairs without outside interference. At the most local level, the parish was the unit of administration, a unit which has survived to this day.

During the nineteenth century, the wide variety of local governing bodies were standardised. In larger towns and cities a single local authority existed, but elsewhere the system had two or even three tiers: the county councils and below them municipal boroughs and perhaps urban districts, or in the countryside rural districts and parish councils.

In the nineteenth century many candidates at council elections were independent citizens concerned with the wellbeing of their town, or county. But during the second half of the century the two main political parties, the Conservatives and Liberals, began to sponsor their own candidates. Today it is almost impossible to succeed even in local elections without representing one of the national political parties. To this extent national politics have modified local democracy and made it an aspect of national politics. Even in the very few rural areas where independents may still successfully stand, they are usually believed to identify with a national party in their thinking.

Consequently, today people usually elect councillors according to their party affiliation, not on the qualities of each individual candidate, an unfortunate fact since local issues are often quite different from national ones, and can make local government unnecessarily adversarial. Sometimes a conflict of loyalty arises for councillors who wish, in spite of their party loyalties and the contradictory directions received from party headquarters, to pursue a policy in the local interest. Some councillors have been expelled from their party for disobedience.

National parties all use local government as a 'nursery' for those ambitious to enter Parliament. Between 1945 and 1979 45 per cent of Labour and 25 per cent of Conservative MPs entered Parliament after service as a councillor in local government. As with the constituency system, the tendency to vote for a party rather than an individual undermines the chief advantage of a localised political process, and it is hardly surprising that most local council elections usually attract barely 40 per cent of the electorate, roughly half that of national elections, and substantially lower than those in other Western European countries. It must be concluded that people either feel local government is unimportant or that it is too remote and party-based to respond effectively to their needs.

A local council election.

How large should local authority areas be? There is a natural tension between the demands of democracy and efficiency. Major changes in population size and distribution, in particular the spread of suburbs and the growth of conurbations (the growth of one town to reach a neighbouring one), made a major restructuring of local government a necessity during the second part of the twentieth century. In the 1960s and 1970s there was a fashion for the creation of larger, regional bodies for overall planning, and for the administration of health, police, fire and water services.

In 1974 a new local government system was introduced by the Conservative government. Many of the old counties were replaced with larger ones which bore new names, for example Humberside, which incorporated parts of Yorkshire and Lincolnshire. The change proved immensely unpopular and also, despite the argument for greater efficiency, increased the cost of local government. The largest conurbations were given special status. A Greater London Council (GLC) was given authority over London itself and many of the suburbs which had previously been administered by the counties in which they found themselves, and the six metropolitan counties, mentioned above, were created.

Although their creation had not been welcomed by Labour in 1974, by the 1980s the councils of the GLC and six metropolitan authorities were all controlled by a Labour majority. In 1986, after a long struggle, the Conservative government abolished these councils, returning the large conurbations to control by local borough councils, which had previously acted under metropolitan authority. Regional boards were established to coordinate particular services like health and transport. It soon became clear that instead of financial savings, this reorganisation increased the costs of the regional boards. The move was strongly criticised in the House of Lords and was unpopular among most of the electorate. Although few had loved the metropolitan authorities, there was a feeling that the government would not have abolished these authorities had they been Conservative controlled and that it was, in spite of the return of powers to local borough councils, an interference with local democracy. One man, Ken Livingstone, who was head of the GLC, personified the struggle against government. He had been seen as a dangerous leftist by many in London, but by a skilful campaign he successfully portrayed himself as a champion of local democracy against what he claimed was an

Ken Livingstone in front of County Hall, the headquarters of the GLC.

oppressive central government. In 1987 he entered Parliament, a good example of the progression of many politicians from local to national affairs.

The size and structure of local government does not satisfy everyone. In particular the breakup of the services provided by the GLC and metropolitan authorities, and the sale of regional water authorities into private hands, are likely to lead to continued restructuring in the 1990s.

One of the most controversial and difficult areas of local government has been the question of funding and expenditure, particularly since local authorities consume about one quarter of all public expenditure, employ three million people, and (in 1980) still owned about 30 per cent of the nation's housing stock. Unlike central government where, in theory at any rate, the Commons may examine and reject the financial programme, local councils are subject to annual audit but not to local democratic examination and control.

During the early 1970s there was a massive increase in local government spending, partly as a result of inflation, partly as a result of the expansion of local services, particularly in education, but also as a result of the 1974 reorganisation. By the end of the 1980s the increase in costs had slowed down. Nevertheless, throughout the 1980s central government made strenuous efforts to reduce and control the spending by local authorities. It claimed, on behalf of local residents, that some local authorities were inefficient and extravagant. It could also have been argued that local residents had voted councils into power and therefore presumably supported council policy. It applied penalties from 1983, by withholding part of the central government grant, from eighteen 'overspending' councils, only two of which were Conservative controlled. This had the appearance of an attack on Labour councils. Government figures in 1989 showed that as many Conservative as Labour-controlled councils had increased rates and expenditure sharply during the 1980s.

The Conservative government also ruled that all local authorities must sell council-owned housing to the tenants if the latter wished to buy. This was particularly offensive to Labour councils, which have traditionally viewed the provision of proper housing for all residents, regardless of wealth, to be the first responsibility of local government. Furthermore, in order to curb spending, it was forbidden to sell land or property in order that the council could benefit financially. Most of the proceeds of all such sales had to be handed to central government. This prevented local authorities from using the funds received by the sale of council housing to build more publicly-owned homes (see page 190). It was also decided that local authorities in receipt of European Community grants would be liable to a reduction in government funding. With regard to capital expenditure, particularly on public housing, the Conservative government achieved a 40 per cent reduction. But in annual expenses the savings were marginal and resulted in much ill feeling in the local authorities.

Since the regularising of local government in the nineteenth century, the local taxation system has been based upon property rather than people. By valuing properties, the local authority could calculate the share each property holder should pay, based upon the relative value of each property.

Everyone agreed the rates system, as it was known, was unsatisfactory, partly because it was complicated to calculate and partly because valuations happened only periodically, the last in 1973. Since 1973 the relative value of properties in different areas, not only nationally, but even inside a single authority, had distorted the fairness of the system. Furthermore, only property owners or occupiers had to pay. Many only paid a reduced sum. On the other hand, the rates provided a rough-and-ready graded local tax on capital wealth.

In the 1980s the Conservative government decided to replace the rates system with a 'community charge', an equal charge on every adult living in each local authority. It argued that since every adult in each authority received its services, each should pay equally towards the costs of these services. As with the rates system, this charge, which rapidly became known as the 'poll tax', varied from one authority to another.

At the time of its introduction (in Scotland in 1989, and in England and Wales in 1990) the poll tax was extremely unpopular, each adult being required to pay substantially more than the government had estimated. But its unpopularity also resulted from a sense of unfairness, since the charge was applied to everyone regardless of ability to pay. In fact higher income residential areas (typically with Conservative voters) tended to benefit from the change while lower income urban areas, where people tended to vote Labour, faced a larger tax bill. To the government's embarrassment, the amount paid by many people in rural areas, which tended to be strongly Conservative, also increased sharply.

The poll tax also proved costly to collect. Only 17 million people paid rates, while 35 million were liable for the poll tax. Fewer than one per cent of property owners had dodged paying their rates, for the simple reason that property does not move. On the other hand, 10 per cent of the population move house every year. The average non-payment rate in 1990 was about 25 per cent, and local authorities faced the nightmare of trying to keep track of people, collecting the correct amount of poll tax, and borrowing money in order to maintain their services in the meantime. Non-payment and the need to borrow both led to an increased charge for those who did pay.

The unpopularity of the poll tax – demonstrators confront the police.

Because of the great unpopularity of the poll tax, the Conservative government that replaced Margaret Thatcher's immediately announced that the tax would be fundamentally revised. It tried to design a new local taxation system, one that avoided the complications of the old rates but also the apparent unfairness of the poll tax system. It proposed a 'council' tax, to be introduced in 1993, which was intended to combine features of the old rating system with a residual poll tax. In fact, whichever government tries to undo the mess and create a simple but fair system, whether it is Conservative or Labour, faces a difficult task. Its political opponents will do everything they can to prove it is unfair or

inefficient. Because ordinary people generally dislike change, any alteration runs the risk of attracting unpopularity, even if it is important. However, the money necessary to pay for services must still be collected.

During the 1980s the Conservative government changed the balance between central control and local autonomy, but failed to bring local authorities under central control. The local authorities still have substantial resources with which to defend their policies and freedoms. Local elections, in which Labour proved generally far more popular than it had done in national elections, were a powerful reminder to a Conservative government that there were limits to the level of interference in local democratic practice. Many Conservative councillors were also unhappy with the behaviour of government.

Government policy in the 1980s has increased the sense of conflict between local and central government. The effects are likely to be felt well into the next century, with the two fundamental problems – a satisfactory national philosophy for the management of local politics and government, and the system of financing – still to be resolved.

On the other hand, during the second half of the 1980s many councils had no single party in a majority. In these hung councils there was a move away from adversarial politics – since these could only lead to stalemate. The result was an increase in multi-party rule, with conscious cross-party cooperation, particularly between Labour and the Liberal Democrats. While decisions were perhaps less predictable, local political life became more open and democratic. It remains to be seen whether this will mark a new trend in asserting more local independence from central party discipline.

Nevertheless, the policy of central government is bound to define the broad philosophy of local government. Labour would probably revive the GLC, but not the other metropolitan authorities, which it never liked. Instead it would probably give back nine large cities (like Bristol, Southampton and Leicester) wider powers, but would eliminate many county or shire districts. It would also probably create a directly elected regional tier for water, transport, police and economic planning. All these are policies on which a Labour government could expect support from the Liberal Democrats.

In the meantime, the sense of instability, ambiguity and confusion, which has been aroused by the efforts of government to bring traditionally local matters under central control, is bound to persist. Reforming local government and stabilising the balance between the centre and localities will remain both difficult and controversial for any future government.

Questions

Section analysis

1 The system: Which of the following people are elected and which are appointed? Which are paid and which give their services free: a councillor, a local government official, a chairman, a mayor, a provost?

2 The system: Decide which of the following services are the responsibility of the county (regional) councils, and which are the responsibility of the district and borough councils: transport, health, fire services, waste disposal, housing, education, environmental health, highways.

3 Central government and local democracy: Why did the Conservative government abolish the central planning body for London? Do you think it was a desirable step to take? Give reasons for your opinion.

4 Central government and local democracy: List the arguments in favour of a local government tax based a) on property and b) on individual people. Which system in your opinion is better?

Chapter analysis and discussion

1 Which of the following is the best explanation of the conflict between local and central government in Britain? Give reasons for your answer.

a There is a permanent, inevitable and natural conflict between locally expressed civic freedoms and the national interest.

b Central government wishes to increase its control, particularly in areas where its political opponents are strongest, while local government seeks to retain its own powers.

c Given the broad sweep of tasks carried out by local and central government, disagreements between the two are hardly worth discussion.

2 Opinions in Britain differ on the following points. What is your opinion?

a Local government should no longer be the nursery for those ambitious to enter Parliament.

b Local government should not be monopolised by the national political parties.

c There should be central planning bodies for the major cities, especially London.

3 Find textual evidence to support these statements:

a Central government pays for more than half the expenditure of local government.

b Local government spending has increased over the past two decades.

c Central government does not allow local councils to keep money gained from the sale of housing or land.

4 In what way does Britain's system of local government differ from the system in your country? Which of the two do you think is better, and why?

Textual interpretation

Consider the following statement: "On the one hand, large units of government are necessary in urban-industrial society in order to achieve efficiency, economies of scale, functional effectiveness and an adequate capacity to plan and organise; on the other hand small units of government are necessary to preserve the attributes of grassroots democracy . . . "

1 Do you think Britain has now found the right balance or not? Find evidence in the text to support your view.

2 Has local government in your country found a better balance?

6 Working Britain

The economic problems

Little more than a century ago, Britain was 'the workshop of the world'. It had as many merchant ships as the rest of the world put together and it led the world in most manufacturing industries. This did not last long. By 1885 one analysis reported, "We have come to occupy a position in which we are no longer progressing, but even falling back. . . . We find other nations able to compete with us to such an extent as we have never before experienced." Early in the twentieth century Britain was overtaken economically by the United States and Germany. After two world wars and the rapid loss of its empire, Britain found it increasingly difficult to maintain its position even in Europe.

Britain struggled to find a balance between government intervention in the economy and an almost completely free-market economy such as existed in the United States. Neither system seemed to fit Britain's needs. The former seemed compromised between two different objectives: planned economic prosperity and the means of ensuring full employment, while the latter promised greater economic prosperity at the cost of poverty and unemployment for the less able in society. Neither Labour nor the Conservatives doubted the need to find a system that suited Britain's needs, but neither seemed able to break from the consensus based on Keynesian economics (see page 7).

People seemed complacent about Britain's decline, reluctant to make the painful adjustments that might be necessary to reverse it. Prosperity increased during the late 1950s and in the 1960s, diverting attention from Britain's decline relative to its main competitors. In 1973 the Conservative Prime Minister Edward Heath warned, "The alternative to expansion is not, as some occasionally seem to suppose, an England of quiet market towns linked only by steam trains puffing slowly and peacefully through green meadows. The alternative is slums, dangerous roads, old factories, cramped schools, stunted lives." But in the years of worldwide recession, 1974–79, Britain seemed unable to improve its performance.

By the mid 1970s both Labour and Conservative economists were beginning to recognise the need to move away from Keynesian economics, based upon stimulating demand by injecting money into the economy. But, as described in the Introduction, it was the Conservatives who decided to break with the old economic formula completely. Returning to power in 1979, they were determined to lower taxes as an incentive to individuals and businesses to increase productivity; to leave the labour force to regulate itself either by pricing itself out of employment or by working within the amount of money employers could afford; and, finally, to limit government spending levels and use money supply (the amount of money in circulation at any one time) as a way of controlling inflation. As Prime Minister Margaret Thatcher argued in the Commons, "If our objective is to have a prosperous and expanding economy, we must recognise that high public spending, as a proportion of GNP [gross national product], very quickly kills growth. . . . We have to remember that governments have no money at all. Every penny they take is from the productive sector of the economy in order to transfer it to the unproductive part of it." She had a point: between 1961 and 1975 employment outside industry increased by over 40 per cent relative to employment in industry.

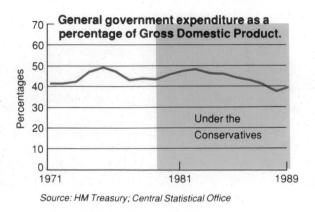

General government expenditure as a percentage of Gross Domestic Product.

Under the Conservatives

Source: HM Treasury; Central Statistical Office

During the 1980s the Conservatives put their new ideas into practice. Income tax was reduced from a basic rate of 33 per cent to 25 per cent. (For higher income groups the reduction was greater, at the top rate from 83 per cent to 40 per cent.) This did not lead to any loss in revenue, since at the lower rates fewer people tried to avoid tax. At the same time, however, the government doubled Value Added Tax (VAT) on goods and services to 15 per cent.

Retail prices index (inflation)

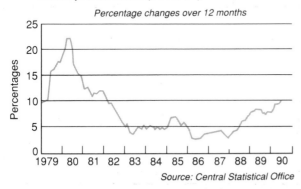

Percentage changes over 12 months

Source: Central Statistical Office

The most notable success of 'Thatcherism' was the privatisation of previously wholly or partly government-owned enterprises. Indeed, other countries, for example Canada, France, Italy, Japan, Malaysia and West Germany, followed the British example. The government believed that privatisation would increase efficiency, reduce government borrowing, increase economic freedom, and encourage wide share ownership. By 1990 20 per cent of the adult population were share owners, a higher proportion than in any other Western industrialised country. There was no question of taking these enterprises back into public ownership, even by a Labour government.

Despite such changes, however, by 1990 Britain's economic problems seemed as difficult as ever. The government found that reducing public expenditure was far harder than expected and that by 1990 it still consumed about the same proportion of the GNP as it had ten years earlier. Inflation, temporarily controlled, rose to over 10 per cent and was only checked from rising further by high interest rates which also had the side

A march to highlight the problem of unemployment.

effect of discouraging economic growth. In spite of reducing the power of the trade unions, wage demands (most notably senior management salaries) rose faster than prices, indicating that a free labour market did not necessarily solve the wages problem. By 1990 the manufacturing industry had barely recovered from the major shrinkage in the early 1980s. It was more efficient, but in the meantime Britain's share of world trade in manufactured goods had shrunk from 8 per cent in 1979 to 6.5 per cent ten years later. Britain's balance of payments was unhealthy too. In 1985 it had enjoyed a small surplus of £3.5 billion, but in 1990 this had changed to a deficit of £20.4 billion.

There were fears that Britain's industrial sector was becoming an assembly economy, serving foreign-owned enterprises. In 1984 the National Economic Development Office reported, "It appears that the UK now enjoys an intermediate status between the AICs [Advanced Industrialised Countries] and NICs [Newly Industrialising Countries], and has features of both types of economy in trade with the other." Certainly the level of commercial interpenetration by multi-national companies greatly increased during the 1980s. A survey in 1987 showed Britain to be the major recipient of foreign investment in Europe. For example, 30 per cent of Japan's total West European investment, and 36 per cent of US investment in the European Community came to Britain. By August 1988 over 1.2 million people, 10 per cent of Britain's workforce, were employed in the top 1,000 foreign-owned companies in the country.

On the other hand, while foreign companies invested over £49 billion in Britain during the decade 1977–87, British companies invested £91 billion abroad. In 1987 alone, British companies spent almost $32 billion buying American companies.

Government policy and the state of the world economy plunged Britain into the worst recession since the end of the Second World War. Britain suffered more than other industrialised countries, its share of world trade falling by 15 per cent in the years 1979–86. To give a comparison, between 1979 and 1984 productivity rose by 20 per cent in Japan, 10 per cent in the United States, 6 per cent in France, 4.3 per cent in West Germany and only 3.9 per cent in Britain. If one discounted income from North Sea oil, Britain's productivity rose by only about 1 per cent. Britain's manufacturing sector shrank by 10 per cent in this period,

while at the same time the import of manufactured goods rose by 40 per cent. As a result, in 1983, for the first time in more than 200 years, Britain imported more manufactured goods than it exported. It did not recover its 1979 manufacturing level for almost ten years, but even so British manufacturing compared poorly with its competitors. Car workers in Germany could produce a Ford Escort under virtually identical conditions in half the time taken in Britain. As a House of Lords Select Committee on Overseas Trade reported in 1985: "It is neither exaggeration nor irresponsible to say that the present situation undoubtedly contains the seeds of a major political and economic crisis in the foreseeable future." By 1988 Britain's balance of payments deficit (the amount by which imports exceed exports) was larger than the total deficit for the previous forty years.

Furthermore, unemployment rose from 1.5 million in 1979 to over 3 million by 1983 and was reduced to 2.5 million by the end of the 1980s mainly by a fall in the workforce and by redefining unemployment. Although some expansion occurred between 1983 and 1989, 60 per cent of all jobs created in this period were part-time.

The 1980s Conservative government believed that only painful restructuring would lead to greater efficiency. It scored some successes, of which the most notable was in steel production. In the early 1980s British Steel was an industry in decline. By the late 1980s its future was bright, the industry having made a profit in 1988 of £410 million, a better result than that of any European competitor, and its own best result since its formation in 1967. This was achieved by shedding most of the workforce, from 130,000 in 1980 to 50,000 by 1987, and improving efficiency. In 1980 the production of one ton of steel had taken 12 man hours. By 1988 it was taking only 3.7 man hours.

However, although in certain areas efficiency was much improved, Britain still compared poorly with worker productivity elsewhere, and the prospects for real recovery remained bleak. In 1988 average productivity per employee was:

Switzerland	$55,700
Japan	$47,500
France	$45,000
United States	$41,700
Italy	$38,200
Britain	$31,400

(Source: Institute for Labour Productivity and Production)

The only real bonus Britain enjoyed was the oil resources discovered mainly in the North Sea, whereby Britain became the world's sixth largest oil producer. It was oil revenue which softened the impact of the recession 1979–85, reaching an annual peak of £12 billion by 1985, but it then began to decline. Much of the oil revenue was spent on social security for those unemployed, and this apparently unproductive use of this precious resource became a hotly debated issue. Many felt that oil revenues distracted Britain from facing economic realities, and that they should have been invested to lay new foundations for Britain's industrial possibilities (see pages 87–8). For example, the Confederation of British Industry (CBI) appealed in the early 1980s for investment in engineering, production, design, managerial and marketing practices: "This probably represents the only route available to the United Kingdom to become a high-income, high-growth economy as the contribution of North Sea oil declines."

There were other areas for optimism during the 1980s. Small businesses began to increase rapidly. By 1984 officially there was a total of 1.4 million small businesses, though the real figure, including the 'black economy', was probably nearer two million. However proportionately there were 50 per cent more in West Germany and the United States, and about twice as many in France and Japan.

Many small businesses fail to survive, mainly as a result of poor management, but also because, compared with almost every other European Community member, Britain offers the least encouraging conditions. But such small businesses are important not only because large businesses grow from small ones, but also because over half the new jobs in Britain are created by firms employing fewer than 100 staff.

It is not as if Britain is without industrial strength. It is one of the world leaders in the production of microprocessors. Without greater investment and government encouragement it is doubtful whether Britain will hold on to its lead in this area. However, it has already led to the creation of 'hi-tech' industries in three main areas, west of London along the M4 motorway or 'Golden Corridor', the lowlands between Edinburgh and Dundee, nicknamed 'Silicon Glen', and the area between London and Cambridge. In the mid 1980s Silicon Glen was producing 70 per cent of British silicon wafers containing the microchips essential for the new information technology. The Cambridge Science Park, symbolised by its

Modernist Schlumberger Building, is the flagship of hi-tech Britain. Beginning in 1969, by 1986 the Park contained 322 hi-tech companies. In the words of a consultant, "The Cambridge phenomenon . . . represents one of the very few spontaneous growth centres in a national economy that has been depressed for all of a decade."

The Schlumberger building.

Central actors in the economy

The most important actors in the economy are, obviously, those who own and manage it, those who finance it, and those who provide the workforce. In the 1950s the government created the National Economic Development Council (NEDC), a consultative body composed of leading industrialists, trade unionists and members of government, with the task of helping to give direction to industrial development. This was the nearest Britain had come since 1945 to a Ministry for Economic Planning. The NEDC has not been successful, partly because its role was only advisory but most importantly because of the inability of either management or union representatives to ensure cooperation among those they represented. During the 1980s the Conservative government almost entirely abandoned using the NEDC, because the idea of government planning and intervention in the economy contradicted its philosophy.

The most important organisation for owners and managers is the Confederation of British Industry, which seeks to support industrial growth and planning. It is Britain's major industrial institution, and has considerable economic authority and influence. Although more sympathetic to

Conservative governments than to Labour ones, in the 1980s it was critical of the Conservative policy of maintaining high interest rates as a means of controlling inflation, since this also made it expensive to borrow money for expansion and so reduced industrial growth. The CBI was also critical of the failure of government to encourage investment rather than consumption. It argued that massive investment was required in new technology, as was innovation in industry and greatly improved road and rail networks. In the 1980s this did not happen. In fact the Director General of the CBI was so depressed in 1984 that he exclaimed, "Britain is falling to pieces!"

As with the trade unions, there has been a process of concentration in terms of capital and power. In 1915 the top 100 manufacturing firms controlled 15 per cent of manufacturing output. By 1950 they controlled about one fifth, and by 1970 they controlled over half manufacturing output. As a result, the number of interest groups controlling the CBI and other business organisations is fewer, and their individual influence consequently greater.

The Institute of Directors, a right wing group of individuals, was more in tune with government in the 1980s. It welcomed the reduction in trade union power, the reduction of public services, and the programme of privatisation. Other groups exist, for example particular professional or trade groups and federations.

The Stock Exchange (above) and the Bank of England (opposite).

The financial sector

The government's most important controlling institution is the Bank of England, a state-owned central bank which works in close cooperation with the Treasury (Britain's ministry of finance). There has been a long tradition of directing the economy through the great financial institutions which together are known as 'the City', which until 1987 were all located in the 'Square Mile' of the City of London. The banks, insurance companies (most notably Lloyds) and Stock Exchange of the City have always played an extremely important role in Britain's economy, not only because they are the nerve centre of national finance but because such a large proportion of Britain's wealth has been invested by the City overseas. Indeed, apart from income from tourism, the City has been mainly responsible for Britain's large annual invisible exports which have done so much for the national economy.

In order to increase the City's role as an international financial centre, the old exclusions which limited who could operate in the City were removed in 1986. This deregulation, the 'Big Bang', as it was popularly known, allowed any foreign financial institution to participate in the London money market. "What we were trying to do," in the words of a former Deputy Chairman of the London Stock Exchange, "was create a new market, not one just oriented toward the UK, but one that can become international." Indeed, it was intended to secure London as the leading financial centre in Europe, and the third in the world (alongside New York and Tokyo).

Many foreign banks and finance houses tried to profit from the deregulation, some by direct competition and others by buying long-established City enterprises. Before the Big Bang all City stockbroking firms were British. By 1990 154 out of 408 were foreign owned. The main investors in British stockbroking are the United States, Japan and France.

Since the Big Bang, the City has seen frenzied financial activity. For example the brokers of the London International Financial Futures Market are responsible for about 25,000 contracts daily. Most of these brokers trading in 'futures' (the future relative values of different currencies) are under twenty-five years old. Very few survive the stress beyond the age of thirty.

Intense competition for a limited market led to painful shrinkage at the end of the 1980s and the City Stock Exchange computer system proved inadequate and old fashioned for the challenge it faced. During the 1990s the City has to prove whether or not it is able to act as Europe's main finance centre.

The emphasis on guiding the economy through the City's financial institutions gives rise to major problems. Those who invest in the City are often concerned with making maximum profit in the minimum amount of time. Many industrial ventures require long-term investment, and show slow profits at first. As a result, industrialists and financiers can have different goals. Banks, insurance companies, pension funds and building societies (which act as banks and lend money to house purchasers) frequently prefer to invest in areas other than industry, in contrast with most of Britain's competitors, for example Germany and Japan, where there is a far higher level of industrial investment. In addition, while the City may like a 'strong' pound (against other currencies), this can be damaging to industry's export efforts. While the political Right sees the City as a highly successful network of institutions earning large sums of money by its trade abroad, the Left fears that the City is a potential drain on national resources, by tempting British capital away from domestic industrial investment, and by exerting political influence through its control of funding and the external value of sterling.

The City has found it increasingly difficult to maintain its reputation for honest dealing after several scandals concerning 'insider trading' – the use of inside financial knowledge for personal profit. In 1988 more than half the banks and financial institutions in the City had been victims of fraud. That year the police investigated £477 millions' worth of fraud, and estimated that an additional 17 per cent of City banks did not bother to report such matters to the police. Government has traditionally left the City to regulate itself. Yet the success of the City depends upon its trustworthiness. Major scandals make it increasingly necessary for government to regulate the City more closely than in the past. Otherwise, in the words of an ex-editor of *The Times*, "The City will gradually wither away if it ceases to be seen as a trustworthy manager of other people's funds."

The trade unions

The other central actor in industry is the trade union movement, the organised labour of Britain. Its main characteristics are 1) the belief in collective bargaining with employers to protect the interests of its members, i.e. negotiations by one or more unions with an employer to achieve satisfactory rates of pay for the employees; 2) a willingness to be militant, using any form of industrial action to be effective; 3) affiliation to and support of the Labour Party.

Originally many of the unions were organised to protect their members not only against employers but often against other workers, especially where a particular skill was involved. In 1868 the Trades Union Congress (TUC) was established as a coordinating body to represent the collective interests of workers with industrialists and with government.

From 1945–79 the number of unions in the TUC decreased while the number of members increased, thus leading to a smaller number of more powerful unions. In 1960 there were 650 unions with 9.8 million members, but by 1980 there were 438 unions with over 12 million members. This centralisation was an inevitable response to the growing concentration of capital power. By the mid 1970s over 25 per cent of the workforce were employed in firms of over 10,000 employees in the private sector alone. The largest union, the Transport and General Workers (TGWU) had 2 million members in 1979. More unions merged during the 1980s, partly because of falling membership, but also to adapt to the increased power of employers to insist on making arrangements with a single union at the workplace rather than several, as had traditionally happened.

During the 1960s and 1970s the unions became politically so powerful that no government could operate without closely consulting them. 'Beer and sandwich' lunches at which trade unionists and Prime Ministers discussed industrial strategy

A TUC conference.

became a well-known feature of life at 10 Downing Street. In 1974 a miners' strike brought down the Conservative government and five years later strike action brought down the Labour government. Throughout the period both Labour and Conservative governments had tried to introduce laws to limit union power, but both had been unsuccessful and decided that voluntary agreements were the only fruitful solution.

The Conservative government elected in 1979, however, was determined to limit union power by law and introduced a series of laws in 1980, 1982, 1984 and 1988. These laws had two main aims. The first was to restrict and regulate the power of unions in industry, and the second was to shift the balance of power within each union, in the belief that ordinary members of unions would moderate the behaviour of their officials. The laws reduced picketing rights (assembling outside workplace entrances to discourage anyone from entering) and the right to secondary action (sympathy strikes or other action at workplaces not directly involved in the dispute); made union leaders liable to legal prosecution if they organised a strike without a secret ballot of membership; weakened the right of unions to insist that all workers at a particular workplace belonged to a union; threatened union funds for any violation of the new laws; insisted that all union leaders should be subject to periodic elections by secret ballot; and required that the members of each union should vote on whether they should have a political fund (a clear attempt to destroy the financing of the Labour Party).

Union power was further weakened by a fall in membership, from 12.2 million (53 per cent of the employed workforce) in 1979 to 8.7 million by 1989. Most of the shrinkage was explained by growing unemployment, and by the shift in the national economy. Union membership was far lower in the new and growing service industries, so the loss in manufacturing was not made up in those industries. Union power was also weakened by the exclusion of the TUC from consultation with government – no more beer and sandwiches at Downing Street.

Finally, changing economic circumstances, not only in Britain but in the industrialised world generally, brought great stress to the union movement, particularly to those most resistant to economic and technological change. In 1984–5 the miners, led by their Marxist leader, Arthur Scargill, fought a prolonged and damaging strike which ended in their defeat at the hands of a triumphant Conservative government. According to one newspaper editorial it ended "thirty years of dominant union power which had consigned this country to a third-rate industrial status". As another newspaper commented:

"Scargill's failure achieved what decades of exhortation did not. It enabled the labour movement to sever its atrophied link with the tribal loyalties of the 1920s, and with the 'them' and 'us' mentality of class war slogans. In splitting his own union, losing its funds, and sending strikers back to work with nothing, Scargill opened the way to a new unionism based upon the ballot box, free of ideological claptrap."

Miners on the march during their strike, 1984/5.

Apart from the damage to trade union morale, this defeat also led to a split in the miners' union, with a small new Union of Democratic Miners being formed in Nottinghamshire. Four years later, in 1988, there were two further blows to union solidarity. The Ford Motor Company decided against building a large car factory in Dundee because the different trade unions involved could not agree on single union representation for the workforce, which Ford had demanded. A few months later the TUC felt obliged to expel one union from the movement because it had reached a special deal with employers which broke TUC guidelines. The union in question had agreed 'single-union' deals and 'no-strike' undertakings with employers, in the belief that its agreement with employers reflected the realities of the modern economy, a view with which at least one other union sympathised.

The tension between such modernists who wish to break away from old-style trade unionism, and provide a fresh type of service to its members, and the left of the trade union movement, which clings to the old working-class ideologies, is likely to continue through the 1990s. It is a struggle that the modernists are likely to win. One reason for this is that a majority of ordinary union members agree with the sense of single-union deals with employers. Furthermore the nature of union membership is changing, with a clear proportionate rise in the number of white-collar union members, a rising proportion of female members, and a dramatically increased proportion (25 per cent) of members who by the end of the 1980s were share owners. Each of these three growing categories is likely to weaken the male-dominated/working-class/leftist ideologies of traditional trade unionism. It is indicative of the change that in 1987 58 per cent of union members voted either Conservative or Alliance (Liberal/Social Democrat). British trade unionism will either adapt to changing circumstances or it will continue to decline.

It is easy to exaggerate the decline of trade union power during the 1980s. In 1988 fewer days were lost through strike action than in any year since 1935. But it is also true that certain groups of workers went on strike successfully throughout the 1980s, particularly in essential services, like nursing, railways, and the ambulance service. With the loss of direct political power, unions become more skilful at winning the sympathy of the public. While the unions are likely to remain bound by legal restrictions, many Conservatives as well as the Labour Party believe the unions must be brought back into constructive cooperation with government. As a result the unions are likely to regain in the 1990s some of the authority they lost in the 1980s.

The TUC itself, however, may never recover its powers because, in the words of one commentator, "The wave of mergers suggests that in a few years five or six mega-unions will dominate the TUC. They will also weaken it because they will need it less."

The trade union movement has often been blamed for Britain's disappointing economic performance since 1945. Many people, even union members, have highly contradictory attitudes towards trade unionism. While a majority in the 1980s felt that the unions had too much power, a majority also believed that without union support most workers would receive worse pay and conditions. Despite a popular impression that trade unions have damaged the national economy, it should be remembered that even during the worst years of strikes, 1967–70, Britain was midway between the most and least strike-affected industrialised countries. The apparent irresponsibility of the unions is partly explained by hostile press reporting. This has concentrated on industrial conflict but ignored other aspects of union activity, its voluntary workers and social assistance to those suffering hardship. A survey in 1979–80 at 2,000 factories and other workplaces, for example, showed that 48 per cent of employees believed management–worker relations were first rate, 34 per cent good, 15 per cent fairly good, 1 per cent not bad and only 2 per cent fairly poor or bad. The fact is that most union members never strike during their working life, and most unions will try every possibility to avoid strike action.

The workforce

By 1991 there were 35.5 million people of working age, one million more than in 1981. There will be no substantial change in the size of the workforce until after the year 2000. But the age pattern will change. By 1994 the number of 16–19-year-olds will have fallen by nearly a

million, compared with ten years earlier. By the year 2000 there are likely to be 1.8 million more people aged 34–54 in the workforce. This will have far-reaching implications. The workforce changes will be felt unevenly during the 1990s, with a loss of 3.3 per cent in Scotland and the north west, and of 4.9 per cent in the north, compared with a growth of 7.6 per cent in the south west and of 10.2 per cent in East Anglia.

There have been significant changes in the labour force. In 1980 one in five jobs was part-time, by 1990 it was one in four. During the decade 1973–83 for the first time in British history white-collar workers outnumbered blue-collar workers, the former growing from 43 to 52 per cent of the workforce. Mass unemployment was a major factor in blue-collar decline. But there has also been a sharp decline in the lower grades of clerical worker. A gap has grown between those sufficiently skilled to operate computers and other hi-tech equipment, and the lower paid manual workers who cannot. This is, today, the real divide between white- and blue-collar classes.

Working from home.

A more flexible employment pattern may grow, with more people sharing jobs on a part-time basis, some people coming back from retirement, and many more women entering the workforce. If this is to happen government will have to help young mothers financially so that they can provide care for young children during working hours. By 1990 only 3 per cent of companies had introduced child-care schemes. Information technology may change the pattern of workplace attendance. On average most workers in London spend over four hours weekly on commuting to work, yet with computer terminals and fax machines at home they might only need to attend their workplace for periodic meetings. A survey in 1988 suggested that by 1995 almost half the workforce could be doing part of their work from home. This would cut down office rents and other office costs. It might also make qualified people in depressed areas of the country more competitive than workers in the south east. It could lead to a decline of payroll employees, and an increased use of self-employed workers hired for particular jobs.

Despite its unhappy reputation for industrial disputes, there is a high level of job satisfaction in Britain. Surveys in 1979 and 1989 show that almost 90 per cent of the workforce are either very satisfied or fairly satisfied with their work situation. Furthermore, a comparative study by European trade unions in 1980 showed that the British worked almost an hour a day more, usually in less favourable work conditions, than elsewhere in Europe. But this does not mean that British workers are either efficient or hardworking. As Ralf Dahrendorf noted in 1982, "Any foreigner who watches the British at work cannot help being amazed at their leisurely pace." In 1990 a senior industrialist put it another way, "The British are insufficiently serious about earning a living."

Throughout the 1980s unemployment was a major problem. But its level varied on a regional and occupational basis. After a decade of mass unemployment, unemployment was below 2 per cent in many prosperous towns of the south by 1989, for example Winchester, Crawley and Tunbridge Wells, compared with a national average of 6.5 per cent. In occupational terms, unemployment among unskilled labourers in 1986 was around 35 per cent, compared with an overall national rate of 13.7 per cent. But in another recession in 1990–92 unemployment again rose sharply, hitting white-collar occupations in the south east hardest of all. During 1990 unemployment rose by 22.5 per cent nationally, but by 51 per cent in the south. By comparison the job losses in the north were well below the national average.

Unemployment, the weakening of trade unions and the reduction of higher rates of income tax have all helped increase the gap between higher and lower rates of pay in Britain. A century ago, in 1889, the first reliable earnings figures were published. They showed that the highest-paid fifth of the workforce earned 143 per cent more than

the national average and the lowest-paid fifth earned 31 per cent less than the average. Exactly a century later official figures showed that, in spite of the policies of the welfare state 1945–79, the gap between top and bottom earners had widened rather than narrowed. In 1989 the top fifth earned 158 per cent more and the bottom fifth 35 per cent less than the national average. Most of this new inequality occurred in the 1980s. At the bottom of the scale, almost six million full-time workers, 37 per cent of the total full-time workforce, earned less than the 'decency threshold' defined by the Council of Europe as 68 per cent of average full-time earnings. At the top of the scale senior executives of British companies in 1988 were receiving salary increases averaging 28 per cent, compared with average earnings increases of 9.25 per cent. Even the increases in average earnings, it should be noted, were substantially above the inflation rate at the time of under 5 per cent.

A highly paid corporation executive (top).

A low-income worker in catering.

Britain's energy industries

A few words should be said about one other major component of the economy – energy. It was Britain's development of coal production which determined its economic leadership of the world in the eighteenth and nineteenth centuries. It remains the single most important source of energy, in spite of its relative decline as an industry, and in spite of the major discoveries of oil and natural gas under the British sector of the North Sea at the end of the 1960s:

British energy consumption in 1987 (million tonnes of coal equivalent):

Oil	109.3
Coal	116.2
Natural gas	85.9
Nuclear power	19.8
Hydroelectric power	2.1
Net imports of electricity	4.7

In short, oil and coal each account for about one third of total energy consumption. Oil was first brought ashore in 1975, five years after it was first discovered in exploitable quantities in the North Sea. By 1980 Britain was self-sufficient in oil. By 1985 oil production reached a maximum output of 2.5 million barrels of crude oil per day, making Britain the sixth largest world producer. Since then output has been in slow decline. Smaller but exploitable oil reserves have been found in Dorset. Since 1977 natural gas has entirely replaced coal gas for industrial and domestic use.

A 'nodding donkey' in a Dorset oil field.

A miner operating roof supports in a coal mine.

British policy makers have insisted over a number of years that energy should be derived from a balance of different sources. Easily the most controversial of these is the nuclear energy prog-ramme. Britain established the world's first large-scale nuclear plant in 1956. It was assumed that nuclear energy would be a clean, safe solution to Britain's energy needs. Successive governments promised benefits which its technology was unable to fulfil. However, public worries grew over the years, because of the difficulties of dealing with nuclear waste and because nuclear power stations had been built without much idea of how to dismantle them safely once their useful life had come to an end. In addition, nuclear development suffered from inadequate research and experience, and this became clear as the government dithered between inadequate British-designed reactors, and the US-developed Pressurised Water Reactor (PWR).

and the go-ahead given for the construction of a PWR at Sizewell in Essex.

It was only when the government planned to sell the electricity industry into private hands that the real costs of nuclear energy became apparent. In 1990 the Energy Select Committee published a report entitled *The Cost of Nuclear Power: What Went Wrong*? which showed that the real commercial cost by 1990 was twice as high as for a coal power station. Needless to say, no private operator wished to take on this highly expensive form of power generation which was so unpopular with the public. In spite of the environmental disadvantages of coal, nuclear energy will probably be phased out, unless a much more efficient and much safer system is designed.

One might have imagined that on account of the growing concern with pollution Britain would be investing heavily in the research necessary for the exploitation of renewable energy. It is officially estimated that the combined onshore and offshore wind energy resources could provide over 60 per cent of the national electricity requirement. Yet the total spent on research in this area in the period 1974–90 was £220 million, a fraction more than the annual research expenditure on nuclear energy. Renewable energy sources are planned to provide 1 per cent of the national energy requirement by the year 2000. Unlike Britain, Denmark, Holland, Germany, Italy and Greece are all pressing ahead with wind energy programmes. Growing concern with pollution may accelerate the development of wind energy.

A nuclear plant on the Cumbrian coast.

The question of nuclear energy became a highly emotive subject, particularly after the US disaster at Three Mile Island and the Soviet one at Chernobyl. In 1988 a major disaster occurred on the North Sea Piper Alpha oil rig, in which over 160 people died. This did not lead to the closure of the other oil rigs. Had a disaster of similar magnitude occurred in a nuclear power station the government would have found it difficult to resist popular pressure for the total abandonment of nuclear energy.

Nevertheless, the Conservative government was committed to nuclear power in the 1980s. At first it announced plans to build a further fifteen nuclear power stations. This was then scaled down to one PWR a year for ten years. As the cost grew the programme was pruned to six, then to four,

Facing the causes of failure

Why has Britain declined so rapidly during the twentieth century from its status as the most powerful nation in 1900, to one of the middle-ranking members of the European Community by the 1990s? This has been one of the hardest questions to answer. Of course the stress of two world wars and the loss of empire, though not unique to Britain, led to difficult adjustments. But it is also true that life is still sufficiently comfortable that people are unwilling to make the painful adjustments that might make Britain more competitive economically.

Among the long-standing reasons for Britain's poor performance, perhaps the most complex ones are cultural. One theory is that Britain never had a revolution that swept away the old order as occurred in many other parts of Europe. Despite the major economic changes of the Industrial Revolution, the old gentry class (the aristocracy and land-owning families) of Britain did not oppose the rising middle class but made skilful adjustments to allow them to share the ruling culture. This was most evident in Britain's private education system, misleadingly called 'public' schools (for a fuller discussion, see Chapter 11). At public schools, most of which were in the country-side away from industrial centres, the sons of successful industrialists and entrepreneurs lived alongside the sons of the aristocracy and gentry, and became 'gentlemen'. Few went into industry like their fathers. On the whole they tended to demonstrate their arrival into the ruling class by living on a country estate and preferring gentle-manly amateurism to middle-class professional-ism. This has changed, but very slowly. Few public schools even in the 1960s encouraged their best pupils to enter industry or business rather than the Civil Service or the professions, such as law, medicine, the armed forces. Even in the 1980s, while the emphasis had changed from the Civil Service to merchant banking, there has been less enthusiasm for industry. For Ralf Dahrendorf, able to observe British society as an intimate member and yet with the eyes of an outsider, "The upper class is relaxed, the middle class is acquiescent and the working class is passive."

Possibly it is for such reasons that Britain has failed to give technical and scientific subjects as much seriousness as its competitors. This is a very long-standing failure. In 1868 a Royal Commis-sion reported, "Our industrial classes have not even that basis of sound general education on which alone technical education can rest." In fact no start was made to provide technical education until 1889. Technical education has remained weak ever since, when compared with Britain's major competitors. In 1977 a government study reported, "In manufacturing industry generally the status of mechanical engineering is low in itself, and production engineers are regarded as the Cinderella of the profession." At the end of the 1970s there were 15,000 professional engineers graduating in Britain each year compared with 70,000 in Japan and 30,000 in France. In 1982 a government report stated that "Britain has one of the least trained workforces in the industrial world."

Many pupils in Britain enter the workforce with-out any qualifications at the age of sixteen; in the United States the average age of entry into the workforce is eighteen, in Japan twenty. In West Germany and France in the early 1980s some 80–90 per cent of school leavers received vocational training, compared with 40 per cent in Britain.

After a century of relative neglect, the government established a major vocational and technical education programme in the mid 1980s. A real effort, for the first time, was made to break down the artificial barrier between education in school and training for employment. Whether this manpower strategy, based upon equipping school leavers with basic skills, will be enough in the long term to make Britain more competitive may not be seen until the end of the century. The change in skills requirement and in the require-ments of the labour market led in 1988 to the establishment of a major adult employment retraining programme.

Such training is specifically geared to job pros-pects. But at university level, too, government in the 1980s cut budgets, thus reducing both the numbers of students and range of courses. In the 1980s only 6 per cent of Britain's labour force had a university degree, compared with 18 per cent in America, 13 per cent in Japan and 10 per cent in West Germany. In addition in the 1980s the government reduced research budgets and put pressure on universities to direct their research towards practical purposes. Both aspects of this philosophy were fiercely opposed in the universi-ties, which continue to claim that Britain's future depends upon adequate research funding and also the freedom to pursue pure research, not applied to immediate industrial needs, but which advance scientific knowledge more broadly.

Britain's failure to treat these matters properly is most clearly seen in the area of Research and Development (R and D), most of which is directed towards immediate and practical problems. Unfor-tunately, British companies spend less on R and D as a percentage of annual revenue than many European competitors. At the end of the 1980s, for example, 71 per cent of West German com-panies, and 35 per cent of Japanese ones, were spending more than 5 per cent of their revenue on R and D compared with only 28 per cent of British companies.

Britain, too, has been less willing than its com-petitors to invest its resources in industry. In the 1970s the rate of capital investment per worker was half that of West Germany and Japan and

Learning building skills: a vocational training programme.

substantially lower than that of virtually every other industrialised country. Consequently Britain has been automating more slowly than its rivals. It has fewer appropriately skilled people to oversee such changes, and both less research and less investment to produce the kind of automation necessary.

One of Britain's most eminent industrialists in the 1980s was Sir Charles Villiers, Chairman of British Steel until 1984. In his view one of the most serious shortcomings of British industry is in the area of management. He argued, and the argument remains relevant, that the workforce is divided into "those who manage and those who are managed. It is the depths of the last division which is unique to Britain. This is the division which damages us most. It holds the key to improvement. . . ." Little effort is made to interest the workforce in the company's wellbeing. A survey in 1982 suggested that one-half of the workforce in larger companies did not know and did not care what profit their company made. Fewer than one-third of these companies had a

bonus or incentive scheme for increased productivity. In such circumstances it is hardly surprising that British workers have a leisurely approach to work. Villiers argued for joint consultation and keeping workers fully informed, a policy taken for granted in some countries.

During the 1990s it may become clearer whether Britain has been able to shake off its long-standing casual approach to economic productivity and to take the uncomfortable decisions to plan and build a more competitive economy.

Questions

Section analysis

1 The economic problems: What were the successes of 'Thatcherism'? What were the failures?

2 Central actors in the economy: What is the CBI? What is its role?

3 The financial sector: Why is the City so important?

4 The trade unions: How far are the trade unions responsible for Britain's disappointing economic performance?

5 The workforce: What happened to the workforce as a result of social changes in Britain in the 1980s? What will happen to it in the 1990s?

6 Britain's energy industries: Should Britain invest more or less in nuclear energy? How does its policy on nuclear power differ from the policy of your country?

7 Facing the causes of failure: Britain's economic power has declined rapidly in the twentieth century. Find three reasons in the text for this decline.

Chapter analysis and discussion

1 Which of the following statements best summarises Britain's economic position today? Find evidence in the text to support your choice.

a The economic changes introduced by Margaret Thatcher have laid the foundations for Britain's economic success.

b The economic changes introduced by Margaret Thatcher have still not solved Britain's fundamental economic weakness compared with its competitors.

c Britain's economic failure is too complex for any solution to be found.

2 Is Britain's economic decline inevitable? Can its economic position improve? Find arguments to support both points of view.

3 Almost 90 per cent of the British workforce say they are very satisfied or fairly satisfied with their work situation. Does this surprise you? Why/Why not?

4 Read the following statements about the British economy and compare them with the situation in your country:

a Britain struggles to find a balance between government intervention in the economy and an almost completely free-market economy such as exists in the United States.

b A more flexible employment pattern may grow, with more people sharing jobs on a part-time basis, some people coming back from retirement, and many more women entering the workforce.

c The question of nuclear energy became a highly emotive subject, particularly after the United States' disaster at Three Mile Island and the Soviet one at Chernobyl.

Visual interpretation

What do these graphs tell you about changes happening within the trade union movement? Which of these graphs are confirmed in the text?

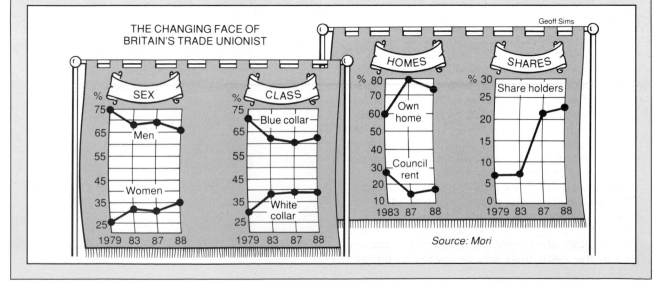

THE CHANGING FACE OF BRITAIN'S TRADE UNIONIST

Geoff Sims

SEX — Men, Women — %: 75, 65, 55, 45, 35, 25 — 1979 83 87 88

CLASS — Blue collar, White collar — %: 75, 65, 55, 45, 35, 25 — 1979 83 87 88

HOMES — Own home, Council rent — %: 80, 70, 60, 50, 40, 30, 20, 10 — 1983 87 88

SHARES — Share holders — %: 30, 25, 20, 15, 10, 5, 0 — 1979 83 87 88

Source: Mori

7 A social profile

It is easy to assume that the population of a Western industrialised country like Britain is stable, but it is a dangerous assumption to make. There is plenty of change going on, even though the population will not reach 60 million, from its present 57 million, until about 2025. As already noted, the population is unevenly distributed across the land, and there has been an insistent drift to the south and south east since the 1980s. But the shape of Britain's population in age and composition has been changing substantially too. Since the middle of the century fertility has fluctuated, rapidly increasing and decreasing (up to 30 per cent variation) in a single decade. This has serious implications for health and education services, and for employment.

Overall, the 'baby boom' that followed the end of World War II, followed by an overall decline in births (to slightly under replenishment level) during the 1970s, is leading to major changes in balance between age groups. The higher birth rate of the 1960s exacerbated unemployment levels in the 1980s, since there were 30 per cent more young people leaving school than a decade previously. In the period 1971–81 the number of infants (0–4 age group) fell by 12 per cent, while those aged 65 or over increased by 34 per cent (to become 17.7 per cent of the total population). Primary school enrolment in 1986 was 26 per cent lower than in 1971.

The British population is already one of the oldest in Europe, and it is slowly getting older. In 1990 the median age in Britain was thirty-six but it will rise to forty-one by 2020. At the end of the 1990s the number of pensioners will begin to rise rapidly, and the workforce will shrink. One result will be that by 2020 there will be twice as many people aged eighty-five or over as in 1990. A disproportionate number of the old, incidentally, choose to retire to the south coast and East Anglia, creating regional imbalances.

In the 1980s there were too many school leavers, but in the 1990s there will be too few to fill the job vacancies created by retirement. This could have important implications for some of the presently unemployed, for the fuller employment of women (see page 96) and for deferring retirement until a later age, a logical step for those who wish to continue working in view of the better health most enjoy today.

Britain is also changing ethnically. There used to be an assumption that the British were nearly all Anglo-Saxon, in spite of the substantial immigration of people from continental Europe during the first half of the century. Since black people from the Caribbean were recruited to fill job vacancies during the 1950s over two million Afro-Caribbean and Asian people have come to live and work in Britain, becoming 5.7 per cent of Britain's population by 1990, but concentrated particularly in

An ageing population: retired people on the south coast.

An Asian community in London.

London and Leicester (where their density is three times the national average), and in Bradford, Slough and Birmingham (where it is twice the national average).

Despite such changes, broad stereotypical views concerning British society persist. Take, for example, the classic family.

Family

"There is no such thing as society," Mrs Thatcher once said. "Only individual men and women, and families." Many people disagree with her, but there remains a strong feeling that the immediate or 'nuclear' family is the basic unit of society, and that traditional family values remain the mainstay of national life.

The nuclear family is usually pictured as a married couple, with two children, ideally a girl and a boy, and perhaps their grandmother, or 'granny', in the background. As a picture of the way most British live, this becomes increasingly unrealistic each year. If the picture includes the traditional idea of the man going out to work while the wife stays at home, it is probably true of less than 10 per cent of the country. Even without such a limited definition, only 42 per cent of the population live in nuclear family households, and even within this group a considerable proportion of parents are in their second marriage with children from a previous marriage. In fact, it is expected that by the year 2000 only half the children born in Britain will grow up in a conventional family with parents already married when they were born and remaining married after they have grown up.

Social attitudes and behaviour are undoubtedly changing. The number of people living alone has risen significantly, from one in ten in 1951 to one in four thirty years later. By the end of the century it is expected to rise to one in three. In the same period the proportion of households containing five or more people has dropped from one in five to fewer than one in ten. The British are clearly becoming a more solitary nation in their living habits. This will have social implications, for example housing needs in the future.

There is an increasing proportion of men and women living together before marriage. For example, in 1961 only 1 per cent of first-time married couples had previously been living together, compared with 24 per cent in 1988. By the year 2000 it is estimated that most couples will live together before marrying. Others living together, or 'cohabiting', never do get married. In 1979 only 3 per cent of all women between the ages of 18 and 49 were cohabiting, but ten years later the level had risen to over 8 per cent.

This does not mean that there are fewer marriages in Britain. Marriages are as popular as ever, with 400,000 weddings yearly. But in 1961 85 per cent of all marriages were for the first time, while today 37 per cent are second-time marriages for at least one partner. This figure implies a high yearly divorce rate, and this has risen to be the highest in Europe. In 1961 the yearly divorce rate was 2 per thousand, but by 1988 this had risen to 12.9 per thousand, almost twice the European average of 6.9 per thousand. In fact, more than one in three first marriages ends in divorce, one quarter of first marriages failing in the first five years. Research shows that the rate is highest among those on a low income and those who marry very young, say under the age of 24.

A traditional wedding.

What happens to those who do not marry? Remarriage may keep up the number of total marriages each year, but there has also been an increase in the number of couples choosing to live together but not marry, and also of women who choose to marry later in life. Only one in seven women aged between 25 and 29 was still single in 1979, compared with one in three by the end of the 1980s. Some, undoubtedly, choose to cohabit, but other women prefer a measure of independence, either by cohabiting or by living

alone, which they fear they will lose by marriage. The preference of pursuit of career rather than marriage was characteristic of the 1980s. Personal development must also partly explain the growing divorce rate. Alongside a social acceptance of divorce greater today than in the 1950s and 1960s, women have been increasingly dissatisfied by the traditonal expectations of the woman's role in marriage. They also frequently want the right to pursue a career. Sometimes the husband's difficulty in adapting to the new situation puts a strain on the marriage.

One inevitable consequence of the climbing divorce rate has been the rise of single parent families. These families often experience isolation and poverty. Single parent families have been increasing, doubling from 8 per cent of all families in 1972 to 16 per cent by 1988. The great majority of single parents are women. Children, of course, are the main victims. One in three children under the age of five has divorced parents. Forty per cent of children experience the divorce of their parents before the age of eighteen.

A single parent family.

There has also been an increase in babies born outside marriage. It is a sign of both increase in numbers and changing social attitudes that these babies, once described as 'illegitimate' (a permanent punishment for the innocent baby), are now described officially as 'non-marital'. In 1961 only 6 per cent of births were non-marital, but the rate rose steeply during the 1980s, from 16 to 23 per cent in the years 1983–87. This rapid rise reflects the increase in cohabitation, which accounts for 48 per cent of non-marital births. Unfortunately, cohabitation is no indication of a long-term stable environment for children. Statistics show that cohabiting parents are three times more likely to split up than married parents.

The remaining non-marital births are to single mothers, with the rate being highest in areas of high unemployment and the greatest poverty, suggesting to some analysts that the birth of a child gives a woman in such circumstances someone to love, a purpose in life and also state assistance. There is also an ethnic dimension. On account of the traditional weakness of family life resulting from centuries of slavery, 43.4 per cent of West Indian families are single-parent families.

What can be made of such evidence? For some members of the Conservative Party, such statistics are evidence of moral decline, and they argue the need to return to traditional values. In the face of the evidence this sounds like wishful thinking, but it is true that during the 1980s, in the words of an official survey, "the pendulum is swinging against the more liberal attitudes of the 1960s and 1970s". By the end of the 1980s there was a more censorious attitude towards sex outside marriage (but not towards sex before marriage), towards homosexuality, the availability of pornography and the provision of contraception for those under the age of sixteen.

Is Britain really in moral decline? It would be safer to say that moral values are changing, with less attention on traditional definitions of immorality, and greater emphasis on personal morality being rooted in kindness and respect for others. Many, however, would disagree with this verdict, pointing to the high divorce and non-marital birth rates as evidence of fundamental failure to be kind or to respect others. One retired school teacher and Devon magistrate has this to say: "You cannot give young people moral tuition in this [sex] area any more. They regard it as an intolerable intrusion into their privacy." Yet, he continues, "I must admit that I also find older children more mature, more responsible, more considerate to each other." It is too easy simply to blame a moral decline on the failure to uphold family values. There are other things which must be considered to understand what is going on in society and why. A fundamental one is the matter of social class.

Social class

Britain has a deeply individualistic society. Nevertheless, it is also described as having a class-ridden one. Is it really true? The answer is not simple. Undoubtedly Britain is a class-conscious society but this does not mean that society is more divided than, for example, in France. Many people feel that class divisions exist less in reality than in the imagination. In part the sense of division probably comes from that love of hierarchy and sense of deference about which Walter Bagehot wrote over a century ago. Not only the Royal Family, but also the surviving titled families and old land-owning families are treated with greater deference than might be expected in a democracy. There can be no doubt that they enjoy special status.

But such people are a very small minority of the population. Most people are classified according to their work occupations, falling into two broad groups, as in other industrialised societies, the middle class (or white-collar workers) and the working class (or blue-collar workers). The kind of work done not only indicates education and how much is earned, but also the kind of social contact that is usual. Most people generally mix socially with the same kind of people as those with whom they work. Manual workers tend to mix with each other, as do professionals (doctors, lawyers and senior civil servants) and managers.

Such a picture suggests a static situation, but in fact there is major movement between classes. Many people move from one category to another or increase their level of responsibility during their working lives. More importantly, the working class is rapidly declining. In 1911 three out of every four employed or self-employed people were manual workers. By 1950 that proportion had fallen to two out of three, but since then has fallen to only one in three. Since the 1950s there has been a massive growth of the middle class.

The middle class embraces a range of people from senior professionals, for example judges, senior medical specialists and senior civil servants, through to clerical workers – in other words, almost all people who earn their living in a non-manual way. To this extent, the middle class embodies much variety and cannot claim a single identity. The sense of social class or group is affected by social circle, education and comparative wealth, although these do not necessarily work together. A relatively poor but highly educated

A working-class person at home (top).

A manual worker.

Middle-class leisure (top).

An art director – a skilled, white-collar worker.

family may find itself associating with wealthier but similarly highly educated friends. An extremely rich but less highly educated family will probably associate with others of similar educational level.

The middle class is the engine room of the economy. Unlike the working class, the middle class has great fluidity and mobility. During the twenty years 1971–91 approximately two million jobs were created in the professional and managerial fields alone, and the whole middle class is constantly expanding. Over half of today's middle class started life in the working class.

Beyond the middle class lies a small but powerful upper class, which survives from one generation to another. Although the upper class seems to be merely an extension of the middle class, it is actually separated by three things: property, networks and power. For example, the top 1 per cent of wealth holders probably own about one quarter of the nation's wealth, a large drop from the two thirds they controlled in 1914, but a larger proportion than one might expect in a

modern democracy. The reason that the top 1 per cent has remained so wealthy is inheritance, which is spread around the family to minimise the effects of taxation. Without inheritance the top 1 per cent would be far less wealthy and would not be able to sustain their position from one generation to another. The core of the class is probably only between 25,000 and 50,000 strong, but they control key areas of capital in the national economy. For example a study in 1976 showed how just eleven people held fifty-seven directorships in the top 250 companies in Britain. Nine of the eleven, through their directorships, linked thirty-nine major companies. Members of the upper class share a very specific identity. The sons all go to public schools, usually the more famous ones. As one sociologist has noted, "The ruling minority has survived all the transformations from medieval to modern society by a long series of concessions and accommodations in return for retention of privileges and property." In fact in the 1980s, after thirty years of a more egalitarian mood, there was a growing nostalgia for the upper-class life style, exemplified by the

A social occasion for the upper classes.

television dramatisation of Evelyn Waugh's *Brideshead Revisited* in 1979, and stimulated by a general political mood which encouraged the acquisition and display of wealth as a symbol of success. Perhaps the wittiest comment on the upper class was the publication of a bestseller in 1982, entitled *The Official Sloane Ranger Handbook*, which parodied the upper classes for whom Sloane Street was the centre of their London life.

Those who think that Britain has a class-ridden society usually think of the contrast between this small group, maintained by its great wealth, property and privileged education, and the shrinking unskilled manual working class, which has been characterised by significantly higher unemployment than other groups. But these two extremes are where there is the least social mobility. Almost half those born into the upper class remain in it, while 40 per cent of sons of unskilled manual workers themselves remain in that class. But among the intermediate categories of people, skilled manual workers, clerical workers, supervisors, managers and professionals, there is a high degree of social mobility.

Nevertheless, the perception of class conflict remains. Since 1964 opinion polls have asked a random sample of people, "There used to be a lot of talk in politics about the 'class struggle'. Do you think there is a class struggle in this country?" In 1964 48 per cent thought so, and this figure increased to 60 per cent in 1975 and 74 per cent in 1984. One reason for this may be the way in which the slow redistribution of wealth from the top 5 or so per cent (which still controls 47 per cent of marketable wealth) has only filtered down through the richer half of society. In relative terms, the bottom 50 per cent has remained almost wholly unaffected.

Gender

Many women would argue that there is a different half of the nation which gets less than its share of power, freedom and wealth: the female sex. In spite of the considerable change in social attitudes since 1945, and particularly since the feminist revolution which began in the 1960s, women are still significantly disadvantaged. It is true that women have entered employment in increasing numbers. In 1971 52 per cent of women between the ages of twenty-five and forty-four were economically active, a figure which rose to 70 per cent by 1989, and is set to rise to 75 per cent or more in the 1990s. Nevertheless, their position relative to men in employment has improved only slightly.

The reasons are complex, but largely to do with the fact that men continue to control the positions of power and of wealth and are slow to share these with women. In spite of having a female monarch, and having had a female Prime Minister for over a decade, the difficulties begin at the top. During the whole of the 1980s Prime Minister Margaret Thatcher only ever had one other female Cabinet minister, and she lasted for less than a year. In 1989 the Labour Party decided to adopt a system of positive action in favour of women, whereby MPs voting on the composition of the Shadow Cabinet would be compelled to vote for at least three women (out of eighteen nominees to Cabinet posts).

Following the 1987 election forty-one women were elected as MPs, more than ever before, but holding only 6.2 per cent of seats in the Commons. The Commons *300 Group* is an all-party national organisation working towards a minimum of 300 women MPs. Even that would be less than representative of the proportion of women (52 per cent) in the country. At least in local government, women hold 20 per cent of available seats.

If one looks at the senior positions of power in the country virtually none are held by women. At the beginning of 1990, of the ten judges who form the highest court of appeal none was a woman, and there was only one (out of 27) at the next senior level. In the Civil Service there was no female Permanent Secretary, the senior rank, although there were an increasing number at senior, but lower, levels. In fact, out of 304 Permanent Secretaries between 1900 and 1990, only two have been women. The situation is not much better in local government. Take, for example, the City of Bradford. Two thirds of the council's workforce in 1983 were female, yet while 22 per cent of male employees were earning over £10,000, only 2 per cent of women did so.

Discrimination ranges well beyond government. No woman has ever been appointed as a police Chief Constable. Fewer than 3 per cent of university professors are women. While 25 per cent of qualifying doctors are women, only 2 per cent of

surgeons are women. Hardly any women have become trade union leaders. An internal report in 1988 commissioned by the largest union of all, the Transport and General Workers' Union, stated that the image of union officials among its white-collar members is "male, middle-aged, somewhat aggressive and sexist".

It is difficult to think of many successful women in business or industry. Those whose names come to mind, Anita Roddick of the Body Shop and the late Laura Ashley, reached their position by creating their own businesses. They did not climb to the top of a career ladder in an already established company. Women in career structures sense that a 'glass ceiling' exists which prevents them reaching the top. As Ann Watts, equal opportunities director at the Midland Bank, remarked, "We can see the opportunities and goals but at the same time something we cannot pin down is holding us back."

The exception to the rule: Anita Roddick, founder of the Body Shop at her factory.

Women are also paid less than men. On average women earn between two thirds and three quarters of men's pay. Although the Equal Opportunities Act, requiring equal pay and conditions for women, came into effect in 1975, little has changed since then. Among police officers under the rank of sergeant, for example, women earn only 93 per cent of men's hourly rate. In nursing, women earn on average 87 per cent of men's wages. The main reasons for the difference is the segregation of employment by gender, so that it is possible to pay those categories of work in which women predominate significantly less, and the confining of women to the lower grades of a particular industry – which then become considered 'women's work'. This is particularly true of clerical work, welfare and primary education.

Another reason is that married women rather than their husbands suffer the career penalties of producing and raising children. A small but growing number of employers ensure that mothers can resume their careers without any damage to their career prospects after having a baby. Few employers provide crèches for young children in order to encourage women to work for them. Even the state provides day care for fewer than one per cent of under-three-year-olds, thus discouraging women from working. Apart from that in Ireland, this is the the lowest level of provision in the European Community.

For those women who do work, there is an added penalty. Although on average they work shorter hours than men (in 1988, 39.7 compared with 44.5), there has been no substantial adjustment of the domestic burden. Women still do almost all the housework, except for household repairs. In the words of a government report in 1989, the "greater acceptance of a woman's right to work outside the home does not appear to have translated itself into a sense of egalitarianism in the allocation of tasks within the home".

The problems begin early with the assumptions made both by parents and by schools. Although girls tend to perform better at school, they are often encouraged to specialise in humanities subjects, for example modern languages, rather than the sciences (see Chapter 11).

Undoubtedly perceptions are changing, but they are doing so mainly as a result of economic pressures, which are likely to encourage more women to work in the 1990s, with the possibility that they may win a fairer slice of the power and wealth that should come with work. In the 1980s the Conservative government encouraged young

mothers to stay at home with their children, but this was largely ignored. By 1985 more than a quarter of mothers with children aged three or under were at work, and almost half of those with children aged four or five. The shortfall in manpower will push public opinion towards giving women greater freedom to work.

The ethnic dimension

The ethnic minority communities in Britain are about 5.7 per cent of the total population but are likely to rise to about 7 per cent in the early years of the 21st century, on account of their higher birth rate. Black immigrants first started coming to Britain in substantial numbers from 1948 onwards, in response to labour shortages. At first almost all came from the West Indies, but during the 1960s and 1970s a large number came from India, Pakistan and Bangladesh. There were already several thousand non-white Britons, mainly in ports like Liverpool, Bristol and Cardiff. Some families dated back to the eighteenth century and slave trading. They were used to discrimination.

Members of ethnic minorities often find themselves in low paid work.

The immigrants arriving in waves in the 1950s and after soon discovered that they were the target of discrimination in class and status. Black people have generally had the worst paid jobs, lived in the worst housing and encountered hostility from white neighbours. The initial view that black immigrants would assimilate into the host community was quickly proved wrong. In the mid 1960s the government introduced the first of three Race Relations Acts in order to eliminate racial discrimination. The 1977 Race Discrimination Act sought to prevent discrimination in employment, housing and other areas, and to prevent the publication of any material likely to stir up racial hatred. At the same time, however, laws were introduced to restrict immigration. Although these laws were not specific, it was difficult to avoid the conclusion that they were particularly aimed at coloured or black immigrants. Over the years the situation for the ethnic minorities has not improved.

Before she came to power, Margaret Thatcher promised that a Conservative government would "finally see an end to immigration". Implicit in these words was the aim of bringing to an end the arrival of coloured or black immigrants, for she also spoke sympathetically of the fears of white Britons that they might be "swamped by people with a different culture". During the 1980s her government restricted immigration further, and ended the automatic right of anyone born in Britain to British citizenship.

Mrs Thatcher's provocative remarks angered the country's 2.5 million people of ethnic minority origin and contributed to the level of hostility many of them felt in Britain, for she had touched upon a widespread but ill-informed view of immigration, which has been persistently echoed in the press, that the problem is one of immigration into an already overcrowded island. For people either living in areas of poor housing or in need of their own home, there is understandable resentment at the idea of immigrants competing for a scarce resource. But immigration has been dropping steadily since its peak year in 1967 and, although this is not widely known, in the thirty years up to 1982 750,000 more people left Britain permanently than entered to settle. Since then immigrants and emigrants have nearly balanced. There is anger too, because the processing of applications for immigrants and for those seeking political asylum can take years because of bureaucratic inefficiency.

The other charge frequently levelled against the ethnic minority communities is their "failure to integrate". Integration is difficult in a hostile climate. The ethnic minority communities feel that they face hostility not only from the white people amongst whom they live but also from the authorities. In 1989 the Joint Council for the Welfare of Immigrants claimed that each month hundreds of black people were stopped at random by the police to check whether they were illegal immigrants. A Home Office survey of two police stations indicated that in some areas a young black man was ten times more likely to be stopped in the street by police than the average white citizen. Black people feel harassed by such treatment, particularly since a growing number of black youths, the main target of the police, were born in Britain. There is also clear evidence that the police more readily arrest blacks than whites. A study in 1989 showed that although only 6 per cent of the population, blacks made up 20 per cent of those held in custody in England and Wales, and 38 per cent of those held in custody in London. Blacks, it seems are both twice as likely to be held in custody before trial and twice as likely to be acquitted once their case is heard by a magistrate.

Discrimination, or at least a failure to involve the ethnic minority groups adequately, is apparent in many institutions. The army is a good example. In 1988 only 1.6 per cent of applicants were black, and only one out of 881 people recruited as officers was black. Moreover, it was only after Prince Charles had drawn attention to the absence of black recruits in the Brigade of Guards, which performs most of London's ceremonial and royal parades, that any attempt was made to recruit members of the ethnic minority communities. By 1988 two black guardsmen had been recruited, one of whom complained of "intolerable racial abuse and bullying". These cases were not unique. Other cases of racial bullying and abuse in the army and the police force were periodically reported in the press.

Because the police force is perceived as hostile to the ethnic minority communities, and because of the racial abuse experienced by the few who have joined, recruitment is very low. By 1989 coloured police officers made up only 0.9 per cent of the police in England and Wales. Even in the trade union movement, which has made many statements on racial equality, blacks are underrepresented. In 1988 the Transport and General Workers' Union had only one out of 500 full-time officials who was black. Like women, ethnic minority workers tend to be concentrated in particular areas of work, in declining industries or in unpopular night-shift work. Like women, too, non-manual black workers on average earn only about three quarters of the wages of white colleagues.

At a popular level Afro-Caribbeans and Asians experience disadvantage. It may merely be that they find greater difficulty getting a job. One controlled experiment, using two actors, one white, the other black, demonstrated that a white is ten times more likely to obtain a job than a black. The unemployment figures confirm this. In 1982 unemployment among whites was 13 per cent, and 25 per cent among Afro-Caribbeans. A government survey in 1986 found that among white youths aged 16–24, 17 per cent were out of work, compared with 32 per cent of Afro-Caribbeans and 43 per cent of Pakistanis and Bangladeshis. A black is likely to find it harder to obtain credit from a bank or a loan to purchase a house. Even in the provision of housing, there is widespread discrimination, with a tendency for councils to allocate their better housing to whites. Two London borough councils during the 1980s were warned by the Commission for Racial Equality (a monitoring organisation) to stop discrimination in housing allocation.

At a more serious level Afro-Caribbeans and Asians are frequent targets for verbal abuse, harassment or even attack. A government report in 1981 estimated that Asians were fifty times, and Afro-Caribbeans thirty-six times more likely to be victims of a racially motivated incident than whites. The experience of the Meah family from Bangladesh is a good example. Mr Meah had been in London since 1963 but brought his family to Britain in 1981, and obtained a council flat. Within weeks, gangs of white youths began to spit, swear and jostle Mrs Meah and her daughters whenever they left their flat. Their car windscreen was repeatedly smashed. Sometimes they were hit or had their hair pulled. Volunteers stayed with the Meah family to give them support and to call for help. Eventually the ringleaders were taken to court and the Meahs were left alone. But elsewhere many Asian people go on suffering harassment. One in four Asian households has direct experience of harassment. In Leeds, for example, a survey in 1988 showed that 45 per cent of victims of racial harassment had been forced to alter their pattern of life, for example by not letting their children play outside. A relatively small number of activists, sometimes in specifically right wing groups like the National Front, create most of the trouble. But a far greater number of whites will either sympathise with such activists, or look the other way.

Difficulties for ethnic minority children begin when they go to school. Most members of the ethnic minorities live in deprived inner city areas where the quality of the schools is worse than elsewhere and where teachers may have lower expectations. Low expectations from their teachers and a sense of alienation from the majority white community are serious disadvantages. Afro-Caribbeans are expected to remain at the bottom of the economic scale. Asians, who do better in formal education than Afro-Caribbeans and many white children, are often resented when they surpass whites.

It is hardly surprising that those aged between fifteen and twenty-five feel the greatest anger. They discover prejudice at school and on the streets, and when they leave school they find it is far harder for them to find work than it is for whites. In 1981 there were serious riots in two deprived inner city areas: Brixton in south London and Toxteth in Liverpool. Four years later there was another outbreak of rioting in a number of poor urban areas across Britain. In all these cases – the result of poor housing, poor education, poor

Blacks are often allocated the least desirable public housing.

Inner city anger.

The exception: Bill Morris at the top of his trade union.

employment expectations and finally of insensitive policing – there was a major ethnic element.

In some places the barriers have begun to be broken down, but it has required determination. When the Afro-Caribbean footballer, John Barnes, began to play for Liverpool Football Club, he was met with racist abuse from spectators. When play took him to the edge of the pitch he was spat upon and showered with bananas. Barnes refused to react, and slowly won the respect of the crowds. More black players have become a frequent sight in football matches. But the suspicion remains, in the words of one newspaper that, like other black players, Barnes "has not so much been accepted as being black as forgiven for it".

Economic success has helped a number of Asians move into a more secure position in the middle class. Some remain firmly committed to the Labour Party, traditionally more sympathetic to the position of the ethnic minority communities than the Conservatives. But an increasing number of successful Asians have begun to vote Conservative. At the end of the 1970s nine out of ten Asians were Labour voters. By 1987 one in four Asians, and half of those in the middle class, voted Conservative. Nevertheless, a number of successful Asians and Afro-Caribbeans continue to challenge the situation for the ethnic minority communities through support of the Labour Party. A few enter Parliament, like Keith Vaz, who was elected to represent Leicester East in 1987. Others enter local government where, like women, they have stronger representation. In 1984 the Lord Mayor of Bradford, for example, was an Asian.

Successive governments have introduced legislation that promises absolute equality for non-white British citizens. But the promise has remained unfulfilled. Government has not done enough to implement functional equality in the areas over which it has direct control, and white Britons have not yet accepted Afro-Caribbeans and Asians who are born and grow up here (now more than 40 per cent of their communities) as being as British as themselves. Reporting on the Brixton riots of 1981, Lord Scarman wrote, "We must create a black British middle class . . . black and brown as well as white faces must be seen not only on the production line but also in positions of authority and influence at all levels of society."

Questions

Section analysis

1 Since the middle of the century, fertility in Britain has increased and decreased significantly. What effect does this have on employment?

2 Family: Why is the number of 'non-marital' births increasing?

3 Social class: Are class divisions in British society real or imagined? Find evidence in the text to support your argument.

4 Gender: Women are still disadvantaged in employment in Britain. In what ways are they disadvantaged? How does the position of women in Britain compare with that in your own country?

5 The ethnic dimension: Ethnic minority communities in Britain have always been the target of discrimination in Britain. From the text, find evidence for discrimination in the following areas: relations with the police, the armed services, employment, housing, education, sport.

Chapter analysis and discussion

1 Many British people feel that they do not enjoy their rightful share of power and wealth. Who do you think they are? Why do they feel as they do?

2 The traditional picture of the British family, with a married couple and two children is becoming increasingly unrealistic. In what major ways is the family changing? Are similar changes taking place in your country?

3 What predictions can you make about British society? In what ways is it likely to differ from today by 2010?

4 Both women and ethnic minorities suffer disadvantages in Britain. Do you think those disadvantages are comparable?

Visual interpretation

What does this graph say about the changing role women play in politics?

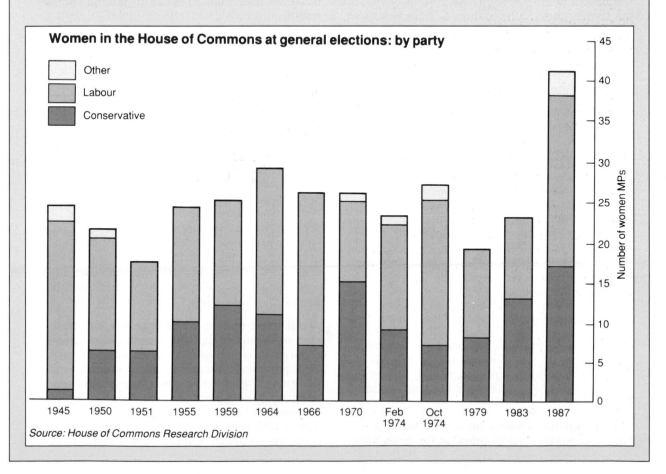

Women in the House of Commons at general elections: by party

Other
Labour
Conservative

Number of women MPs

1945 1950 1951 1955 1959 1964 1966 1970 Feb 1974 Oct 1974 1979 1983 1987

Source: House of Commons Research Division

8 Culture and style: national self-expression

How do these aspects of British society express themselves? Like any other society, the British like to create an agreeable picture of themselves. The majority like to think the important national values are things like tolerance, decency, moderation, consensus and compromise. They are uncomfortable with terms which polarise, such as: ideology, liberation, bourgeois, capitalist, collectivist. They like modesty and understatement, and they prefer practical common sense to pure logic. One writer, contrasting England with neighbouring France, says, "At times it seems that the French and English national characters could be expressed in a series of antitheses: wit/humour; logic/tradition; gallantry/courage; thrift/expenditure; taste/comfort; town/country; vanity/pride." Unlike elsewhere in Europe, someone described as an 'intellectual' usually feels embarrassed rather than flattered.

Community and the individual

In spite of having been a centralised state for longer than most European countries, British society is also deeply individualistic in a way which is inseparable from ideas of liberty and localism. This has a long history. According to one sociologist, "Individualism is built into 'custom and practice', into local work places and community organisations."

There is a feeling that it is the ordinary people, standing up for their rights *in spite of* government, who safeguard freedom, in contrast with France where in theory it is the state which upholds liberty. According to Ralf Dahrendorf, "There is a fundamental liberty in Britain not easily found elsewhere."

In part this liberty stems from the growth of a variety of institutions in previous centuries, which have strongly resisted the authority of central government. The tradition continues. Unlike in many other countries, local government clings both to local identity and style. For example, the reorganisation of the old counties in 1974 still causes fury where much-loved identities have been removed. Locally, many people refuse to recognise the reorganisation and deliberately use old county names, sometimes with the support of local councils. Some people have formed lobby organisations to persuade central government to recognise their right to return to the old county system.

This local response illustrates another long-standing characteristic of the British. They have a strong civic sense and participate in public affairs as their birthright. It is at the local level that British democracy is most meaningful. Writing eighty years ago, Elie Halevy, a French writer on Britain, spoke enthusiastically of Britain as "the country of voluntary obedience, of spontaneous organization". It is as true today.

The impulse to organise oneself and one's neighbours in some cause is a strong British tradition. William Beveridge, the wartime architect of Britain's welfare system, wrote at the time, "Vigour and abundance of Voluntary Action outside the home, individually and in association with other citizens, for bettering one's own life and that of one's fellows, are the distinguishing marks of a free society."

About seven million Britons are involved in some kind of voluntary activity, ranging from urban community action groups of the political left, to local preservation societies, associated with more traditionally-minded people. Choirs, local dramatic groups, shelters for homeless people, the provision of the lifeboat service around Britain's shores, and many other things besides, depend upon the voluntary impulse. There are 160,000 charities officially registered with the government, and another 200,000 voluntary organisations, including sports clubs, trade unions, rambling clubs, protest groups and other societies which are not. Most charities operate with less than £1,000 yearly. Only a handful operate with more than £1 million. One of the largest of these, the Third World development agency Oxfam, has a network across Britain of over 800 shops selling second-hand goods and Third World products, staffed by unpaid volunteers. These organisations, great or small, all depend upon time, skill and money given voluntarily.

A sponsored walk to raise money for Third World development.

The fine distinctions of speech

A picture of the British as both individualist and yet community-minded is a cosy one, and in many respects the British have a deep sense of cultural cohesion and unity. Yet, in the words of a leading educationist, "The trouble with the British is that they accept and enjoy the nice distinctions of social class. They love hierarchy and see nothing wrong in the deferential attitude that it breeds." Nowhere is this clearer than in the question of speech. For the way English is spoken gives away not only regional identity but to some extent class status too. It is, for one sociologist, "the snobbery which brands the tongue of every British child".

Since the days of Shakespeare, the English of south east England has been considered the 'standard', for no better reason than that the south east is the region of economic and political power. The emergence of an upper and upper-middle-class mode of speech, 'received pronunciation' (RP), was systematically established through the public (in fact private) school system attended by the boys of wealthier families. RP persists as the accepted dialect of the national élite.

Broadly speaking, there are two kinds of RP. One is 'unmarked' RP, which suggests no more than that the speaker is well-educated (although of course many equally well-educated people speak with a regional accent). This is the dialect of the BBC, and thus it has a kind of authority. Through radio and television unmarked RP is becoming a more widely spoken accent. Then there is 'marked' RP, which indicates high social class and is spoken, for example, by many army officers who come from upper-class families. At the time of the Falklands War, marked RP was very fashionable, since it suggested leadership and authority at a time of national crisis. Although spoken by less than 5 per cent of the population, RP has immense influence. Those who speak it enjoy a social authority that contradicts democratic ideals. As long as RP remains suggestive of authority, some job advertisements will demand 'well spokenness', and some ambitious politicians will hide their regional accents with RP.

Regional accents exist, in class status terms, below RP. But even they have a hierarchy. Scottish, Welsh and Irish are generally the more popular regional accents. Then come northern, Yorkshire and west country accents, and at the bottom of the list come the least popular ones of the great conurbations, London, Liverpool, Glasgow and the West Midlands. Significantly the television news is read by RP speakers, while the weather forecast following the news is often read by someone with a regional accent. Is there an implicit difference in the importance and status of news and weather?

Do dialect (a matter of grammar and vocabulary) and accent enrich or impoverish? This is a continuing matter for debate among linguists. Some argue that regional accents enhance the sense of local community, and that to abandon them is to give way to the accents of the ruling class. Others argue that regional dialects, given their class associations, are socially divisive. Dialect is unlikely to disappear and the debate is likely to continue.

The culture of violence

The sense of unity and community is also disturbed by a gradual erosion of the consensus on acceptable social behaviour. Society seems to be more openly violent. The urban riots of 1981 and 1985 and the violence of football crowds, which give British soccer fans such notoriety in continental Europe, are not the only evidence. Among poorer young people there has been growing anger at financially successful young professionals, or 'yuppies'. The second half of the 1980s saw increased violence in wealthy country towns in southern England. In 1987 there were 251 incidents of public disorder in rural areas involving no fewer than 36,000 people.

Violence on the football pitch.

Does this represent a new breakdown in social values? It is probably nearer the truth to recognise that the law and order achieved during the years 1900–60 was exceptional, and resulted from a stronger (and accepted) class system, the loss of many young men in war, and the hard grind of economic survival. We know that urban violence was a regular feature of nineteenth-century Britain.

Apart from the abuse of alcohol, the reasons for the present growth in violence may include: the widespread destruction of traditionally close-knit communities when the old slums were replaced by modern housing estates; the decline of the working-class cultural solidarity; the growth of the middle class, in which individualism is more important than community solidarity; and possibly most important of all, the vastly increased mobility of individuals who can no longer feel they are deeply rooted in one particular community.

Hooliganism may appear uncivilised and purposeless. Those who have studied football hooliganism, however, believe that it represents an attempt to find a group identity. Gangs find their identity through loyalty to a particular club, and controlling the area around the club stadium. "Our violence," one gang member explained, "is all about defending and invading territory." When England played in West Germany in 1988, police identified seven gangs involved in the violence, with names like The Intercity Firm (West Ham), The Headhunters (Chelsea) and Bushwhackers (Millwall).

Although football hooliganism has been a cover for the demonstration of the 'hardness' expected of young men on rough public housing estates, it is not confined to any one social group. One researcher found a gang which included two solicitors' clerks, an insurance underwriter, a bank manager and some soldiers on leave. As a twenty-six-year-old financial adviser told a joint research study by five European countries, "Whilst away representing my country, England, [at the 1988 European championships] I had one of the biggest 'buzzes' of my life. The adrenalin that was pumping through my body, aching with pride from the moment we landed was something I have never experienced in my life before." According to the same study, the typical British hooligan travelling to the European football championships was a single man, aged seventeen to thirty-three, and living in the south east, probably a skilled worker or badly paid clerk.

Football matches provide the potential enemy and the environment in which people can organise themselves to express their frustration or alienation violently. Violence, one should note, is not confined to hooligans. Violent methods have been increasingly used by the police to maintain order since the 1980s (see page 61). Furthermore, government has been less tolerant of those who do not conform to social norms.

The rural ideal

While many might agree that the characteristics and behaviour mentioned above are recognisably British there are, of course, many cultures reflecting age, class, gender, ethnicity and social outlook. Broadly speaking there is a divide between the cultures of the controlling majority and those of the protesting minority, people who feel comparatively weak.

A thatched cottage: the rural dream.

One of the most striking aspects of popular mainstream culture in Britain is the love of the countryside. Many people, whether they live in a suburban house or in a flat in a high-rise block, would say their dream home was a country cottage with roses growing over the door. In 1977 a collection of Edwardian amateur watercolours and sketches of wild flowers and simple rural scenes were published under the title *The Country Diary of an Edwardian Lady*. To the surprise of the publishers this proved to be the best selling book of the next ten years, selling over 2.6 million copies in thirteen languages, and £75 million worth of associated merchandise. It appealed to romantic (and upper-class) nostalgia for the countryside. *The Archers*, radio's longest running serial soap opera (over thirty-five years so far), Laura Ashley's highly successful decor and fashion shops, and the fashion for unpainted pine furniture, all tap deeply into the British rural imagination.

As a nation, the British have made a mental retreat from the urban environment. They have a deep nostalgia for an idealised world of neat hedgerows, cottages and great country houses, surrounded by parkland, that clever eighteenth-century style of gardening that looked 'natural'. The nostalgia stems partly from a sense of loss which has lingered since the Industrial Revolution two centuries ago, and from a romantic love of nature which has been such a powerful theme in English literature. The National Trust, which owns or manages hundreds of country estates, stretches of countryside and great country houses, was founded a century ago on the rising nostalgia for a lost rural paradise. Its growth in membership during the late 1970s and 1980s, from 315,000 to 1.3 million, illustrates its success in encouraging a love of the country and of the past. It too easily becomes an exercise in national nostalgia.

A basic reason so many town dwellers wish to live in the suburbs is to have a garden in which to grow flowers. Indeed, many suburban houses imitate a cottage style. Even in the heart of London, its great parks, such as St James', Hyde Park and Kensington Gardens, are informal, recreating a rural ideal, and city-dwelling children often know the names of wild flowers and birds.

St James' Park recaptures the countryside.

Britain is a country where over 80 per cent of the population live in towns of 50,000 inhabitants or more. Yet most reject the urban industrial culture, viewing life in the city as an 'unnatural' economic necessity. It is perhaps only in Britain that the Home Secretary (responsible for civil order) could retire to his country estate following the most serious urban riots since 1945 (the Brixton riots of 1981), and frankly tell the nation that he took heart as he looked out across the countryside, "the *real* England", as he actually put it. In another country such a remark might have seemed so absurd a response to urban riots as to require his resignation. In an urbanised Britain that still dreams of the countryside it touched the heart of the nation.

This sense of nostalgia and traditionalism is also expressed in appearances. The 1989 British Interior Design Exhibition contained twenty-seven example room sets, the majority of which were traditional, pretty and uncontroversial, and were mainly some version of the English country house. Laura Ashley floral wallpapers and fabrics decorate suburban and even high-rise homes all over the land.

Dress codes

Being so traditionally minded, the British are less fashion-conscious than other Europeans. The majority dress conservatively rather than fashionably. For example, the upper and upper middle classes tend to dress 'safely' in the well-tried styles of the past fifty years or so. During the 1980s this style appealed to a wider clientele which, inspired by the romance of the upper classes, particularly by the Royal Wedding (Prince Charles and Lady Diana Spencer) in 1981, began to imitate them. For all its simplicity, this old-fashioned style of the upper and upper middle class is distinctively exclusive. As one fashion writer, speaking of the disappearance in 1989 of the European 'powersuit', observes:

"Meanwhile, the pin-striped men of London do not care what is happening to the suit in Paris. . . . It is from the sober tailoring of the Victorian power-lord and from mediaeval heraldry that the British suit takes its imagery of power and control. It is not an ostentatious display of wealth and privilege but a discreet system of signals . . . [through which] the subtle working of the establishment is revealed. At official functions throughout the land, the tie, the suit's colours, signal to the assembled company the allegiance of the wearer – which school or university he attended, which club or company he belongs to. . . . And those who imagine that the code has become redundant in the modern world do not understand the strength of the patriarchal system in this country."
(Charlotte Du Cann, *The Independent*, 18th May 1989)

It is a question of breeding not wealth. The suit is the uniform of traditional Conservative MPs, while Labour MPs wear the clothes of the ordinary *middle* middle classes, the suburban look of off-the-peg suits from a major retailer like Marks and Spencer. There is, of course, an equivalent dress for women. For those who want to understand the mystique of the upper class, all is revealed in Peter York's book which popularised the style of the 1980s:

"THE OFFICIAL SLOANE RANGER HANDBOOK explains *precisely* how to decorate your house, how to wear your clothes (and what clothes to wear), how to word your letters and how to educate your children. If you are a Sloane Ranger, you'll recognise the form. Mummie and Daddy will have done a proper job on that years ago. But It Never Hurts To Be Sure."

For those 'Young Fogeys' as they are known in Britain, who want to wear the clothes of 'good breeding', there are a number of shops which specialise in the look, like Hackett's.

Hackett's: specialists in upper-class clothes.

Most people, of course, do not imitate top society. Nevertheless, the 1980s was a decade when wealth and power were strongly expressed, for example in 'power dressing', an echo of the dominant political ideas of the Thatcher decade, as Peter York noted:

"To grow into her role as a leader of men, she [Margaret Thatcher] had . . . to turn to a power symbol – the warrior queen. . . . She wears career lady suits with lapels and those bows and cravats which are a kind of pretend tie. Her hair is lacquered into Britannia's golden helmet, her voice is stronger, slower, deeper. . . . I think Margaret Thatcher mastered the nation by style, by projecting strength and certainty when people wanted it."
(Peter York, *Modern Times*, p.15)

The old upper class will continue to dress as it always has, but there may be a swing in the 1990s back to a more classless informal look more in keeping with Britain's greater integration into Europe. This is what the leading fashion writer, Charlotte Du Cann, had to say in 1989: "Eurostyle does not come from a reactionary mould. Eurostyle comes out of the sixties, it is both optimistic and modernist. It does not serve the greedy individual but the free citizen. It believes in the citizen's right, for example, to equal education, new architecture and culture."

That does not mean that the British are merely going to adopt 'Eurostyle'. As noted, Britain has a strongly individualistic culture. The British may be among the least smartly dressed people in Europe, but they wear *what* they want *when* they want. There is as great a tolerance of personal appearance as anywhere in Europe. As Charlotte Du Cann baldly states, "They frankly don't give a damn when it comes to the rule book." She explains, "In the years of high-spirited street style [the 1960s and 1970s] the British were heralded as the saviours of fashion. In the subsequent era of serious work dressing [the 1980s], they were denounced as 'embarrassing' and 'amateur'." But with the change in mood at the end of the 1980s, British fashion designers like Vivienne Westwood, Jasper Conran, Katherine Hamnett, John Galliano and Rifat Ozbek, made a comeback. They emphasise individuality because the British hate the idea of appearing the same.

British fashion designs.

Nostalgia and modernity

However, there is an important and sometimes destructive tension between nostalgia and individualism. Tradition and creativity are in conflict. Much of Britain, its creeping Neo-classical revival, its love of the country-cottage look, the old-fashioned dress style of the upper class, says much about the way the British perceive themselves. Because the past is glorious for the British, they prefer its reassurance to the uncertainty of the future. Speaking of fashion in its wider sense, Charlotte Du Cann notes the price the British pay for their nostalgia: "Those who come to Britain want to buy what we sell with utter conviction: our cosy comforting past. The handcrafted nostalgia that we market so desperately robs contemporary design of its rebellious energy."

During the 1980s British nostalgia grew more than ever. Forty-one 'heritage' centres were established. More people than ever went to visit England's historic houses, 67 million such visits in 1985 alone. Why? In the words of *The National Trust Book of the English House*, "They [English country houses] look back to periods of apparent stability and order that, to some people, seem preferable to the chaos of the present." In 1986 there were 2,131 museums in Britain of which half had been established *since* 1971. But as one museum curator warned, "If you are not careful you will wallow in nostalgia, in this sort of myth that the past was wonderful. I personally believe the past was awful."

Anti-Modernism has been a prevalent theme in British culture this century. The popular culture of the urban working class, expressed for example, in cinemas, dance-halls and football stadiums, has been a poor relation. Britain has a far weaker modernist culture than exists in France or Germany, because the British feel less certain about the relationship between architecture, art, design, craft and manufacture. It is safer to live with the quiet authority of a rural past, than the uncertainties of the urban present.

Nowhere was this tension more fiercely debated at the end of the 1980s, than in the field of architecture. There was a strong revolt against the use of bare concrete, and against the high rise buildings which had been so popular in the 1960s and early 1970s. But it was also a protest against the unfamiliarity and apparent brutality of Modernist architecture, as it is called. This was popularly associated with cheap public housing and office blocks. In the late 1980s Prince Charles openly championed a return to traditional architecture and building materials. For example, he intervened to prevent a Modernist addition to the National Gallery, an early nineteenth-century building, and to prevent the construction of what he called a 'Glass Stump', designed by the great Modernist architect, Mies van der Rohe, in the City of London. Prince Charles' interventions and his book on the subject, *A Vision of Britain*, created a major debate, in which the popular mood was clearly in sympathy with his views.

The attack on modern architecture tended to concentrate on the worst examples and to ignore more exciting modern work. Modernist architects had no intention of defending the poor architecture of many cheap modern buildings. As the

Modernist architecture at its worst is depressing and brutal.

Richmond Riverside Development hides offices behind a pretty exterior.

leading architect James Stirling remarked, "The housing architecture of the 1960s was simply a matter of building more and more houses for less and less money until you ended up with a sort of trash."

Many architects watched with dismay as important sites were developed in Post-Modernist decorative, 'Toytown' styles, as for example in much of the housing in London's redeveloped Docklands; or in copies of the Classical style, for example Quinlan Terry's Richmond Riverside Development, which carefully but dishonestly disguised modern offices behind 'tasteful' mock-Classical facades. The Modernists, of whom Richard Rogers was a leading champion, insisted that buildings should be, and appear, true to their purpose.

These styles, Post-Modern and Neo-Classical, were associated in people's minds with private development in the way that high-rise cheap concrete buildings were thought of as the architecture of the welfare state. Thus, Post-Modern and Classical (which are too expensive for low-income families) were associated with the Thatcher decade.

At a deeper level, it is difficult to avoid the conclusion that the Post-Modern and Classical challenges to Modernism were a popular revolt against the demands and reality of the modern world. The argument goes beyond stylistic conservatism. The retreat from bold modern planning and buildings implies hesitancy in contrast with, for example, the self-confident modern buildings in Paris. More seriously, it suggests a fear of change, and apprehension rather than enthusiasm about the future.

However nostalgic the British may be, foreign modern influences have been immensely important in shaping popular culture since 1945. As a result of the US presence during and after the war, Britain was invaded by American culture – symbolised by chewing gum, jazz, flashy cars and mass production. It spoke of material wealth and social equality, and seemed highly subversive to adults, who accepted the existing social order, but highly attractive to the young. By 1959 almost 90 per cent of all teenage spending was conditioned by a rapidly Americanising working-class taste. It was not destined to last. In the 1960s Britain was more influenced by the apparent sophistication of the Continent – Italian, French and Spanish cuisine, espresso bars, Scandinavian design, Modernist architecture, and even holidays in the sun. This, too, implied a more egalitarian country than Britain traditionally had been.

In the 1960s this mixture of influences that made up a new popular culture exploded in a distinctly English type of pop music – exemplified by the Beatles, the Rolling Stones and many others – and a revolution in dress and style, expressed most strikingly in the mini-skirt and the exotic range of clothes that expressed social liberation, on sale in London's Carnaby Street. The revolution became permanent as this popular culture seeped into even the upper-class reaches of Britain's youth. Nevertheless, the tension between the popular modernism of rebellious young people and the traditionalism of a staid, silent majority persists.

Urban sub-cultures

Rebellion and dissent belong on city streets. Among those who rejected the English cottage culture in favour of a popular urban culture, some remained deeply dissatisfied with their place in society. Teds, Mods, Rockers, Bikers, Skinheads, Punks and Rastafarians, the sub-cultures of the politically or economically weaker segments of society, all have their roots in the poorer parts of towns. They reflect a refusal to conform in post-1945 society. Like the rural dream of the majority, some of these sub-cultures are based on nostalgia for a lost world, for example, an imagined traditional working-class culture for the Skinheads, or an idealised Africa for Rastafarians.

The single greatest influence for all these rebel sub-cultures has been Afro-Caribbean. Afro-Caribbean immigrants, and more particularly their children, have felt excluded from mainstream British society. Many feel they have exchanged one colonial situation for another, as a cheap and marginalised labour force. As they were largely confined to depressed urban areas, many whites associated Afro-Caribbean youths with violence and disorder. In 1981 and 1985 riots in London, Bristol, Birmingham and Liverpool were to a considerable extent an expression of Afro-Caribbean frustration with their lot. One of the most colourful of their celebrations is the annual Notting Hill Carnival. The rich and lively expression of Afro-Caribbean identity is what the Carnival is really about, yet the media tend to

A Rastafarian.

record the event in terms of the violence or good humour of the occasion.

At a spiritual level many Afro-Caribbeans, like those still in the Caribbean, dreamed of a golden age in Africa before the slave traders came. Their text was the Bible, which had traditionally been used by a dominant white culture to tame them. They reinterpreted it according to their own experience of racial suffering, viewing Britain as part of the Biblical 'Babylon', the land of slavery, and Africa, especially Ethiopia, as the 'Promised Land'. These Rastafarians began to wear distinctive clothes, camouflage jackets, large hats in the red, gold and green colours of Ethiopia, and put their long, uncut hair in 'dreadlocks'. They took to speaking in a special 'patois', or dialect. This was defiance and revolt, until Rastafarians became a recognised and legitimate minority group at the end of the 1980s.

Most important, however, for its cultural impact, has been the black music which came into Britain mainly through the Rastafarian movement. Two particular types, ska and reggae, evolved in the Caribbean and United States but were developed in Britain during the 1970s. 'Break-dance' music came direct from the United States as did 'Hip-hop'. "Nowhere in the world," according to the style writer Peter York, "is black American dancing music more cherished than in England." At first the music spread through informal channels, and home-made tapes. By the mid 1980s there were over 100 different independent reggae 'labels', or companies making tapes and records of reggae music. These types of music were powerful expressions of dissidence.

Black dissident music was adopted by other rebel sub-cultures, even those which were openly hostile to the ethnic minorities. Indeed, it is through music that the black and white cultures have fused. The Skinheads, for example, who developed in the 1970s out of an older cult, the Mods, copied black mannerisms and fashions and danced to reggae. According to Ronnie Am, a retired black disc-jockey, "White teenagers loved the music and copied the clothes. This was the biggest adoption of black fashion by white people." Yet Skinheads were closely identified with extreme right wing views of Afro-Asian immigrants. In general they have tolerated Afro-Caribbeans more willingly than they have the Asian minority. Such a number of Skinheads have been violent to blacks and homosexuals, or gays, that they are widely considered to be virtually fascist. They wear heavy boots, jeans and braces, and shave their hair or cut it very short. They aggressively seek to recover a crude working-class identity which their parents' generation has largely abandoned. As a movement the Skinheads are now in decline.

Notting Hill Carnival: a celebration of black vitality.

A broader movement, a reaction to the glamour of the pop star world of the 1960s, is that of the Punks. Punks, like the Skinheads, are reactionary, but they are passive and politically apathetic. Their real appeal to the young has been their ability to outrage middle-aged opinion, particularly among the guardians of social values, like the police and other civil authorities. They have done this by using foul language, dressing in torn clothes, wearing Union Jacks, swastikas, mutilating their bodies with safety pins, wearing chains and even articles suggestive of urban waste like black plastic dustbin liner shirts. Punk, too, used black music, particularly reggae, to inspire its own Punk sound. Unlike Skinheads, however, many Punks openly identified with Black Britain. After almost twenty years, Punks too are in decline.

'Heavy metal' is the music of failure, and the fact that it is widely despised by those who enjoy pop, reggae or soul, is its appeal. Unlike other rebel cults, though, the followers of heavy metal have the manner of victims, and some wear gothic script and grinning skulls, suggestive of morbid interests. The capital of heavy metal is Birmingham, one of Britain's least loved cities.

Such cults arise and disappear over periods of a decade or two. Two such youth cults which arose in the 1980s were Ragga and Gothic. Raggas are essentially American-inspired, as their clothing: baseball caps, tracksuit trousers and chunky trainers indicate. Gothic is a home-grown British style – a mixture of 1970s Punk and 1960s Hippie. Typically 'Goths' wear their hair very

Punk hairstyles: an innocent form of protest.

While the rock star culture of the 1960s proclaimed a classless society, Punks, Skinheads and Rastafarians, each in their own way, were insisting that they inhabited a world divided, as they saw it, by class and race.

Who is attracted to such cults? Generally it has been young people with low self-esteem, who have done poorly at school. Joining a gang is a means of finding status, and of defying the conventional world in which they have been defined as failures.

An Acid House party.

long and dyed black, and dress in cheap, loose, black clothes, sometimes embroidered in black and frequently torn. Both boys and girls wear make-up, looking pale with mascara around the eyes. They tend to be non-violent, and seem nostalgic for the youth culture and music of the 1960s.

At the end of the 1980s the fashionable sub-culture was Acid House, which attracted thousands of adolescents who had not previously belonged to a cult. Unlike the more angry cults such as the Punks and Skinheads, Acid House promised fun and all-night dancing. It came ready-made with its own music, another variation on black music from America ('House' music), and a special drug, 'Ecstasy', which created a powerful sense of wellbeing. By 1990, however, partly because the police repeatedly broke up large Acid House parties, this too was in decline.

Such sub-cultures follow a cycle. They create initial shock and provoke a strong response, particularly from the police. Adherents are frequently portrayed as 'sub-human' or 'just animals'. Their addiction to drugs is sometimes exaggerated as a major threat to society. As the sub-culture gathers momentum it attracts youth in search of a rebel identity (often merely to irritate their parents). Many, perhaps most, adopt it for fun, conforming to the requirements of conventional society during working hours, and playing at rebellion in their leisure time. Meanwhile, the fashion designers commercialise the look and sell it in the clothes shops. The sub-culture rapidly ceases to express serious dissent, let alone being a threat to society. In the end, of course, it becomes another accepted and colourful part of urban culture.

Each new culture also blends with existing ones in a kaleidoscope of style. According to one black teacher in south London, "Unlike any other time I can remember, black and white children in working-class areas are wearing identical kits, of the black groups they idolise."

On the other hand, many blacks in the late 1980s were wearing totally different clothes which had no connection at all with reggae or with black America, but which were Italian 'designer label' suits. Finally, one cannot be sure that those whose clothes suggest violence are necessarily aggressive. As one Skinhead remarked, "Most Skinheads drink hot milk with their mothers at night, you know. We're not half as hard as we look."

The culture of sport

Britain was the first country to organise sport as a national activity. In the second half of the nineteenth century it organised and exported a number of games, notably football, rugby football and cricket. The initial purpose behind organised sport was to provide an outlet for youthful energies at public schools. It was generally believed to have character-building qualities for future leaders. But it was not long before local businessmen began to organise football and other sports as recreational activity for their workforces. Football clubs quickly sprang up in towns and cities all over Britain, and football was rapidly taken into working-class culture. The Saturday afternoon match was an occasion which working class men would attend, supporting their local team.

Supporters of a local football club.

From the 1960s, however, the character of football (and other national sports) began to change. A fundamental reason was financial. As match attendance dropped, clubs sought external help from sponsorship and advertising. Commercial companies found this profitable. For example, Cornhill Insurance began to sponsor English 'test' cricket in 1980 at a cost of £4.5 million. Beforehand only 2 per cent of the population had heard of Cornhill, while by 1985 20 per cent had done so, and Cornhill had almost doubled its turnover.

More seriously, however, the decline in spectators forced club managers to make their sporting events less occasions for local support and more displays of spectacular skill. Football clubs started buying and selling players. In the 1950s football heroes, like Stanley Matthews, remained in their traditional communities. From the 1960s, many football stars moved into expensive suburbs and displayed their newly acquired wealth. Supporters became primarily consumers, remaining supporters but with no involvement in the club they supported. Few members of the teams they supported were genuinely local people. High transfer fees, the glamorous lives of some players, and the lack of participation in the control of clubs, have undermined the traditional involvement and loyalty of supporters. A process of alienation has taken place between supporters and clubs. Increasingly supporters have demonstrated loyalty through their own action, by invading the football pitch and controlling the surrounding streets, inevitably leading to violence.

Meanwhile the clubs have desperately tried to remain profitable. In 1982 only twelve out of ninety-two football league clubs in Britain made a profit from spectators. If football (and other sports) were not run as business enterprises, they might enjoy greater local participation and less violence. Even though football has become such a spectator sport, in the mid 1980s 1.6 million British were playing it as recreation, more than ever before. It remains a truly national game.

Over a century ago, the novelist Anthony Trollope listed the sports "essentially dear to the English nature". These included hunting, shooting, rowing and horse racing. He was, of course, referring to the 'gentleman class', which through the public school system established football, rugby and cricket as national games. But hunting, rowing and horse racing, because of the expense involved, have remained primarily upper-class pastimes. Attendance at Henley Regatta, the high

Paul 'Gazza' Gascoigne exemplified the glamour of the football star in 1990.

point of the rowing season, and Royal Ascot, for horse racing, remain the pinnacles of the upper class summer season.

Despite these areas of exclusivity, sport remains one of the areas in which members of ethnic minorities have demonstrated their ability in a white-dominated society, particularly in athletics, cricket and soccer. However, no black has yet been invited to captain an English cricket or football team. And there is well-founded black resentment that sport, music and show business are virtually the only areas in which their excellence is acceptable in a predominantly white society. For none of these activities confers durable power.

Royal Ascot: the upper classes at play.

The arts

As has been seen, there is much in Britain's culture to cause unease. But curiously enough, like the discussion of Britain's intellectual life, the British find discussion of their national artistic life faintly embarrassing. As the great British art historian, Nikolaus Pevsner, himself a refugee immigrant, remarked over thirty years ago, "None of the other nations of Europe has so abject an inferiority complex about its own aesthetic capabilities as England." This inferiority complex owed much to the rise of the Modern Movement which was so strongly rooted in continental Europe, particularly in France and Germany.

Yet Britain today has much to be proud of, though its artistic achievements are frequently better appreciated, and known, abroad than at home. In 1976 the American artist Ron Kitaj (now resident in Britain) argued that there were "artistic personalities in this small island more unique and

strong and, I think, more numerous than anywhere in the world outside America's jolting artistic vigour". Examples easily come to mind. Henry Moore exhibited more widely than any previous artist. Until his death in 1992, Francis Bacon was frequently described as the greatest living artist. Lucien Freud has been described as "the greatest living realist painter". David Hockney has been described by one critic as "one of the most original and versatile artists of his generation anywhere in the world". Howard Hodgkin and Carel Weight, too, are possibly as well-known abroad as at home.

As in fashion, so also in art, the British seem to enjoy breaking the rules of the current Modernist style, and this perhaps is what gives it such originality. As one art critic wrote in 1988, "British artists, who are currently enjoying the highest international standing, have been singularly unaffected by the much vaunted internationalism of the Modern Movement. English art is perhaps

A Bigger Splash *by David Hockney (opposite).*

beginning to escape from insularity and provincialism through a rediscovery of its Englishness."

So, too, there is much fine architectural work, in spite of the controversy between Modernists and Post-Modernists at the end of the 1980s. Richard Rogers, Norman Foster and James Stirling are much in demand, abroad perhaps more than at home. In Glasgow the fame of Sir William Burrell's amazing art collection owes much to Barry Gasson's architecture in which it is housed.

However, there are areas of the arts in which Britain more confidently excels. British theatre is among the liveliest and most innovative in the world. Some would argue that the quality of theatre is a good register of a country's democratic values. For it is on the stage that some of the most painful questions can be asked about the way we live, both as individuals and as a community.

Over 300 commercial theatres operate, 100 of these in London, and about 40 of them in London's famous West End. However, the real vitality of British theatre is to be found less in the West End than in the regional, 'fringe' and pub theatres all over the country. West End theatres are essentially commercial. They stage what will fill the house, which means there is an emphasis on musicals, comedy and other forms of light entertainment. They depend on foreign tourists to fill up to 40 per cent of seats.

Much of the liveliest theatre, however, has grown out of 'rep', the repertory movement, which experienced a major revival from 1958 when the Belgrade Theatre in Coventry was built, the first new regional theatre for over twenty years. During the next twenty years forty theatres were built, rebuilt or extensively renovated. These theatres, however, did not follow the classical

Modernist architecture at its best: Barry Gasson's architecture for the Burrell Collection, Glasgow.

tradition of repertoire, a much repeated cycle of well rehearsed plays. Nor did they offer a menu of uncontroversial light entertainment, like dramatised versions of Agatha Christie thrillers.

Instead they presented seasons of plays, each running for about four to six weeks after which they would not be re-staged. Certain theatres have become particularly famous for their presentation of new plays and powerful, sometimes controversial productions of classic ones. Among the better known of these energetic centres of dramatic talent are the Glasgow Citizen's, the Sheffield Crucible, the Bristol Old Vic, the Manchester Royal Exchange, in London the Royal Court and the Lyric Hammersmith, and others, too, in Leeds, Liverpool, Nottingham and elsewhere. It is these theatres, rather than those in the West End, which stage most of the best innovative British drama today.

Theatre is a powerful instrument of education as well as art and culture. Another significant feature of British theatre is the way in which

actors have taken drama to young people, even into primary schools. This has broken down some of the traditional barriers between formal stage drama and the community.

Much of the excellence of these theatres is a result of the intensive preparation and speed with which productions are staged, and their short performance lifespan, usually four to six weeks. Their intensity and freshness is not allowed to grow stale. Another important feature, however, is the youthfulness of many of the best productions. Length of experience in Britain is not allowed to stand in the way of talent, and as a result young people, some recently from drama school, perform many leading roles. The most obvious young star at the end of the 1980s was Kenneth Branagh who, while still in his twenties, was hailed – perhaps unfairly – as a new Lawrence Olivier, Britain's most celebrated twentieth-century actor.

In 1988 Branagh illustrated a growing development in British theatre, by forming his own company for small-cast productions of Shakespeare, in which he both directed and performed. By 1990 there were three touring companies staging Shakespeare, with small casts but great vigour. Thus, alongside the formal and talented presentation of Shakespeare by the Royal Shakespeare Company at the Barbican in London, and in Stratford-on-Avon, other companies provide highly stimulating and sometimes controversial alternative productions.

The theatres already discussed almost all receive some government subsidy, but significantly less than most theatres in continental Europe. Some theatres have been unable to continue, and have closed. Most are forced to mix their more adventurous productions with safer, more commercial productions. Nevertheless, even though British theatre laments the lack of support, inadequate financing creates a permanent sense of tension and hardship in which some of Britain's best drama is staged. Fringe and pub theatre doubled in size during the 1980s, becoming a popular form of less conventional theatre. These theatres, like the Gate in Notting Hill Gate and the Bush in Shepherd's Bush (both in west London) operate entirely without subsidy. Many operate in the informality of a room above a pub, seating an audience of only 50 or 70 people, and with the actors often receiving little more than their travelling expenses. Why do actors work for so little or no money? One reason is that actors like to keep in practice in the sometimes long periods between other engagements, but a more serious reason is that many actors can only earn a living in film or television, performing meaningless and unrewarding roles in thrillers and so forth. Many became actors to perform serious drama. If they cannot do it for a living, they do it when they are free for little or no money. This is a measure of the very high level of artistic commitment in British theatre. What is worth seeing and what is not? Many people rely on the critics in the press, or buy *Time Out*, a magazine devoted to listing and recommending current drama, music and other arts in Britain each week.

Since the 1960s Britain has achieved a special position in music. While Britain's operatic, dance and classical music performances compare well with top international standards, it is in the field of popular music that Britain has achieved a particular pre-eminence. Britain remains at the forefront of pop music. In 1985 alone twelve out of twenty-seven top single records in the US were British, making Britain "the undisputed leader of youth culture" as *The Economist* put it.

At the start of the 1990s, British pop music seemed to be rediscovering the spirit of the 1960s. Liverpool and London had been the musical power-houses of the 1960s, but in 1990 the new pop generation took root in Manchester's clubland, the birthplace of Acid House music, and young people started wearing trousers flared not from the knee, but the waist, dayglo colours and ethnic styles. Why Manchester? According to one commentator, "Large enough to support a cultural infrastructure, yet small enough to form a community, the city has fused the styles of Ibiza, Chicago, Detroit and London into something recognisably, tantalisingly, new."

The new music marks a departure from the unrelaxed mood of the 1980s, and a declaration of freedom. Ian Rose, singer for one of the leading new groups, the Stone Roses, put it this way: "The Eighties were cynical. People didn't want to participate. You can wake up in the morning and feel negative or positive. Why feel negative? It's better to be optimistic, to connect. . . . Anything is possible. . . . People coming together can always change things." Among the successful leading Manchester groups of 1990 were Candy Flip, the Stone Roses and the Happy Mondays. Ironically, the greatest danger such groups face is the pressure of success and the destructive media attention which accompanies it.

For an older generation, however, which enjoyed giant flared trousers and clogs in the 1960s, the music of groups like the Stone Roses may not appeal. Such people are conscious of the generation gap. In the words of Charlotte du Cann, "The happening scene of pop in the Nineties, it seems, has suddenly become too young and too close to home for thirty-something hipsters. . . . Pop has begun to make them feel old, a been-there. A gap has widened where they thought one was never possible." For them, "Jazz is the perfect music for Nineties attitude. . . . Jazz suggests the lifestyle of liberty. . . "

Culture for the community

On the South Bank of the Thames, opposite Whitehall, stands the capital of Britain's cultural life, with three concert halls, the National Theatre (containing three theatres), the National Film Theatre and the Hayward Art gallery. A fairly recent addition is the lively Museum of the Moving Image. The South Bank receives two and a half million paying visitors each year, while many others come to see free exhibitions and use its restaurant facilities.

The South Bank enjoys both the strengths and weaknesses of its position as a national cultural centre. The buildings, by leading architects of the 1950s, 1960s and 1970s, are in the bare and uncompromising concrete so favoured in the period. It is planned to hide their brutalism behind glass and soft stone textures in the early 1990s. This is an interference with the intentions of the architects which says much about the way officialdom can often treat artists. Officialdom likes life to be bland and uncontroversial, "Do not upset the populace", it seems to say.

On the South Bank one can hear the greatest sounds of classical music, and some of the finest acting in the world. But for artistic vitality one may be more successful in a fringe theatre or pub. For it is the level of popular participation which makes British artistic life so distinctive. All over the country there are millions of people engaged in amateur music, art and theatre. For example, for more than two hundred years the Royal Academy in London has held an annual Summer Exhibition, for which any painter or sculptor may enter their work. In 1988, for example, 12,500 works were submitted, of which only 1,261 were actually exhibited. Virtually every town and suburb has some form of amateur music group, a choir, an orchestra or

The South Bank: the capital of British artistic culture.

even neighbours who form a string quartet. All over the country there are amateur choral groups, ranging from the local village church choir through to highly selective and internationally known choirs, like the Bach Choir. Then there are all the amateur dramatic groups across the country. There are an estimated 6,500 separate amateur companies, involving roughly 75,000 aspiring actors. Such local activities take place everywhere.

Take Stranraer, as an example, a town of 15,000, on the south-west tip of Scotland. Its amateur drama and opera groups put on a major opera and a play each year, plus a pantomime and one or two minor productions. It has youth choirs based in local schools, a youth brass band and two pipe bands, one for entertainment and one for bagpipe competitions. It also has an annual dance festival. Stranraer may be geographically far from the mainstream of national life, but such activities suggest real community participation.

In many market towns and cities all over Britain, roughly 200 cultural festivals are held each year. The choice of what music or drama to perform may not always be very adventurous, nor the quality very high, but these festivals provide a lively form in which local people can celebrate not only their own local arts and culture, but also invite visiting performers of national standing. Ludlow in Shropshire, for example, started having an annual festival in 1960. It is entirely the result of local initiative and effort. The main event each year is a Shakespearian play staged against the castle walls. But local singers perform in the parish church, and there are cricket matches, jazz bands, string quartets and a fair. Fundamentally, such festivals are really celebrations of community.

People do these things for fun. But there are more serious conclusions to draw. In the words of the Director of the National Theatre, "The arts help us to make sense of the world, they help us to fit the disparate pieces together; to try to make form out of chaos."

Questions

Section analysis

1 Community and the individual: List eight examples of the type of voluntary activities in which many ordinary British people engage.

2 The fine distinctions of speech: Some people want to encourage different dialects of English because they admire their richness. Other people think they are socially divisive and should be abandoned. What is your opinion?

3 The culture of violence: Has Britain got a violent culture? Give arguments for and against.

4 The rural ideal: Is Britain's nostalgia for life in the countryside harmless, or damaging? State your opinion and support it with evidence from the text.

5 Dress codes: The British are perhaps less fashion-conscious than other Europeans. Why?

6 Nostalgia and modernity: "Tradition and creativity are in conflict [in Britain]." Give examples from the text to support this view.

7 Urban sub-cultures: Why do young British people join sub-cultures? What sub-cultures exist in your own country?

8 The culture of sport: In what ways has the character of football as a national sport changed in the last thirty years?

9 The arts: Why are many of the best British theatrical productions to be found in the smallest theatres?

10 Culture for the community: What is distinctive about artistic life in Britain?

Chapter analysis and discussion

1 William Beveridge remarked that the vigour and abundance of voluntary action "are the distinguishing marks of a free society". Do you agree? Is it true of Britain? Is it true of your country? Give reasons for your opinions.

2 British society is strongly individualistic. Find examples of the ways in which this individualism is expressed in the following areas: violent behaviour; dress; urban sub-cultures; the theatre.

Textual interpretation

Consider the following two quotations. Do you think there is a connection between them? Can you find evidence from the chapter to support your view?

"The English football warrior is more than a 'mindless' lawbreaker for whom simple disobedience is a goal in itself. Rather, his anti-social fury is fuelled by a conception of self-worth based firmly on long-established notions of national pride. The thug thinks of himself as a super patriot, and his fanaticism is contagious."

"The point of the British is that they do not behave. They neither dress nor act according to the rules, though they know them perfectly well." [taken from a fashion page]

9 The importance of not being English

A Canadian touring Britain in 1989 discovered, in his own words, "There's no such thing as the British, only English, Irish, Welsh and Scots." There is considerable truth in his remark. The sense of difference from the English is more than a thousand years old. It dates from the time when Anglo-Saxon invaders from the European continent drove the Celtic people out of what we call England today and into what we now call Ireland, Scotland and Wales. In fact, almost one in five of today's British is not English.

The English habit of considering Wales and Scotland to be extensions of England is an old one. In the sixteenth century William Shakespeare spoke of England as "This royal throne of kings, this scepter'd isle", even though much of this isle was not English. Since 1945 there has been a growing dislike in the Celtic countries of the habit of defining the 'island race' as English.

In 1969, in response to growing regional feeling, a constitutional Royal (Kilbrandon) Commission was established to examine relations between the different parts of the United Kingdom, and in its report in 1973 it proposed greater autonomy for Wales and Scotland, where nationalist sentiment seemed to be growing. In both countries, however, when a referendum on the proposal was put to the Welsh and Scottish electorates, an insufficient number of voters supported the proposals, which were abandoned as a result. However, the sense of difference has not disappeared. The English, for their part, sometimes feel resentful that, as the wealthiest member of the United Kingdom, England subsidises the others.

Northern Ireland

Nowhere has the sense of conflict with the English been stronger than in Northern Ireland, where the population is composed of Protestants and Roman Catholics. The Protestant Unionists, or Loyalists, certainly do not feel English, but they claim Ulster (as most Protestants prefer to call Northern Ireland) as an integral part of Britain. The Catholic population feel more Irish than British and some, the Nationalists, would prefer to be part of the Irish Republic. Both communities feel considerable frustration with the English. Today there are probably approximately 980,000 Protestants and 650,000 Catholics in Northern Ireland. There are another 3.5 million Irish south of the border, in the Republic.

The story of England's involvement with Ireland is an unhappy one. English adventurers began colonising parts of Ireland 900 years ago. In the sixteenth and seventeenth centuries England brought the whole of Ireland under systematic rule. While England became Protestant at that time, Ireland did not. In order to strengthen its political and economic hold on Ireland, the government in London encouraged thousands of Protestants, both English and Scottish, to settle in the more fertile parts of Ireland. In the north-eastern part, Ulster, the Protestants soon outnumbered the Catholics.

Inspired by the French Revolution of 1789, the Irish began their struggle to be free from England. Many of the new Irish nationalists were Protestant. However, the majority of the Protestants, particularly in Ulster, felt threatened by the Irish Catholic majority, and formed the Orange Order, a solidarity association of 'lodges', or branches. The title 'Orange' refers to William of Orange (or William III) who defeated an attempt by the Irish to throw the Protestant settlers out of Ireland. William, or King Billy as Protestant Ulstermen call him, defeated a Catholic Irish army at the River Boyne in 1690. It says much about entrenched sectarian attitudes, that both Loyalists and Nationalists prefer to forget that King Billy's army contained a large number of Catholic soldiers.

When the Irish finally persuaded England in 1920 that it could no longer go on governing Ireland, the Protestants of Ulster warned that they would fight rather than be part of a Catholic-dominated state. Rather than take the risk, London persuaded the Irish nationalists to accept independence for all Ireland *except* the six counties that made up Ulster. Here the Protestants were 67 per cent of the population.

In 1921 London decided to allow the Northern Irish to govern themselves. It was hoped, perhaps naively, that if they were not governed by the English, the Protestants and Catholics would find a way of living happily with each other. This was not to be. Every election for the Northern Irish government at Stormont, from 1921 onwards, was about Ulster's future – whether it should remain part of the United Kingdom, the Protestant position, or become part of the Irish Republic, as many Catholics wanted. The consequence was that the Protestants, as the majority, kept the Catholics completely out of government the whole time. Ulster Loyalists were determined to keep the province under British rule, fearing that any Catholic participation in government might lead to what they feared most, incorporation into the Irish Republic.

Northern Ireland was already the poorest part of the United Kingdom, but this poverty was not equally shared. Catholics were significantly disadvantaged. In autumn 1968 the Catholics, supported by many Protestants, demonstrated on the streets, demanding fair participation in political and economic life. Ulster Loyalists confronted them and the Ulster police force, which was almost entirely Protestant, was unable to keep order. The violence soon resulted in deaths, some caused by the police, most by the paramilitary groups in each community. At first there was considerable sympathy in Britain for the Catholic population, particularly in view of the pro-Protestant police force. When the army was

The landscape of Northern Ireland.

deployed in summer 1969 to maintain law and order, many hoped that this sympathy, even within the army itself, would reassure the Catholic population. But the honeymoon did not last long, and the disorders increased. In 1972 the Stormont government was suspended and the province brought under direct rule from Whitehall. During the next few years the number of deaths increased rapidly, among both the government forces and the civilian population.

The measures brought in to satisfy Catholic civil rights claims were too few and too late. The violence on the streets, particularly the shooting dead of thirteen demonstrators by the army in early 1972, allowed the extremists on both sides to establish a strong hold on their respective communities. Paramilitary forces, on the Nationalist side the Irish Republican Army (the IRA) and its offshoots, and on the Loyalist side the Ulster Defence Association and Ulster Volunteer Force, used violence and terrorism to advance their aims.

A Loyalist mural in Belfast (top) and the Nationalist retort.

Over the years the IRA evolved from a handful of street thugs into a sophisticated fighting force, with enough modern weapons, including advanced firearms, ground-to-air missiles and tons of Semtex explosive, to sustain their present level of war well into the twenty-first century. In the words of one security expert, "They are the most professional terrorist organisation in the world today."

The British government and army were soon seen as part of the enemy by the IRA and by Catholic Nationalists, but were also suspected by Protestants of being willing to surrender to Irish Nationalism. During the 1970s it slowly became clear that no solution was in sight. The IRA would accept nothing short of Ulster becoming part of the Irish Republic, and the Loyalists refused any measure that allowed the Catholics to share power, or which implied recognition of Dublin's interest in the fate of Ulster.

The position of the government in Dublin has not been easy either. Although it has always claimed Ulster as part of Ireland, it does not want to inherit the sectarian conflict. It prefers the idea of unity to remain a dream. Any prospect of Britain abandoning Northern Ireland is a political and economic nightmare for Dublin, but is one it can hardly admit. As one leading member of the Irish political establishment, Conor Cruise O'Brien, once remarked of the British army presence in Ulster, "Please say you're going, but for God's sake stay."

The minority on both sides of the divide in Ulster have been willing to use violence, but the vast majority of people have preferred a democratic and constitutional solution. On the Loyalist side the Official Unionist Party and the Democratic Unionist Party have both sought to keep Ulster within the United Kingdom. Most Catholics have supported the Social and Democratic Labour Party, which wants Ulster eventually to become part of the Irish Republic by democratic and lawful means.

But in the 1980s the political wing of the IRA, Sinn Fein (pronounced 'shin fayn'), began to participate in elections, receiving one third of the Nationalist vote. Although Gerry Adams, Sinn Fein's leader, was elected to the Westminster Parliament, he refused to take his seat. But it was clear that the lack of any apparent political progress by Westminster made Sinn Fein more popular with the Catholic community.

The Reverend Iain Paisley, leader of the Democratic Unionist Party.

Gerry Adams, leader of Sinn Fein.

Fear of growing support for Sinn Fein and frustration with the refusal of the Unionists to allow power sharing or any compromise with the Catholic community persuaded the British government to negotiate an Anglo-Irish Agreement with Dublin in 1985. By this stage Dublin's sympathy for the Nationalists was mixed with a dislike of the IRA and a fear of any attempt to bring Protestant Ulster into the Republic unwillingly. Dublin reluctantly accepted the need for British troops to keep order in Ulster. As Garret Fitzgerald, Irish Prime Minister at the time, said:

"The reason why I and many others in Irish politics are opposed to British withdrawal in advance of arriving at an agreed resolution of the north–south problem is the evident danger that such a departure, or indeed even the announcement of the intention to depart, could unleash violence on a scale hitherto unknown in Northern Ireland, and lead eventually to the re-partition of the area by force."

The Anglo-Irish Agreement allowed Dublin a consultative role in the government of Ulster, and also recognised that to some extent Dublin represented the Catholics of Ulster. The crucial clause read: "If in the future a majority of the people of Northern Ireland clearly wish for and formally consent to the establishment of a united Ireland, they [the London and Dublin governments] will introduce and support in the respective parliaments legislation to give effect to that wish."

This implied that London was not determined to keep Ulster in the United Kingdom if a majority of its people wished to become part of a united Ireland, while Dublin also showed it was willing to abandon its claim to Ulster until its people were themselves ready for union. This weakened the IRA/Sinn Fein position which argued for immediate withdrawal of British troops and unification with the south. But it was also intended to weaken the position of the Protestant Unionists, warning them that Dublin and London would work together in spite of Unionist fears.

An uneasy relationship: the Prime Ministers of Ireland and the United Kingdom in 1991.

In practice relations between London and Dublin have proved less happy. Dublin has repeatedly criticised British security forces' practices, in particular for a 'shoot-to-kill' policy, for the wrongful imprisonment of innocent people, and for the physical and psychological abuse of arrested Nationalist suspects. London has been angry at the unwillingness of Dublin to hand over terrorist suspects to British security forces.

By the late 1980s the level of violence had been brought down to a level where fewer people died in terrorist killings than in traffic accidents. But although the British government has contained the violence, at considerable expense, a solution is no more apparent than it was twenty years earlier.

Yet by 1990 there were modest signs that the Unionists might moderate their position slightly, and they seemed more ready to consider power sharing with the Catholics. At the same time Sinn Fein seemed to be in crisis. In Northern Ireland its electoral appeal was in decline from 11 per cent, while in the Republic it attracted less than 3 per cent of support. Its military wing, the IRA, was faring even worse. Its bombing campaigns had borne no fruit, and fewer members of the Catholic population seemed willing to support it. The IRA leadership was bitterly divided between 'hawks' and 'doves', while there was an overall collapse of morale in the organisation generally. The bombing and shooting incidents in Britain and on the Continent, in which innocent civilians were killed, suggest not only the destructive abilities of the IRA, but also its desperation.

One day London may well find itself negotiating with Sinn Fein. But it is now clear that this will not happen unless the IRA abandons its campaign of violence. For London and Dublin are determined that there shall be no change in the status of Northern Ireland until a majority of its people wish it to be so. In the meantime, the 'troubles' cost both governments an annual total, estimated in 1990, of £410 million.

There is no foreseeable solution to the problem of Ulster. In 1920 the Catholic population was one third of the population. Today it has increased to two fifths. In theory there could be a voting Catholic majority by the year 2040, if the higher Catholic birthrate does not continue to fall. But this is fifty years away, and in the meantime Catholic growth is slowed down because more Catholics than Protestants emigrate in search of work.

In any case it has been a popular misconception that the majority of Ulster's Catholics want to live in a united Ireland. Most apparently do not. Opinion polls since 1970 have suggested that a varying proportion of Ulster's Catholics, between one quarter and just under one half, would like to live in a united Ireland. Percentage variations

Patrolling the city of Belfast.

reflect the level of Catholic frustration (or relative satisfaction) with political progress. An opinion poll in 1988 indicated that more than half Ulster's Catholics had *never* felt any sympathy for Sinn Fein.

Even in the Republic, opinion polls indicated that the idea of Irish unity in 1987 attracted only 67 per cent support, and this would probably fall substantially if the incorporation of Ulster involved significant cost. Altogether, the people of all Ireland are probably almost evenly divided between those who want a united Ireland and those who do not.

More Ulster Catholics would wish to live in a united Ireland if the Republic was not significantly poorer than Northern Ireland. British government public expenditure in Northern Ireland is 50 per cent higher than it is in England, in an attempt to improve the weak economy of the province. Put another way, the rest of Britain provides one third of public expenditure in Ulster. In a united Ireland, the people of Ulster would lose this subsidy and face worse economic prospects, higher taxes and a share of Ireland's large national debt.

Sadly, the prospect of a solution has diminished rather than grown as the years have passed. The idea that, if (or when) 51 per cent of the people of Ulster vote for union with the Republic, the problem will be solved, is simplistic. If the remaining 49 per cent, or a large enough number of them, are determined to fight to prevent this happening, the problem will not be solved.

More important, therefore, is the far harder task of building confidence between the two communities themselves. In 1968 there were a number of mixed areas as well as strongly Protestant areas (e.g. Shankhill, Belfast) and Catholic areas (e.g. the Falls Road, Belfast). But within a year of the outbreak of the troubles, walls and wire-mesh fences were erected to separate the warring communities. Many mixed communities separated as the pressures to demonstrate sectarian loyalty outweighed individual neighbourliness between Catholics and Protestants. In any case, the mixed areas became the battlegrounds for the youths of both groups.

Here is another major problem. Most of those who fight and throw stones are young men and teenagers who cannot remember a time before the troubles. With little for youngsters to do, there is strong pressure to join the junior branch of a paramilitary force. As one young man admitted to a reporter in 1989, "In riots, people say you're a coward if you wouldn't throw a brick." As another explained: "If all your mates start throwing [stones], you feel left out. Last summer your friends would say, 'Shall you go up to the

Communities divided in the countryside.

Shankill riot?' nearly every day. There was a riot whenever you felt like one or you saw one. There's been that many you forget them."

The immediate task of government is to contain violence and eliminate terrorism. Until that time the army's 10,000 troops are likely to stay. The presence of the army may not be liked by Catholics, but the majority of them probably accept it as an unpleasant necessity. However, the army is likely to remain a target for bricks – and worse.

Governing Northern Ireland has tended to bring out the least attractive qualities in the British conduct of affairs. For more than twenty years the IRA has committed many outrages in which many innocent bystanders have been killed, but governments always have the responsibility of upholding high ethical standards and the rule of law. Such standards have not always been upheld. In 1974 the Prevention of Terrorism Act allowed the security forces to hold suspects without charge for up to seven days. Between 1974 and 1987 6,430 were detained under this Act, of whom 5,586 were released without any charge.

Inevitably there has been disquiet at the excessive force sometimes used in searching homes, interrogating suspects and in guarding convicted terrorists. In the early 1980s six IRA suspects were shot dead although they were unarmed, giving rise to the suspicion that British security forces had adopted a shoot-to-kill policy. In 1988 another three IRA members were shot dead in Gibraltar.

They, too, although clearly planning a terrorist act, were unarmed. The way in which enquiries were handled in both cases reinforced the suspicion that security forces were operating without regard for law.

A number of outrages committed by the IRA encouraged the authorities to neglect the full requirements of law. In 1989 the convictions of four Catholics for the bombing of a pub in Guildford in 1974 were quashed and the prisoners freed. It was revealed that all four had been forced to make 'confessions' at the time (see page 61). In 1990, the convictions of the 'Maguire Seven', imprisoned for running a bomb factory in the 1970s, were quashed and the remaining prisoners released. Then, in 1991, the Birmingham Six, accused of bombing a Birmingham pub in the 1970s, were also released when their convictions were found unsound. How does a government make amends for such wrongful convictions?

In 1989 the government reduced civil rights in Ulster in two ways. It banned direct broadcasts by Sinn Fein or other 'terrorist' spokesmen, thus reducing the level of democracy. It also abolished the right to silence in court in Ulster, a right which defendants in the UK have traditionally enjoyed.

The problem for any British government is to balance short-term interests, which may require tough measures, against the long-term interest of persuading everyone in Ulster that Britain is

The release of the Birmingham Six, 1991.

determined to ensure and protect full democratic rights as well as the rule of law in all parts of the United Kingdom. The British government is caught in a dilemma. Violence frustrates any political initiative and the lack of such an initiative increases the danger of violence. A progressive reduction in civil liberties in Ulster also threatens civil liberties in all Britain. If there is no solution in sight, the long-term struggle for 'hearts and minds' becomes increasingly important.

One long-term problem is that Catholics and Protestants live apart far more than they did before 1968. It is very difficult to rebuild trust. One way might be to insist on mixed schools, so that children can learn about the other community at an early age. But the Roman Catholic Church particularly wishes Catholic children to be educated in a Catholic environment. Protestants, on the other hand, are deeply suspicious of the power of the Catholic Church in Ireland.

It is also vitally important to end the economic discrimination from which many Catholics have suffered. For one aspect of the conflict is the problem for both Catholic and Protestant people who have low incomes, suffer from high unemployment and are too poor to escape the conflict. So far, successive governments have failed to eliminate these economic aspects. In the past twenty years the economic gap between Catholics and Protestants has hardly closed at all. In 1984 Catholic unemployment was 35 per cent compared with 15 per cent for Protestants. Although the government has encouraged an end to employment discrimination, employers have preferred to recruit solely within one community to avoid conflict in the workplace. This has worked decisively against the Catholics. For example, even at the main university, Queen's University, Belfast, which is publicly committed to a policy of non-discrimination, it was found in 1989 that Catholics made up only 18 per cent of locally recruited academic staff, 11 per cent of administrative and executive staff, and only 7 per cent of blue-collar employees.

In 1988 the government required all companies in Northern Ireland to complete annual statements concerning their employees. The intention is to force companies to employ a proportionately acceptable number of Catholics. But this can only be done as job vacancies occur, and must be done in a way that will not lead to increased Protestant unemployment. This is difficult because of the generally poor economic prospects for Northern Ireland. Full employment for the Catholic community, including the creation of new industry in Catholic areas, is probably a vital requirement for peace.

Can Unionists become less fearful of an eventual integration into the Republic? This is possibly the greatest problem of all. Because of centuries of Protestant oppression, the Catholic Church has an important symbolic and moral role in the Irish Republic. Unionists would feel less fearful if the Republic began to distance itself from the Church. While people on both sides of the divide feel passionate about the wrongs of yesterday, it will be difficult for genuine integration between Protestants and Catholics to happen.

It is easy to conceive of false solutions to the conflict. For example, the province could be repartitioned by British withdrawal from the predominantly Catholic areas on the west and southern edges of Ulster. This could reduce the Catholic proportion of Northern Ireland by about half. But it would not really solve anything since it would not remove the siege mentality of Ulster's Protestants, nor would it satisfy Sinn Fein, particularly its most fervent supporters who live in Catholic West Belfast. It would only reduce the scale of the security problem. It is a solution which ignores the fact that the real border is not geographical but runs through the minds of the people.

Whatever the long-term solution may be, one can at least look forward with modest optimism to the progressive political and economic unity of the European Community. The importance of 'flag-waving nationalism' may diminish, and the Catholics and Protestants of the province may slowly find a common identity to displace the old tribalisms.

Wales

Wales was conquered and incorporated into a single political and administrative system with England seven hundred years ago, but the Welsh sense of difference survived and has become more persistent during the present century. Welsh cultural self-consciousness was awakened in the mid nineteenth century, through the flourishing of literature in the Welsh language and the literary and music festivals, *eisteddfods*, for which Wales became famous. But it was also awakened through the establishment of higher education colleges which emphasised Welsh identity and culture. From 1900 onwards Welsh identity was expressed as well through rugby football, which became a sport of national, almost political, importance.

A rugby match between Wales and England.

Welsh society in the nineteenth century was divided between the dominant Anglo-Welsh culture of the rich land-owning class, and the real Welsh culture of the ordinary, mainly Welsh-speaking people. Dissent from the Anglo-Welsh landowners, and from mainstream English life, has remained a vital aspect of Welsh identity. Until the Second World War its religious expression was through 'non-conformism', attendance at Methodist and Baptist chapels rather than at Anglican churches. Political dissent was expressed in the nineteenth century through support for the Liberal Party, and in the twentieth the Labour Party, rather than the Conservative Party, the party of the ruling English establishment.

In the 1890s many Welsh demanded autonomy, or 'home rule', but the movement shrank, and did not revive again until the 1960s, when there was growing disappointment with both the Conservative and Labour Parties. This was mainly on account of the economic recession in the second half of the 1950s which hit South Wales, the Welsh industrial region, particularly hard. Between 1957 and 1959 twenty-three Welsh coal mines stopped production. There was also a sense of loss as the closure of mines led to a collapse of close-knit valley communities. In the words of one Welsh historian: "The neighbourliness of old communities gave way to the alien impersonality

of housing estates or commuter suburbs. Much of the vital culture of the Welsh heartland disappeared with them." One veteran nationalist wrote in 1968, "We Welsh are not just being denied self-expression as a nation today . . . we are fighting in the last ditch for our very identity." Plaid Cymru, the Welsh National Party, had attracted 11 per cent of the Welsh vote by 1970, and gained three parliamentary seats following the 1974 election.

The London government responded to the rise in Welsh national feeling by delegating some administrative responsibility, most significantly with the appointment in 1964 of a Secretary of State for Wales. But it also used the Royal Family as a symbol of British unity. In 1969 Prince Charles was invested Prince of Wales at a ceremony in Caernarfon Castle. Caernarfon Castle had been built by the English King Edward I in his conquest of the Welsh, and inside its walls he had proclaimed his own baby son Prince of Wales in 1284. The investiture ceremony itself was only invented in 1911, to channel growing Welsh national feeling back to loyalty to the United Kingdom. Not surprisingly, some Welsh find the ceremony symbolic of English rule rather than Welsh identity. Indeed, the 1969 ceremony was completed amid tight police security and fears of Welsh nationalist protest.

A powerful new Welsh Development Agency was founded, and given substantial government funding. However, when the Welsh were asked by referendum in 1979 whether they wanted the proposed legislative devolution and the creation of a Welsh Assembly in Cardiff, they overwhelmingly rejected it – only 11.8 per cent for it, and 46.5 per cent against. Plaid Cymru lost some of its credibility and declined in popularity as a result.

One reason for the Welsh retreat from devolution was that the government had released economic figures in 1971 which gave weight to the belief that Wales benefited from its integration with the rest of the British economy. Then, following the international oil crisis of 1973 there seemed to be improved prospects for the coal industry. However, during the 1980s closures in both the coal and steel industries resumed, and deep alienation from the Conservative government took place. In the 1987 election the Conservatives won only eight out of the thirty-eight Welsh seats.

There are only 2.7 million Welsh, and they have struggled hard to maintain their distinct identity in the second half of the twentieth century. They

The end of an era: the closure of valley coal mines.

have had to do this not only against the political might of London, but also the more dangerous erosion of Welsh culture through the media of radio and television. This erosion is most apparent in the use of the Welsh language. At the end of the nineteenth century over 50 per cent still used Welsh as their first language. Since then the decline has been dramatic:

1911	44 per cent
1921	39 per cent
1931	37 per cent
1951	28 per cent
1961	25 per cent
1971	20 per cent
1981	19 per cent

Because of fears that the language might disappear completely, Welsh language study has become compulsory in Welsh schools, and there is now Welsh medium radio and television. Such efforts have slowed the decline but are unlikely to prevent it, since they promote Welsh as an academic language, known by many but only used by a few. Welsh remains a functional language among 500,000 people in north west and mid-Wales, but could almost disappear from daily use by 2010.

The survival of the Welsh language is a good deal more important than it may initially seem, for it is the most notable way in which the Welsh keep their special identity. The cultural divide between Anglo-Welsh and Welsh Wales a century ago has been replaced by new divides (see over):

1   'Welsh-speaking Wales', those parts of western Wales which still retain the Welsh language as a living culture. It is only in Welsh-speaking Wales that Plaid Cymru candidates have been elected to Westminster.
2   'Radical Wales', the southern industrial valleys of Wales, where Welsh is no longer spoken but Welsh identity is still expressed through dissent, by voting for Labour *within* the wider context of Britain.
3   'English Wales', the far south-west tip (Pembrokeshire) and a broad belt of Wales adjacent to England, which has been heavily settled by the English, and where about half the population no longer think of themselves as Welsh. It is only in English Wales that the Conservative Party remains a significant political force.

The sense of invasion by the English, many of whom have bought holiday homes, is felt acutely.

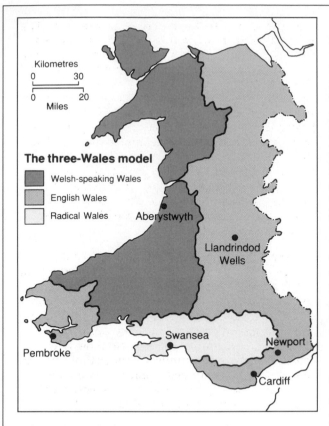

The three-Wales model

- Welsh-speaking Wales
- English Wales
- Radical Wales

Kilometres
0 — 30
0 — 20
Miles

Aberystwyth

Llandrindod Wells

Pembroke

Swansea

Newport

Cardiff

It has forced up the price of many country cottages beyond the means of local Welsh people. A small militant group set fire to almost 200 of these English-owned homes during the 1980s. While the majority of Welsh people condemn the methods, they do not necessarily disagree with the aims, feeling angry at the way in which the English are taking Wales over.

Where Scottish nationalism has been mainly a political movement, Welsh nationalism has been expressed primarily in cultural terms. The language, eisteddfods, and in the 1960s and 1970s the dominance of the Welsh in international rugby football were the symbols of Welsh identity and pride. So, too, were the heavy industries – coal mining and steel – that made South Wales important in the nineteenth century. In 1950 there were still 130,000 coal miners. By 1989 only 8,000 were left. Seventy-two thousand steel workers in 1970 were reduced to fewer than 20,000 by the end of the 1980s. Many Welsh have a terrible sense of retreat.

Politically, Welsh nationalism has not yet really become significant. Plaid Cymru remains a rural party with little prospect of gaining majority support in Wales. Labour, for which most Welsh people vote, has remained unionist like the

Conservatives, in spite of greater sympathy for nationalist feeling. Yet the nationalist issue is unlikely to disappear. An opinion poll in 1987 indicated that 52 per cent of the Welsh might now be in favour of an Assembly, a higher level than was registered even at the height of nationalist feeling in the early 1970s. The progressive decline of Welsh culture (as expressed in the language) awakens a wider sense of loss, and also possibly greater resentment towards their larger neighbour. This may well encourage the Welsh to seek a more political way of securing their identity, which will allow the loss of language to seem less of a tragedy. As one Welshman has written, "There should not be too much surprise if the Welsh discover, some time in the 1990s, that the kind of modest political arrangement . . . that would have established a Welsh Assembly, would be the most natural way to accommodate themselves to the changing patterns of the last part of the twentieth century."

Scotland

On 17th March 1990 Scotland and England played their most important rugby football match since internationals had begun a century earlier, for three championship titles were at stake. However, for Scotland (as it would have been for the Welsh) it was a good deal more important than these three championship titles. It was a question of national dignity against an overbearing neighbour. Scots at the match wore T-shirts marked 'Remember Bannockburn 1314', recollecting Scotland's greatest victory over a more often successful English army.

Scotland was never conquered by England. In fact, when Queen Elizabeth I died childless in 1603, the Scottish king James VI inherited the English throne. But London was always politically and economically more powerful than Edinburgh, and he and his successors ruled from London, effectively becoming English. In 1707 England and Scotland were formerly united as Great Britain. The government in London insisted on this union for political reasons, and the Scots could not refuse for economic reasons. The Scottish Parliament was suspended, and the new Parliament of Great Britain assembled in Westminster.

At the 1990 rugby international two national tunes were played, the British national anthem (for England) and a new national song, The Flower of Scotland. Many Scots were overcome with emotion as they sang their national song. Many also booed the British national anthem, for this was an explicit way in which the English use 'British' to mean 'English'. Being described as 'British' seemed a subtle way of denying the Scots their identity. An opinion poll in the mid 1980s revealed that approximately 70 per cent of Scots identify themselves as Scots before classifying themselves as British.

Unlike Wales, Scotland after 1707 kept three distinctive institutions: its own legal system, its own education system and its own church, or 'Kirk', the Presbyterian Church of Scotland. All three are important symbols of Scottish identity and difference from England. In part they reflect Scotland's closer relationship to continental Europe. Scottish law is discussed in Chapter 4. In education the Scottish universities were closer to the European model, and some still have a four- rather than three-year undergraduate cycle.

However, the most important of Scotland's distinctive institutions is the Kirk, which is closely identified with Scottish national feeling. This is because of its role in national life since the Scottish Reformation in the late sixteenth century. The Kirk at that time insisted that all adults in Scotland should be literate, so as to read the Bible themselves. In practice this laid the foundations for a strong education system and also, inevitably, a strongly democratic tradition. The head of the Kirk, or Moderator, is elected by the General Assembly each year. When the king unsuccessfully tried to enforce English church practices on Scotland in the mid seventeenth century, the Kirk became a symbol of Scottish nationalism. Unlike the Church of England, it never allowed the Crown a position in the Kirk. Even in a secular age, the Kirk remains an important focus for national feeling. Twenty-five per cent of Scots are 'communicating', or practising members of the Church of Scotland.

However, the image of Scotland as one nation can be misleading. As with Wales, the threat from outsiders, particularly the English, has tended to unite Scotland. In reality, Scotland "has no unity except upon the map", as the nineteenth-century Scottish novelist, Robert Louis Stevenson, wrote. "Two languages, many dialects, innumerable forms of piety, and countless local patriotisms and prejudices," he continued, "part us among ourselves more widely than the extreme east and west of that great continent of America."

A view of Edinburgh.

The Rotunda Restaurant and Finnieston Crane, Glasgow.

There is a big cultural as well as geographical divide between the Lowlands and Highlands. The Lowlanders are thought of as quiet, moral and hard-working, the Highlanders as exuberant, carefree and unreliable. If there is some truth in this, it is to be seen in another division, that between Scotland's two great and rival cities, Edinburgh and Glasgow. In the words of one Scottish writer, "For all her elegance and lofty-mindedness, Edinburgh is a reserved, plain, cautious and thrifty city. She is more Lowland, in these respects, than Highland. Glasgow is . . . an expansive, extravagant, romantic, less tight-laced city."

As in Wales, there has been growing resentment during the twentieth century because of the concentration of political power in London and the resentment bred of economic neglect. As with Wales, so also with Scotland, the government in Whitehall made some effort to take account of Scotland's distinctive position in the United Kingdom. A Scottish Office was established in 1885, and since 1945 education, health, agriculture, roads, transport, planning, housing and public order have all been handled by departments within the Scottish Office. In 1975 a Scottish Development Board was established to concentrate on reviving Scotland's economy.

During the past half-century the Scots have seen the giants of their economy, particularly the shipbuilding industry on the river Clyde, disappear. In 1913 Clyde shipbuilding employed 60,000 men. Today the industry barely exists. The closure of Scottish shipyards, coal mines and steel mills, and the consequent high levels of unemployment in Scotland, are in the popular view, closely associated with London government.

The economies of Scotland and England have become increasingly interdependent. By 1979 only 40 per cent of Scots in manufacturing were working for Scottish controlled companies. The rest were working for English, American, Japanese or other foreign-owned enterprises. In 1982 the Monopolies and Mergers Commission reported, "We believe that an important factor in Scotland's economic difficulties has been the progressive loss of morale which the taking over of large companies has caused, and we accept that this is damaging to Scotland."

In the years 1979–81 alone, there was a fall of 11 per cent in Scottish industrial production, and a 20 per cent drop in manufacturing jobs. The Ravenscraig Steel Strip Mill, built in 1963, was the last major capital development undertaken by private enterprise in Scotland. Although financially uneconomic, it was one of the most efficient steel mills in Europe. Even after its neighbouring steel plant, Gartcosh, closed in 1986, Ravenscraig remained open. It became symbolic of the government's residual commitment to industry in Scotland. In 1990 British Steel admitted it intended closing down the whole Ravenscraig complex, with a loss of at least 11,000 jobs, before 1995. In fact it did so in 1992. This, and the insensitive way in which the government introduced the poll tax into Scotland a year before England and Wales, is likely to damage Conservative Party interests in Scotland severely for several years to come.

Since 1981 the Scottish Development Agency's 'Locate in Scotland' campaign has somewhat offset the deteriorating economic situation. A third of the 300 foreign firms with Scottish bases in 1988 had set up within the previous seven years, while 14,500 of the 64,000 jobs provided by foreign companies were created between 1981 and 1987.

One consequence of the "progressive loss of morale" has been the lower state of health in Scotland, and the higher rate of heart disease, alcohol and drug abuse than elsewhere in Britain. Alcoholism, for example, is four times higher than in England. Another consequence is emigration.

Emigration has been a long-standing feature of Scottish social history. Throughout the nineteenth century, the collapse of the Highland clan system led to chiefs selling off clan lands, and allowing their clanspeople to be driven off the land, in what became known as the Highland Clearances. Between 1871 and 1901 half a million Scots emigrated. Emigration has remained an enduring feature. In 1980 alone, over 16,000 Scots emigrated, nearly 10,000 to other parts of Britain, the rest abroad. Scotland's population is in slight decline, 5.1 million today, but likely to fall to 5 million by the year 2000.

Once the Highlands had been stripped of the majority of their inhabitants, the great landowners set aside their estates for sport: the hunting of deer. In the bitter words of one Scot, Iain Finlayson:

"Since the Highland Clearances, the Scottish aristocracy has had very little to do with the day to day life of Scotland. . . . The smart McSloanes [see page 106] have contrived to keep at least a foothold on their ancestral estates, and the most ingenious have never lost the ancestral castles or shooting lodges. It suits the smart McSloanes very well to rent out a few days' shooting every season to [the] rich . . . in order to pay for the rest of the season's shooting to be enjoyed privately and in gentlemanly manner by the owner and his friends."

Stalking deer in the west highlands.

The vast majority of Scotland's great landowners do not live on their estates, and many neither live in Scotland nor are Scottish. Bitterness at this situation reflects the contrast between day-to-day life in the Highlands, and the romantic tourist picture of jolly kilted Highlanders playing bagpipes or participating in Highland Games.

The Highlands, the greater part of the land area of Scotland, have become largely deserted. By the 1960s there were fewer than 300,000 people living in this large area. In the words of a retired forestry expert and Highlander, John McEwen, "Most of the land is held for sport, so the less developed and the less populated it is the better, and it suits absentee landlordism admirably." Since the 1960s the population of the Highlands has slowly grown, to 340,000 by 1990, with encouragement from the Scottish Development Board.

Some Scots, however, believe that no real revival is possible without land reform, to put the land back to use for those who live there. McEwen found that no official land register had been made in Scotland since the nineteenth century. In 1977, at the age of ninety and after much deliberate obstruction by landowners, he finally published his own research which showed that of Scotland's 19 million acres only 2.5 million acres belonged to the state, only 4.5 million acres was in private estates of 1,000 acres or less, but that two-thirds of all Scotland, 12 million acres, was in private estates of over 1,000 acres in size. Scots have good reason to claim that too much economic power is held by people who do not live in Scotland.

In such circumstances, it is hardly surprising that Scottish national feeling has continued to grow since 1945. In the late 1960s the Scottish National Party (SNP) began to attract serious support, and in 1974 won eleven of Scotland's seventy-one seats. In 1979 the Scottish electorate failed to vote decisively for devolution, 32.9 per cent in favour (less than the required 40 per cent), 30.8 per cent against.

Dismay at the progressive integration with England has led to growing cultural expression. Gaelic, still spoken by a small number of people chiefly in the Hebrides, has attracted the interest of a growing number of students. Great awareness and pride in the Scots dialect of English was recently expressed in the translation of the Bible into Broad Scots – part of a resurgence of Scottish identity against the authority wielded by Standard English.

As a result of Conservative government policy in the 1980s Scottish devolution is likely during the 1990s. Prime Minister Margaret Thatcher was strongly hostile to devolution, unlike her predecessor, Edward Heath, who had proposed devolution to Scottish Conservatives in 1968. Heath had recognised the significance of Scottish feeling. It is possible he also recognised its significance for the Conservative Party. In 1955 Conservatives won thirty-six of the then seventy-one Scottish seats in the Commons, the last time they had a Scottish majority. Conservative decline increased dramatically during the 1980s. In the 1979 election the Conservatives won twenty-three seats, but in 1987 they kept only ten, compared with Labour's fifty Scottish seats.

For most Scots, the idea that Scotland should be governed from London by a party which failed to attract more than 14 per cent of the Scottish vote is unacceptable. In 1988 one opinion poll reported that 35 per cent of Scots wanted full independence, 42 per cent wanted a Scottish Parliament within Britain, and only 20 per cent wanted things to remain unchanged. By 1992 another poll indicated that 50 per cent wanted independence, but it remained unclear whether this was a gesture of protest at an unrepresentative government in London, or indicated a genuine move towards independence.

In the 1970s it was the SNP which benefited from irritation with London. In the 1990s it is as likely to be the Labour Party, which after many years' hesitation finally faced the conflict between British and Scottish identities. In 1989 fifty Scottish Labour and Liberal Democrat MPs, leading Scottish churchmen and other community leaders met, significantly, in the Church of Scotland's General Assembly buildings in Edinburgh. Here they unanimously signed a 'Claim of Right':

"We, gathered as the Scottish Constitutional Convention, do hereby acknowledge the sovereign right of the Scottish people to determine the form of government best suited to their needs, and do hereby declare and pledge that in all our actions and deliberations their interests shall be paramount. We further declare and pledge that our actions and deliberations shall be directed to the following ends. To agree a scheme for an Assembly or Parliament for Scotland; to mobilise Scottish opinion and ensure the approval of the Scottish people for that scheme; and to assert the right of the Scottish people to secure the implementation of that scheme."

At a later meeting, a majority of the Scottish Labour Party voted in favour of the introduction of proportional representation. What happens in Scotland promises to be of constitutional significance for the rest of Britain.

If, as seems likely, Scotland succeeds in establishing its own Assembly during the 1990s, Wales is likely to follow its example. If proportional representation is used as the method of election, this is likely to influence more British (not only Scottish) Labour MPs to favour PR for the whole of the United Kingdom.

Finally, there is one more possible influence that Scotland may have on constitutional development. The basis of the English Constitution, as explained in Chapter 2, is the unlimited sovereignty and legal powers of the Crown in Parliament. This was the result of the Glorious Revolution of 1688, *before* the formal 1707 union with Scotland. In Scotland sovereignty resided in the community, in the will of the people. This was the great secular and democratic achievement of the Kirk. The Scots have never been as fond of the Crown as the English have. If the British people decide they need a Bill of Rights, it is possible that Scotland's constitutional view may prove as influential as the English one of the Crown in Parliament.

Questions

Section analysis

1 Northern Ireland: Why were both the Ulster Unionists and Sinn Fein opposed to the Anglo-Irish Agreement of 1985?

2 Northern Ireland: What was your view of the Northern Ireland problem before you read this section? Has your view changed? If so, why?

3 Wales: How has Welsh cultural identity weakened over the second half of the twentieth century?

4 Wales: What has the British government done to contain Welsh nationalism?

5 Scotland: Scotland has always retained its own distinctive institutions. What are they and how do they differ from similar institutions in England?

6 Scotland; Why do you think many Scots resent the concentration of political power in London?

Chapter analysis and discussion

1 Strong local nationalisms are felt and expressed in Northern Ireland, Wales and Scotland. Do these movements result from similar or different causes? Are they expressed in similar or different ways? Find evidence from the text to support your views.

2 Which of the following statements refers to Northern Ireland, which to Scotland and which to Wales? Find evidence from the text to support your choice.

a Nationalism is mainly expressed in cultural and linguistic terms.

b Nationalism is increasing the divisions between communities, and the gaps are becoming harder to bridge.

c Nationalism has increased as industrial power has declined, and nationalists have clear economic as well as political goals.

3 In what ways do you think membership of the European Community could affect the nationalist aspirations of Northern Ireland, Wales and Scotland?

4 Are there regions of your country with strong nationalist feeling? If so, are their aspirations expressed in political parties? How do these parties compare with Sinn Fein, Plaid Cymru or the SNP?

Visual interpretation

Examine this map which shows the demographic distribution of Northern Ireland's Catholic minority. What conclusions can you draw regarding the search for a political solution?

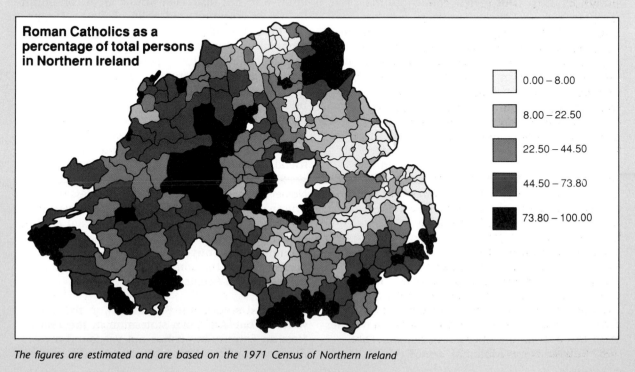

Roman Catholics as a percentage of total persons in Northern Ireland

0.00 – 8.00

8.00 – 22.50

22.50 – 44.50

44.50 – 73.80

73.80 – 100.00

The figures are estimated and are based on the 1971 Census of Northern Ireland

10 A view of Europe and the world

Britain's foreign policy dilemmas

All countries foster myths about themselves, for they are essential to a national self-image. One of Britain's myths is to do with its world position, based on the lingering after-glow of a bygone glory. For two hundred years, until the 1950s, Britain's view of the world was dominated by its overseas territorial possessions and trade. Britain was reluctantly involved in continental Europe, usually only when its own security was directly threatened. Since the disappearance of its empire and the comparative decline in its power, Britain has adjusted its world view with difficulty. In 1959 the Prime Minister asked his intelligence services to review the likely world position of Britain by 1970. This review challenged the maintenance of a nuclear weapons programme, foresaw that the Commonwealth would become increasingly useless as an economic unit, and forecast that Britain would be dwarfed politically and economically by the new European Common Market. But the conclusions were watered down by senior civil servants before they reached the Prime Minister. They contradicted too many assumptions of Britain's world position. There are still occasions when Britain acts as if it were of greater importance than perhaps it is. In the words of one retired diplomat, once ambassador to Paris and then to Washington, "We don't brag as some countries do, but we do tend to assume we'll be treated as a great power."

As a result, Britain's foreign policy tended to lag behind the reality of its world position and to conflict with its true economic interests. It has repeatedly adjusted its overseas political and military commitments since 1945, by troop reduction or political withdrawals, but after rather than before these had become a burden. The 1982 Falklands/Las Malvinas armed conflict is a good example. Britain could no longer afford to defend these islands, and had been discussing with Argentina over several years how to resolve their status. But there had been no sense of urgency. In 1981 the Ministry of Defence economised on the defence of the islands before the Foreign Office had resolved their status with Argentina. This fatally gave the wrong signal to Argentina and resulted in war. The recapture of the Falklands was costly, not only in direct expenditure, roughly £10 billion, but also in lost economic opportunities in Latin America. After its victory Britain was in a far more difficult position for resolving the status of the Falklands in line with British economic resources and political status.

The legacy of empire, exemplified by the Falklands war, has distracted Britain from concentrating on its economic and political future. During the 1970s Britain was dogged by a sense of economic and political weakness, and by the apparent inevitability of post-imperial decline. During the 1980s Margaret Thatcher resolved to reverse the process, and claimed, "Once more Britain is confident, strong, trusted. . . . Strong, because our economy is enterprising, competitive and expanding. And trusted, because we are known to be a powerful ally and a faithful friend."

Not everyone agrees with such an assessment. Britain's military strength (discussed below) has been achieved at the expense of the civil economy. Moreover, even with economic prosperity, Britain's comparative world position is bound to decline during the coming decades on account of the rise of the Pacific economies.

To some it seems as if Britain has, in the hard words of one American statesman in the 1960s, "lost an Empire, but it has not yet found a role". At the end of the 1980s Britain was still uncertain

During the 1980s there were signs in Britain that the relationship was weakening, as the implications of growing political and economic unity in Western Europe became harder to ignore.

British troops in the Falklands/Las Malvinas.

where its primary interests lay, whether it was with the United States, its most important military ally, or with the European Community, its most important economic arena. Because of this uncertainty it was slower than its European allies to respond to the liberalisation of Eastern Europe, slower to invest economic and political effort in the newly free countries, and more anxious than others that America's defence of Western Europe should not decline.

Britain fears the dangers of instability and of dismantling its defences. It also fears that without East–West confrontation, its own pivotal position in the North Atlantic Treaty Organisation (NATO) alliance will disappear, and that it might return to what it was until the seventeenth century, an offshore island on the edge of European affairs.

Ever since the Second World War, Britain has believed in a 'special relationship' with the United States. This relationship is based upon a shared language and Anglo-Saxon culture, and upon a strong alliance forged by Churchill and Roosevelt during the war. In the 1980s Margaret Thatcher spoke of the "very very special relationship" with the United States, partly because she consciously imitated the Churchillian style and partly because she got on particularly well with President Reagan. But the United States has seldom valued the special relationship as highly as Britain has done.

For Britain the relationship was vital to its own world standing. For the United States it was useful for strengthening the European commitment to NATO. The special relationship will only last if both countries have something to gain from it.

A special relationship? John Major and U.S. Secretary of State, James Baker.

Britain in Europe

In the long term Britain is bound primarily to Europe, despite its sometimes unenthusiastic view of the European Community (EC). Unlike the founder members, Britain had not suffered the horrors of armed invasion, so it did not have the same passion to create an economic and political network which would ensure harmony between the market economies of Western Europe. Britain joined the Community in 1973, but it remained diffident, with several MPs of both main parties believing membership to be a mistake. By 1980 it was still possible that Britain could leave the European Community, on account of the dispute over its contribution to the Common Agricultural Policy.

By 1990, even though it remained one of the most argumentative members of the Community, there was no longer any question of Britain giving up membership. But it continued to show it was less enthusiastic than other major members about accepting the implications of membership – a single monetary system and reduced individual sovereignty. The European Monetary System (EMS) was created in 1979, but Britain joined it only in late 1990. British resentment and fears of interference from Brussels in the mid 1980s were well expressed by one Conservative MP: "Almost overnight and largely unnoticed by our fellow citizens, Britain's right to decide many practical matters, even her own destiny, is being surrendered to the majority vote and the interests of other nations, not all of whom share our parliamentary traditions."

Against such attitudes the British Commissioner to the European Community argued that, "Only on a European rather than a national basis can we hold our own in the world." By 1990 few could disagree with this assessment. Britain's economy is closely interrelated with the other members of the Community. Most large companies now operate across frontiers, making the idea of national economic sovereignty meaningless. At a time of world economic crisis, effective decision-making must be transferred from individual members to the European Community as an economic bloc. Without the economic dimension, national political sovereignty has reduced meaning.

Yet this issue produced the crisis within government which led to the downfall of Margaret Thatcher in November 1990. While her ministers had sought compromise with European partners, Mrs Thatcher continued to make defiant statements concerning loss of national sovereignty until the moment she left office. Even after her departure, the issue of national sovereignty remained an important one. At the Maastricht summit in December 1991 John Major agreed to the new EC treaty, but insisted on Parliament's right to 'opt out' of the proposed single European currency at a later date. He also declined to sign the Social Charter safeguarding minimal employment conditions throughout the Community.

Europe occupies two distinct positions in popular esteem. For a long time there has been strong middle-class support for membership of the European Community, based not only upon Britain's pragmatic interests, but also upon interest in European culture. Many middle-class Britons take their holidays exploring different parts of Europe. They are largely pan-European in outlook. However, there is also another category of British visitor to the Continent. These are the young holidaymakers and hooligans who enjoy drunken violence, for example, on Spain's Mediterranean coast, or following English football teams. Their behaviour is not solely to do with social problems in Britain. It also reflects the contemptuous attitude they have for those who are not British. Although these people express themselves drunkenly or violently, it is also true that many other British people do not yet feel culturally European.

The Commonwealth

Beyond its immediate foreign policy priorities, its ties with Europe and the United States, Britain has important relations across the rest of the world. The Commonwealth of countries previously governed by Britain provides an informal forum, unlike the formality of the United Nations, for international issues to be discussed. By 1990 there were fifty member countries of the Commonwealth, with the re-admission of Pakistan (which had left in 1972) and the entry of Namibia. The Queen is titular head of the Commonwealth, actual head of eighteen countries, and an ardent supporter of the Commonwealth idea. There were only eleven members in 1960, twenty-one by 1965, and membership has more than doubled since then.

However, the growth of the Commonwealth is not necessarily a sign of its success. The greatest strength of the Commonwealth in the 1960s and early 1970s was the intimacy of this varied club. Today that intimacy has been largely lost. The larger the Commonwealth becomes, the less effective it is as a place for the uninhibited exchange of views.

The heads of government of all Commonwealth countries meet every two years, and sometimes issue a Declaration of Intent, enshrining agreed ideals or principles. In 1971 the Singapore Declaration stated, "We believe in the liberty of the individual, in equal rights for all citizens regardless of race, colour, creed or political belief, and in their inalienable right to participate by means of free and democratic political processes in framing the society in which they live." As with the United Nations, many members fall short of their undertaking. In 1979 the Lusaka Declaration urged the eradication of racism as a priority for the Commonwealth. Some members feel that Britain's position on South Africa during the 1980s violated the Declaration's intent. On the other hand British critics of the Commonwealth suggest that Britain no longer has any relationship of value with many members, and point to the absence of democratic values of some members. The disagreement in the 1980s over South Africa prompted some Conservative MPs to call for Britain's withdrawal from the international organisation it had created.

The Commonwealth conference, Zimbabwe, 1991.

Today there is no longer the strong sense of Commonwealth purpose that there was thirty years ago. For Britain this is partly because the Commonwealth is now much less important economically than the European Community. The dramatic reduction of Britain's overseas aid during the 1980s, much of which went to Commonwealth countries, and the raising of education fees for overseas students in Britain, have both weakened Britain's Commonwealth ties.

Despite ambivalent attitudes to the Commonwealth, it is most unlikely that Britain would withdraw except in an extreme situation. But if the Commonwealth gently weakens, it is unlikely Britain will do very much to revive it. Unless member countries feel there is some reason for perpetuating an organisation which represents historical accident rather than common purpose, the long-term future of the Commonwealth must be in doubt.

Hong Kong

Margaret Thatcher's claim that Britain was a "powerful ally and a faithful friend" is viewed with scepticism in the Crown Colony of Hong Kong. Most people in Hong Kong feel dissatisfied with the agreement Britain reached with China for the handover of Hong Kong to China in 1997. They believe that Britain has failed in its obligations. The 1984 accord with Peking guaranteed that after 1997 the Legislative Council for the ex-colony would include 30 per cent directly elected representatives. But a fully elected Assembly will not be created until 2007, and may not even occur then.

In 1990, in order to calm Hong Kong's nerves, Britain offered British citizenship to 50,000 key Hong Kong civil servants and their families. But this may well prove the worst of all worlds. It has possibly offered insufficient passports to ensure the survival of Hong Kong as a stable society or dynamic economy, but offered enough that many of those who get them will seize the opportunity to get out. In fact 3.25 million of Hong Kong's 6 million residents have United Kingdom passports. It might have been wiser to have adopted the higher risk strategy of offering all of these the right to live in Britain, since this would more probably have reassured the Hong Kong Chinese that Britain would not abandon them.

The armed forces

The British have mixed feelings about their armed forces. There is pride in their abilities and bravery, demonstrated in the 1982 recapture of the Falkland Islands/Las Malvinas and in the Gulf War. There is also pride in the history and traditions of the Royal Navy, the Royal Air Force, and the regiments of the Army, many of which are over 250 years old. On the other hand the authority required in, and imposed by, an army is deeply disliked by a nation of individualistic and anti-authoritarian people. Any use of the armed forces in mainland Britain to maintain order would provoke a major popular protest. As a result of these two distinct attitudes, the armed forces are the object of both pride and mockery.

After 1945 it was clear that Britain was no longer the foremost power it had been previously. In order to secure "the right to sit at the top of the table", as one Prime Minister put it, Britain

An infantryman in the Gulf War.

In line with its view of itself as the most important member of NATO after the US, Britain has maintained a nuclear deterrent and substantial armed forces in spite of its declining economic power. In 1990 Britain was spending 4.3 per cent of its gross domestic product on defence compared with West Germany's 3 per cent, although both countries were spending roughly the same amount of money. This provided Britain with a nuclear deterrent and a force of 300,000 soldiers, sailors and airmen (and 175,000 civilians providing services for them) at an annual cost in 1990 of £20 billion. During the 1980s Britain also decided to replace the Polaris system with US Trident missiles. These are scheduled to come into service in the 1990s and last until about 2020, at a cost estimated in the late 1980s at £10,000 million. In fact Trident gives Britain a nuclear capacity greatly in excess of its true deterrent requirement. Each of four submarines will carry eight missiles, with each missile capable of carrying fourteen independent warheads. Each submarine will carry a potential total of 128 warheads, compared with 48 warheads in the Polaris system, an almost threefold increase in destructive capability.

A cruise missile base.

invested in the development and deployment of nuclear weapons. It soon found it could not afford production costs and became dependent on US-supplied weapons. From 1962 it purchased US Polaris missiles for its submarines. Whether Britain needed a nuclear deterrent for security rather than to increase its political influence has always been a matter for debate.

As in the political sphere, Britain has adjusted militarily too slowly to its changing circumstances. In spite of the progressive contraction of its commitments, it remains over-extended. In the 1970s it withdrew from its military 'east of Suez' role, but it would probably have been prudent to withdraw ten years earlier. Although the bulk of British forces in 1990 were stationed in Germany as part of the NATO defence, there were also smaller forces in Belize, Brunei, Cyprus, the Falklands, Gibraltar and Hong Kong.

Are such costs worth it? The first Secretary General of NATO forty years ago was British. He privately described NATO's purpose: "To keep the Russians out, the Americans in and the Germans down." Such a view can hardly have a place in modern Europe. However, Britain in 1990 was less willing than its allies to reduce its military expenditure. It still has difficulty in giving up its nostalgic self-image of a great military power.

Nevertheless Britain will have to review and reduce its military capability during the 1990s, partly in response to the momentous changes in

Europe but also because it cannot afford to invest so much in the non-productive sector of a struggling economy. Take, for example, the cost of its fleet. A report in 1990 showed that out of the twenty-year life expected of the average naval vessel, only five years were spent at sea. For the rest of the time the ship was in port, being repaired or refitted, or with its crew on leave. The final maintenance bill might well be two or three times the initial purchase price. Or look at air force costs. Britain and Israel both have about 550 combat aircraft. Britain uses three times as many people to keep them in service, mainly because it deploys them on more airstrips. But in 1990 it also had many aircraft sitting unused: "While all air forces like to have reserves," as one defence correspondent noted, "no other in NATO has such a high proportion of its aircraft gathering dust." The pressure to significantly reduce both the size and cost of Britain's armed forces cannot be ignored.

The armed forces are likely to become a smaller more flexible force during the 1990s. Tanks, heavy artillery and the equipment suitable for a major European war are likely to be reduced, in favour of more helicopters and transport planes to produce a highly versatile rapid deployment force which can be used anywhere in the world. This need for greater flexibility was confirmed by the Gulf War in 1991.

There is a commercial aspect to the strategic changes in Europe. Britain has encouraged the development of a strong arms industry to supply the armed forces and also to make profitable sales internationally. During the 1980s Britain became the largest international arms trader after the United States. With the likely decline in orders from the British armed forces several major companies face the choice of increasing arms sales to the Third World or diversifying into the much more competitive civil sector.

One further point needs to be made about the Army in particular. It is a deeply 'tribal' institution. Infantry regiments, with 200 or more years of history, regard themselves as families. Many officers are the sons or grandsons of men who also served in the same regiment. The officer culture tends to be old-fashioned and conservative in its values and political outlook. It is also, particularly in the smarter regiments, like the Guards, cavalry, highland and rifle regiments, distinctly upper class in a way seldom found outside the Army. The sons of great landowners sometimes pursue an army career, for example in

a Guards regiment, until they inherit the family estate. It almost goes without saying that most officers in such regiments were educated at public schools.

The Guards may represent the upper-class élite in the Army, but the Special Air Service (SAS) represents the tough operational élite. It was established during the Second World War to work behind enemy lines. After the war it continued to exist, but was deliberately hidden from publicity. Men could only join the SAS from other army units after the most rigorous selection procedure for physical and mental ability. They sometimes operated in other countries to support regimes considered friendly to Britain. They also operated in Northern Ireland from 1969 onwards, though it was seven years before the government admitted to this.

In 1980 the SAS became highly visible when some of its men stormed the Iranian Embassy in London to release embassy staff taken hostage. During the 1980s the SAS was repeatedly in the news. It captured the imagination of many for its daring, skill and secrecy. It was this image of a tough, 'go anywhere', secret élite that stimulated such interest.

The SAS storming the Iranian Embassy.

The question of security

Secrecy is a very British obsession. Britain is possibly the most secretive country in the West. Virtually every other country admits it has a secret service of some kind, but Britain has pretended it does not. The air of mystery fascinates the public, both in Britain and elsewhere. The success of Ian Fleming's hero James Bond and the novels of Len Deighton and John Le Carré owes much to this fascination.

Roger Moore as James Bond in a scene from A View to a Kill.

Secrecy may be romantic but there are serious implications in a democracy. Parliament is unable to know what is undertaken by Britain's security services, on the grounds that some parliamentarians would be a security risk. It is a strange argument for a parliamentary democracy to use, since it implies that neither Parliament nor people are sovereign, and that someone else, whose identity we cannot be sure of, knows best.

Secrecy provides a protection against public accountability. It also gives the secret services a powerful hold on the country. In 1968, a Labour minister was falsely accused by MI5 (see below) of marrying a 'Soviet agent'. With his career destroyed, he left politics and Britain with his Russian-born wife to live in Geneva. His Prime Minister, Harold Wilson, was repeatedly and falsely accused of being a KGB agent (1963), of concealing the spying activities of his colleagues and of having Soviet agents as personal friends (1971). During the years 1965–80 a leading trade unionist was falsely accused of being a Soviet agent, to prevent him getting any government post. During the 1980s an investigation by *The Observer* newspaper suggested that official phone tapping rose to a level of 30,000 individual lines each year, without the knowledge or consent of Parliament.

In spite of government silence it has been common knowledge that two main organisations, MI5 and MI6, exist. MI5, which was officially acknowledged in 1989, is responsible for Britain's own security and the detection and arrest of foreign spies. MI6 (also known as the Secret Intelligence Service (SIS)), which the government only officially acknowledged in 1992, runs Britain's spy network abroad. But for many years, MI6 and the identity of its director has been well known to other governments. British diplomats are coy. They refer to MI6 simply as 'the Friends'.

MI5, MI6, the police Special Branch and Signals Intelligence (SIGINT) are all coordinated by the Joint Intelligence Committee (JIC), which is composed of senior civil servants and intelligence chiefs responsible to the Cabinet Secretary and the Prime Minister. The rivalry between these different intelligence networks is most in evidence, it is said, at meetings of the JIC.

During the 1980s several important incidents occurred which demonstrate the British obsession with secrecy. In 1984 Clive Ponting, a senior civil servant, believed his ministers were deliberately concealing information from an interested MP, and from the Parliamentary Select Committee for Foreign Affairs, not on the grounds of secrecy but because it would reveal that the government had been deliberately misleading Parliament for the preceding two years. It concerned the sinking of the Argentinian warship the *Belgrano* in 1982. Ponting decided to send crucial evidence to this MP showing that he and Parliament were being misled. Ponting was prosecuted for violating the Official Secrets Act. The jury found Ponting not guilty. They felt he had acted in the public interest, and justified his disclosure. Afterwards, the government introduced a new Official Secrets Act which specifically stated that the disclosure of secrets "in the public interest" was no defence.

The security services received far more public exposure than many politicians wanted. In 1986 an ex-MI5 operative, Peter Wright, tried to publish the story of his career, *Spycatcher*, but was forbidden to do so by the government, on the grounds that he was sworn to secrecy. When the publisher decided to publish in Australia, the British government tried to prevent it. But the widely publicised case (which Britain lost) created huge interest in the book, causing it to become a bestseller.

The war against the IRA provided another arena in which official secrecy became a highly sensitive issue. During the period 1984–86 a senior police officer, John Stalker, was instructed to investigate the circumstances in which Ulster police had made up stories concerning their shooting of six unarmed men. In spite of obstruction by the Ulster police, Stalker found that MI5 and police Special Branch were closely involved in the incidents. When he demanded a vital secret tape-recording to establish the truth he was suddenly removed from the case, suspended from all duties and himself made the subject of an investigation of malpractice. It was widely believed at the time that he had been removed as a result of pressure by the security services.

In 1988 three unarmed members of the IRA were shot dead in Gibraltar by four soldiers from the SAS. The shootings, coming after the Stalker inquiry, provoked enormous public concern. The government decided to hold an inquest into the deaths to allay public anxiety about the legality of the killings. But it guaranteed anonymity and public-interest immunity for the four SAS men. This ensured that their identity would not be revealed and that they were entitled to remain silent on matters of national security or intelligence sensitivity.

The Government Communications Headquarters (GCHQ) in Cheltenham operates one of the most important parts of the security apparatus, its communications surveillance, known as SIGINT (see above). The system is linked to similar operations in the United States, Canada, Australia and New Zealand. As with other aspects of its secret services, the government is shy about its existence. But during the 1980s it decided that the staff of GCHQ could no longer enjoy trade union membership, on the grounds that the possibility of strike action endangered national security. The decision caused resentment among GCHQ staff since their union offered a promise that it would never call a strike at GCHQ.

The Conservative government in the 1980s may have championed secrecy more than its predecessors, but almost every government this century has acted undemocratically in areas of national security. During the 1970s successive Prime Ministers implemented a programme to upgrade the Polaris nuclear missiles to keep them effective into the 1990s. 'Chevaline', as the programme was known, proved far more costly than expected, and unnecessary in the view of some defence experts. The cost rose from £175 million in 1972 to £530 million (at 1972 prices) ten years later. Yet the most significant feature of the programme was its secrecy. Only a few senior members of the Cabinet and the minimum number of defence staff and civil servants knew of the programme. Parliament, which should have had the opportunity to debate such a programme, only learnt by chance in 1980 of Chevaline, largely as a result of investigative journalism. More open discussion would have given the critics a chance to challenge it, and an enormous wastage of money could have been avoided.

The trouble is that the desire for secrecy in British government goes beyond the need to protect national security to the protection of politicians in power from embarrassment. Whitehall's standard security handbook reads: "Precautions are needed . . . to prevent foreign powers and subversive organisations from obtaining unauthorised information and to avoid disclosures which would cause embarrassment hampering good government . . ." However, private government, effectively what took place in the case of Chevaline, is clearly bad government as well as undemocratic. The ability to conceal the truth, as in the case of the *Belgrano*, is an irresistible temptation for a government under attack from the opposition. Yet the process is corrupt and undermines the democratic principle. In 1980 the Civil Service set out regulations (known as the 'Osmotherly Rules') for civil servants appearing before the new select committees (see page 36) which state, "Any withholding of information should be limited to reservations that are necessary in the interests of good government or to safeguard national security." The explanatory notes following this rule effectively deny MPs any real knowledge of the inside workings of Whitehall, thus preventing Parliament or the electorate making government truly accountable for its conduct.

It is, perhaps, never possible to strike a final balance between secrecy in the interests of national security or good government, and openness in the protection of democratic values. It is only by constant challenge and debate that the public (and Parliament) can keep governmental secrecy within reasonable limits.

Questions

Section analysis

1 Foreign policy dilemmas: Which of the following sentences do you think best illustrates the basic problems of British foreign policy?

a Britain still cannot abandon a self-image of imperial greatness.

b Britain has always been late in scaling down its foreign policy commitments in line with its real political and economic power.

c Britain's fundamental problem is whether to back the European Community fully or to pursue a wider role as a junior partner of the United States.

2 Britain in Europe: Britain has ambiguous feelings about the European Community. a) What is it that Conservative governments particularly fear losing? b) What are the two positions that Europe occupies in popular esteem? Who holds them?

3 The Commonwealth: How has the change in size of the Commonwealth since 1960 affected its effectiveness?

4 Hong Kong: Why might the people of Hong Kong have reason to doubt Margaret Thatcher's statement that Britain is a "faithful friend"?

5 The armed forces: Why has Britain had difficulty in reducing military expenditure?

6 The question of security: The British are preoccupied with secrecy. In what ways is this bad for democracy? Do you think officials should legally be able to disclose secrets "in the public interest"? How does the British government's attitude to secrecy compare with that in your own country?

Chapter analysis and discussion

1 Do you think the following reflect a particular state of mind?

a Britain's concern to "sit at the top table"

b Its reluctance to reduce its armed forces as much as its European allies have done

c Its ambiguous attitude to Europe and its concern with secrecy

Do you think these characteristics are more to do with a) a sense of superiority b) fear of the future c) pragmatic realism d) a lack of self-confidence?

2 Think about basic British attitudes regarding Britain's international role, its relations with the United States and Europe, and the use of its armed forces and security services. What broad changes would you propose if you were Prime Minister?

Visual interpretation

The following table shows the percentage of those who expressed an opinion in 1989 on the idea of a united European government by 1992:

Country	For	Against
Italy	94	6
Portugal	93	7
Spain	92	8
Belgium	87	13
France	84	16
Greece	83	17
Ireland	82	18
Netherlands	80	20
– – – – EC Average	77	23 – – –
Luxembourg	68	32
Germany	66	34
United Kingdom	52	48
Denmark	26	74

Do you see grounds for a pro-Europe British government taking comfort from these figures?

11 Educating the nation

Education has been a controversial area of national life periodically since 1945, subject to major changes as successive governments have tried to improve it. Government policy (both Conservative and Labour) has been bitterly criticised for providing a system which is either too élitist or insufficiently so, which is wasteful of human resources, which is insufficiently demanding of the nation's children, or which simply fails to compete with the education systems of other industrialised countries. During the 1980s, the Conservative government sought to eliminate some of these criticisms, according to its political philosophy. The results, yet again, have been controversial, but they are likely to have a continuing effect on the quality of Britain's education system at least until the end of the century. The controversy surrounding education results partly from particular historical developments, briefly described below, but also from fears for the quality of the system in the future.

Schooling is compulsory for twelve years, for all children aged five to sixteen. There are two voluntary years of schooling thereafter. Children may attend either state-funded or fee-paying independent schools. In England and Wales the primary cycle lasts from five to eleven. Generally speaking, children enter infant school, moving on to junior school at the age of eight, and then on to secondary school at the age of eleven. Roughly 90 per cent of children receive their secondary education at 'comprehensive' schools (see below). Secondary school lasts either until the end of the compulsory attendance cycle, or includes the two final years of secondary education, generally known in Britain (for historical reasons) as the 'sixth form'. In many parts of the country, these two years are spent at a tertiary or sixth form college, which provides academic and vocational courses.

Two public examinations are set, on completion of the compulsory cycle of education at the age of sixteen, and on completion of the two voluntary years. At sixteen pupils take the General

Children at a primary school.

Certificate of Secondary Education (GCSE), introduced in 1989. It replaced two previous examinations: the Certificate of Secondary Education (CSE), which indicated satisfactory completion of secondary education, and the General Certificate of Education (GCE) which was for higher academic achievers. The new GCSE was introduced with two main intentions: to provide one examination whereby the whole range of ability could be judged, rather than having two classes of achievers; and to assess children on classwork and homework as well as in the examination room, as a more reliable form of assessment. The new GCSE remains controversial, partly on account of the rush with which it was introduced, and it is possible that it will be substantially revised during the 1990s. During the two voluntary years of schooling, pupils specialise in two or three subjects, and take the GCE Advanced Level, or 'A level' examination, usually with a view to entry to a university, polytechnic or other college of higher education, discussed later. New examinations, Advanced Supplementary (AS) levels, which were introduced in 1989, are intended to provide a wider range of study. The examinations are not set by the government, but by independent examinations boards, most of which are associated with a particular university or group of universities.

Scotland, with a separate education tradition, has a slightly different system. Children stay in the primary cycle until the age of twelve. They take the Scottish Certificate of Education (SCE) usually at the age of sixteen, and instead of A levels, take the Scottish Higher Certificate which is more like continental European examinations, since it covers a wider area of study than the highly specialised A level courses. Scots pupils who wish to continue their studies beyond the Higher may take the Certificate of Sixth Year Studies (CSYS).

For less academically inclined pupils, a Certificate of Pre-Vocational Education was introduced in 1986, as a qualification for a further year of full-time education after sixteen to prepare for work or vocational courses.

The academic year begins in late summer, usually in September, and is divided into three terms, with holidays for Christmas, Easter and for the month of August, although the exact dates vary slightly from area to area. In addition each term there is normally a mid-term one-week holiday, known as 'half-term'.

The story of British schools

It might seem as if the educational system is comparatively simple. For largely historical reasons, however, it is complicated, inconsistent and highly varied. Most of the oldest schools, of which the most famous are Eton and Winchester, are today independent, fee-paying, public schools. Most of these were established to create a body of literate people to fulfil the administrative, political, legal and religious requirements of the late middle ages. From the sixteenth century onwards, many 'grammar' schools were established, often with large grants of money from wealthy men, in order to provide a local educational facility.

From the 1870s it became the duty of local authorities to establish elementary schools, at the expense of the local community, and to compel attendance of all children up to the age of thirteen. By 1900 almost total attendance had been achieved. Each local authority, with its locally elected councillors, was responsible for the curriculum. Although a general consensus developed concerning the major part of the school curriculum, a strong feeling of local control

continued and interference by central government was resented. A number of secondary schools were also established by local authorities, modelled on the public schools (see below).

The 1944 Education Act introduced free compulsory secondary education. Almost all children attended one of two kinds of secondary school. The decision was made on the results obtained in the '11 plus' examination, taken on leaving primary school. About three quarters of pupils went to 'secondary modern' schools where pupils were expected to obtain sufficient education for manual, skilled and clerical employment, but the academic expectations were modest. The remaining quarter, however, went to grammar schools. Some of these were old foundations which now received a direct grant from central government, but the majority were funded through the local authority. Grammar school pupils were expected to go on to university or some other form of higher education. A large number of the grammar or 'high' schools were single sex. In addition there were, and continue to be, a number of voluntary state-supported primary and secondary schools, most of them under the management of the Church of England or the Roman Catholic Church, which usually own the school buildings.

By the 1960s there was increasing criticism of this streaming of ability, particularly by the political left. It was recognised that many children performed inconsistently, and that those who failed the 11 plus examination might well develop academically later, but through the secondary modern system were denied this opportunity. It seemed a great waste of human potential. In fact, a government report in 1968 produced evidence that an expectation of failure became increasingly fulfilled: secondary modern children aged fourteen were found to be doing significantly worse than they had been at the age of eight. The Labour government's solution was to introduce a new type of school, the comprehensive, a combination of grammar and secondary modern under one roof, so that all the children could be continually assessed and given appropriate teaching. Between 1965 and 1980 almost all the old grammar and secondary modern schools were replaced, mainly by co-educational comprehensives. The measure caused much argument for two reasons. Many local authorities did not wish to lose the excellence of their grammar schools, and many resented the interference in education, which was still considered a local responsibility. However, despite the pressure to change school structures, each school, in consultation with the local authority, remained in control of its curriculum. In practice the result of the reform was very mixed: the best comprehensives aimed at grammar school academic standards, while the worst sank to secondary modern ones.

Pupils at a comprehensive school.

One unforeseen but damaging result was the refusal of many grammar schools to join the comprehensive experiment. Of the 174 old direct grant grammar schools, 119 decided to leave the state system rather than become comprehensive, and duly became independent fee-paying establishments (see below). This had two effects. The grammar schools had provided an opportunity for children from all social backgrounds to excel academically at the same level as those attending fee-paying independent public schools. The loss of these schools had a demoralising effect on the comprehensive experiment, and damaged its chances of success, but led to a revival of independent schools at a time when they seemed to be slowly shrinking. The comprehensive reform thus unintentionally reinforced an educational élite which only the children of wealthier parents could hope to join.

The comprehensives became the standard form of secondary education (other than in one or two isolated areas, where grammar schools and secondary moderns survived). However except among the best comprehensives they lost the excellence of the old grammar schools.

Alongside the introduction of comprehensives there was a move away from traditional teaching and discipline towards what was called 'progressive' education. This entailed a change from more formal teaching and factual learning to greater pupil participation and discussion, with greater emphasis on comprehension and less on the acquisition of knowledge. Not everyone approved. During the 1970s there was increasing criticism of the lack of discipline and of formal learning, and a demand to return to old-fashioned methods.

During the 1960s and 1970s there was also greater emphasis on education and training than ever before, with many colleges of further education established to provide technical or vocational training. However, British education remained too academic for the less able, and technical studies have remained weak, with the result that a large number of less able pupils leave school without any skills at all. By 1988 nine out of ten West German employees had vocational training qualifications based on a three-year apprentice-type course. In Britain only one in ten came into the same category.

The expansion of education led to increased expenditure. The proportion of the gross national product devoted to education doubled, from 3.2 per cent in 1954, to 6.5 per cent by 1970, though during the 1980s this figure fell back to about 5 per cent. These higher levels of spending did not lead to fulfilled expectations. Perhaps the most serious failures were the continued high drop-out rate at the age of sixteen and low level of achievement in mathematics and science among school-leavers. By the mid 1980s, while over 80 per cent of pupils in West Germany and the United States, and over 90 per cent in Japan, stayed on till the age of eighteen, barely one-third of British pupils did so. Surveys of the adult population revealed that half the population could not do simple mathematics or read a railway timetable correctly, and that 16 per cent could not locate Britain on a map of the world. Among ten-year-old primary pupils in seventeen countries, English children were second worst in science. The worst Japanese school was better in primary science than the best 60 per cent of English schools. Although A level science pupils in England are among the best internationally, they are a small group. The damaging fact is the broad ignorance of British children, particularly in science and technology. One reason is that British children, along with American children, spend more time watching television, and there is an established negative association between this and achievement in science and mathematics.

Educational reforms in the 1980s

After 1979 the Conservative government tried to encourage a return to some of the old values. It was critical of the teaching profession and worried by the poor performance of many pupils. Through the Education Act (1986) and the Education Reform Act (1988) it introduced the greatest reforms in schooling certainly since 1944, and in the view of John Rae, a leading educationist and ex-headmaster of Westminster School, the most important reform since the state took responsibility for education in 1870.

Most educational experts saw good and bad features in these reforms. A theme running through most of them was the removal of local authority control, thus striking at the heart of the tradition of localism. In its place the government put greater central government control combined with greater parental choice, based on the philosophy of freedom of choice for the 'consumer'.

The main reforms included the introduction of a National Curriculum making certain subjects, most notably science and one modern language, compulsory up to the age of sixteen. These had frequently been given up at the age of thirteen. The Education Secretary made his views clear: "Boys and girls cannot opt out of technology until they are sixteen, which means that even those who are academically gifted will have to roll up their sleeves and learn some craft. We have for far too long in our country underestimated the importance of craft skills." Many welcomed the creation of national targets for education. John Rae, for example, drew attention to the way France and Japan had both, at a moment of crisis, introduced a system based on national needs. But there was also unease that the compulsory curriculum, taking up over 70 per cent of school time, would squeeze out important wider areas of learning. It also introduced periodic formal assessments of progress, at the ages of seven, eleven, fourteen and sixteen. Independent fee-paying schools (see below), to which Conservative government ministers mainly sent their children, were exempted from teaching according to the National Curriculum. It was unclear to many why these schools did not have to follow the same national objectives.

The other changes were more controversial. In keeping with its philosophy of consumer choice, the government gave parents the right to enrol

The National Curriculum emphasises the importance of science.

their children – given appropriate age and aptitude – at any state school of their choice, within the limits of capacity. This new freedom is generally unlikely to change things much. Parents already sent their children to the local school of their choice. Critics, however, are concerned with two main problems. First, in areas with a large ethnic minority, there was already a desire on the part of many parents, both white and ethnic minority, to have their children educated among their own racial or religious community. Voluntary racial segregation will prove damaging to the social fabric. The other criticism relates to certain urban areas where unpopular schools may be caught in a dangerous downwards spiral, with declining enrolment followed by reduced budgets.

Schools were also given the powers to opt out of local authority control, if a majority of parents wished for this. For successful schools in wealthy areas there are possible advantages in becoming more like a private school, without any local authority control. They will have far greater freedom, and in due course may become highly competitive, like the old grammar schools. There are, however, several dangers. Parents may see education more narrowly than educationists, since they tend to be concerned only while their children are of school age. They may also be more suspicious of progressive education than the local education authority, and keener on more easily measurable evidence of learning. The opting out of the better schools may weaken the general education system locally, which in the past has benefited from shared resources, something of particular importance to weaker schools. If too many schools opt out, the local education authorities, valuable centres of expertise, may disappear altogether. Secondary schools and larger primary schools have also been given responsibility for managing their own budgets. Each school board of governors, composed of parents and local authority appointees, has a greatly increased responsibility, including the 'hiring and firing' of staff. The substantial additional work may well discourage parents from offering themselves as governors, leading to less rather than more parental participation. Furthermore, some critics are unhappy that the school principals do not themselves have full executive powers over staff.

Are these reforms sufficient to produce the skilled and educated population Britain needs if it is to halt its economic decline? The most obvious outstanding problem is the teaching profession. Over the years, its professional standing and recognition has steadily fallen. By 1990, the teaching profession was in crisis, with low morale and self-esteem, and comparatively low pay. The consequence was an accelerating flight from the

The shortage of teachers.

profession. The wastage rate was so high that by 1989 there were as many trained teachers not teaching as teaching. Inadequate pay resulted in teachers avoiding posts in areas where housing was expensive, particularly in the south east. By 1990 teacher vacancies in London primary schools were twice as high as the national average. The worst shortages were in the subjects identified as of greatest national importance: mathematics and science. An official government report indicated that by 1995 the system might be short of 12,000 maths teachers, over half the national require- ment, and 2,300 physics and 3,000 languages teachers. If these projections prove correct it will be impossible for many children to go on to study engineering. In 1989 Britain filled the gap by employing unemployed teachers from Germany, the Netherlands, Australia and elsewhere.

The shortfall is not only in the total number of teachers, but in the inadequate level of qualifica- tion of a high proportion of primary teachers, particularly in science and maths. These problems suggest a need for more attractive career prospects and pay for teachers generally, special recruitment in particular subjects, and intensive in-service training to improve the calibre of teachers with inadequate qualifications. In the words of Eric Bolton, England's chief inspector of schools, "Standards of learning are never improved by poor teachers and there are no cheap, high quality routes into teaching." If this is so, then the most important area of reform may still remain to be tackled.

The private sector

By the end of the 1980s over 7 per cent of the school population attended independent fee- paying schools, compared with under 6 per cent in 1979, and only 5 per cent in 1976. By the year 2000 the proportion is expected to rise to around 9 per cent, almost back to the level in 1947 of 10 per cent. The recovery of private education in Britain is partly due to middle-class fears concern- ing the comprehensive experiment, but also to the mediocre quality possible in the state sector at the present level of funding.

Although the percentage of those privately edu- cated may be a small fraction of the total, its importance is disproportionate to its size, for this 7 per cent accounts for 23 per cent of all those passing A levels, and over 25 per cent of those gaining entry to university. Nearly 65 per cent of pupils leave fee-paying schools with one or more A levels, compared with only 14 per cent from comprehensives. During the 1980s pupils at independent schools showed greater improvement in the examination results than those at state-maintained schools. In later life, those educated outside the state-maintained system dominate the sources of state power and authority in government, law, the armed forces and finance.

The public (in fact private fee-paying) schools form the backbone of the independent sector. Of the several hundred public schools, the most famous are the 'Clarendon Nine'. Their status lies, for the British, in a fatally attractive combination of social superiority and antiquity, as the dates of their foundation indicate: Winchester (1382), Eton (1440), St Paul's (1509), Shrewsbury (1552), Westminster (1560), The Merchant Taylors' (1561), Rugby (1567), Harrow (1571) and Charterhouse (1611).

Pupils at Eton College.

The golden age of the public schools, however, was the end of the nineteenth century, when most were founded. They were vital to the establishment of a particular outlook and set of values by the dominant professional middle classes. These values were famously reflected in *Tom Brown's Schooldays* by Thomas Hughes, written in tribute to his own happy time at Rugby School. Its emphasis is on the making of gentlemen to enter one of the professions: law, medicine, the Church, the Civil Service or colonial service. A career in commerce, or "mere money making" as it is referred to in *Tom Brown's Schooldays*, was not to be considered. As a result of such values, the public school system was traditional in its view of learning, and deeply resistant to science and technology. Most public schools were located in the countryside, away from industrial cities.

After 1945 but before the introduction of comprehensives, when state-maintained grammar schools were demonstrating equal or greater academic excellence, the public schools began to modernise themselves. During the 1970s most of them abolished beating and 'fagging', the system whereby new boys carried out menial tasks for senior boys, and many introduced girls into the sixth form, as a civilising influence. They made particular efforts to improve their academic and scientific quality.

Demand for public school education is now so great that many schools register babies' names at birth. Eton maintains two lists, one for the children of 'old boys' and the other for outsiders. There are three applicants for every vacancy. In 1988, for example, there were 203 names down for only 120 places at Radley School in the year 2000. But such schools are careful not to expand to meet demand. In the words of one academic, "Schools at the top of the system have a vested interest in being élitist. They would lose that characteristic if they expanded. To some extent they pride themselves on the length of their waiting lists." This rush to private education is despite the steep rise in fees, for example 31 per cent between 1985 and 1988. In order to obtain a place at a public school, children must take a competitive examination, called 'Common Entrance'. In order to pass it, most children destined for a public school education attend a preparatory (or 'prep') school until the age of 13.

The independent schools remain controversial. The Conservative Party believes in the fundamental freedom of parents to choose the best education for their children. The Labour Party disagrees, arguing that in reality only the wealthier citizens have this freedom of choice. In the words of Hugh Gaitskell, the Labour leader in 1953, "We really cannot go on with a system in which wealthy parents are able to buy what they and most people believe to be a better education for their children. The system is wrong and must be changed." But since then every Labour government has hesitated to abolish them.

There can be no doubt that a better academic education can be obtained in some of the public schools. But the argument that parents will not wish to pay (by 1990 average boarding public school fees were over £7,000 annually) once state schools offer equally good education is misleading, for it suggests a simple solution. The background from which pupils come greatly affects the encouragement received to study. Middle-class parents are likely to be better able, and more concerned, to support their children's study than low-income parents who themselves feel they failed at school.

State-maintained schools must operate with fewer resources, in more difficult circumstances, particularly in low-income areas. In addition, the public school system creams off many of the ablest teachers from the state sector. A survey in 1989 revealed that nearly a third of teachers recently appointed by public schools had been recruited from the state sector, where this increased the acute shortage of mathematics and science teachers. As the head of one teachers' union remarked, "If the independent sector recruits some of the most able state school teachers, then the outlook for the larger maintained sector is very bleak indeed."

Public school facilities: an Eton College boating ceremony.

The most serious complaint against the public school system is that it is socially divisive. Intentionally or not, it breeds an atmosphere of élitism, leaving many outside the system feeling socially or intellectually inferior, and in some cases intimidated by the prestige attached to public schools. In 1988 a television documentary was made of an exchange for two weeks between pupils at Rugby School and at a Liverpool comprehensive. Horror was expressed by both groups at the alien culture of the other. The Liverpuddlian pupils spoke 'Scouse', the dialect of Liverpool, while Rugby's pupils spoke RP, the accent of the educated upper middle class. Rugby boys found the comprehensive school and its environment characterless, as indeed much of Britain must seem to children coming from highly privileged backgrounds. The comprehensive pupils regarded Rugby as old-fashioned, formal and rigidly disciplined. Neither side liked what they found. In the words of Anthony Sampson, himself an ex-pupil of Westminster, the public school élite "reinforces and perpetuates a class system whose divisions run through all British institutions, separating language, attitudes and motivations".

The old public schools still dominate public life, and because of their recovery in the late 1970s, seem likely to do so for some time to come. In 1983 Eton produced the Governor of the Bank of England, the Chief of the Defence Staff, the Editor of *The Times*, and the heads of the home Civil Service and of the diplomatic service. Winchester continued to produce a substantial number of senior judges. As Sampson asks, "Can the products of two schools [Winchester and Eton], it might be asked, really effectively represent the other 99.5 per cent of the people in this diverse country who went to neither mediaeval foundation?"

Alongside the criticism that public schools are socially divisive must also be the fact that the very best intellectual material is not necessarily among the independent school 7 per cent. Even a century after it tried to turn its pupils into gentlemen, the public school culture still discourages, possibly unconsciously, its pupils from entering industry. "It is no accident", as Sampson comments, "that most formidable industrialists in Britain come from right outside the public school system, and many from right outside Britain." Britain will be unable to harness its real intellectual potential until it can break loose from a divisive culture that should belong in the past, and can create its future élite from the nation's schoolchildren as a whole.

Higher education

Only about one third of school leavers receive post-school education, compared with over 80 per cent in Germany, France, the United States, and Japan. However, it must be borne in mind that once admitted to university relatively fewer (15 per cent) British students fail to complete their degree course.

Fourteen per cent of 18- and 19-year-olds enter full-time courses (degree or other advanced courses higher than A level), and it is hoped that this will rise to about 20 per cent by the end of the century. These courses are provided in universities, polytechnics, Scottish central institutions, colleges of higher (HE) and further (FE) education, and technical, art and agricultural colleges. In 1985/86, for example, a million students were enrolled in full-time courses, of whom 300,000 were at universities, 300,000 on advanced courses outside universities, and another 400,000 were on non-advanced vocational training and educational courses. In addition there were 3.2 million part-time students, of whom half a million were released by their employers. Over 90 per cent of full-time students receive grants to assist with their tuition and cost of living. However in September 1990, the government, while still providing tuition fees, froze the grant for cost of living expenses, and set up a new system whereby students were to take out loans to cover the shortfall.

Today there are forty-seven universities in Britain, compared with only seventeen in 1945. They fall into four broad categories: the ancient English foundations, the ancient Scottish ones, the 'redbrick' universities, and the 'plate-glass' ones. They are all private institutions, receiving direct grants from central government.

Oxford and Cambridge, founded in the thirteenth and fourteenth centuries respectively, are easily the most famous of Britain's universities. Today 'Oxbridge', as the two together are known, educate less than one tenth of Britain's total university student population. But they continue to attract many of the best brains, and to mesmerise a greater number, partly on account of their prestige but also on account of the seductive beauty of many of their buildings and surroundings.

Both universities grew gradually, as federations of independent colleges most of which were founded in the fourteenth, fifteenth and sixteenth centuries. In both universities, however, new colleges have been established, for example Green College, Oxford (1979) and Robinson College, Cambridge (1977).

Scotland boasts four ancient universities: Glasgow, Edinburgh, St Andrews and Aberdeen, all founded in the fifteenth and sixteenth centuries. In the Scottish lowlands greater value was placed on education during the sixteenth and later centuries

Kings College, Cambridge seen from 'the Backs'.

Graduation day, Queens College, Cambridge.

than in much of England. These universities were created with strong links with the ancient universities of continental Europe, and followed their longer and broader course of studies. Even today, Scottish universities provide four-year undergraduate courses, compared with the usual three-year courses in England and Wales.

In the nineteenth century many more redbrick universities were established to respond to the greatly increased demand for educated people as a result of the Industrial Revolution and the expansion of Britain's overseas empire. Many of these were sited in the industrial centres, for example Birmingham, Manchester, Nottingham, Newcastle, Liverpool and Bristol.

With the expansion of higher education in the 1960s many more plate-glass universities were established, some named after counties or regions rather than old cities, for example Sussex, Kent, East Anglia and Strathclyde. After some initial enthusiasm for them, they had become less popular by the 1980s than the older institutions. There is also a highly successful Open University, which provides every person in Britain with the opportunity to study for a degree, without leaving their home. It is particularly designed for adults

who regret missed opportunities earlier. It conducts learning through correspondence, radio and television, and also through local study centres.

University examinations are for Bachelor of Arts, or of Science (BA or BSc) on completion of the undergraduate course, and Master of Arts or of Science (MA or MSc) on completion of postgraduate work, usually a one- or two-year course involving some original research. Some students continue to complete a three-year period of original research for the degree of Doctor of Philosophy (PhD). The bachelor degree is normally classed, with about 5 per cent normally gaining a First, about 30 per cent gaining an Upper Second, perhaps 40 per cent gaining a Lower Second, and the balance getting either a Third, a Pass or failing.

Thirty polytechnics in England and Wales provide a range of higher education courses, up to doctoral studies. (In Scotland there are similar institutions.) But their real purpose was to fill the gap between university and further education work, providing an environment in which equal value was placed on academic and practical work, particularly in order to improve Britain's technical and technological ability. The polytechnics produce excellent quality, but by aspiring to provide the same kind of courses as universities, they have not entirely succeeded in their purpose. Indeed, if one compares the mechanical and electrical engineering work of Britain and its competitors in 1987, in West Germany 134,000 people qualified, in France, 98,000 and in Britain, only 30,000.

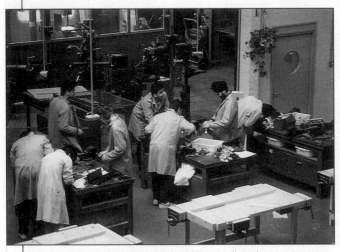

A BSc course in engineering: an almost all male pursuit.

In spite of the high fees, Britain's universities and polytechnics continue to host a large number of foreign students. In 1986 there were 39,000 overseas students at British universities, and another 24,000 in polytechnics and other higher education centres. Half of these came from Commonwealth countries or other ex-dependencies of Britain.

There has been a considerable change since the 1960s in the proportion of undergraduate places taken by women. In the mid 1960s they were only 28 per cent of the intake, but had become 41 per cent by the early 1980s. But comparatively few still stay on for post-graduate work: 21 per cent in the mid 1960s, rising to 32 per cent by 1983. Moreover, there is still an unfortunate separation of the sexes in fields of chosen study. Almost certainly this arises from occupational tradition and social expectations. For example, in 1984 girls accounted for only 21 per cent of A level passes in physics, but 75 per cent in French. It is hardly surprising, either, that women took only 4 per cent of engineering and technology places on further education courses, yet 70 per cent of medical, health and welfare courses at this level. Caring for others is still a 'proper' career for women; building bridges, it seems, is not. Unless one believes women's brains to be better geared to

medicine and men's to bridge-building, one must conclude that social expectations still hinder women from realising their potential.

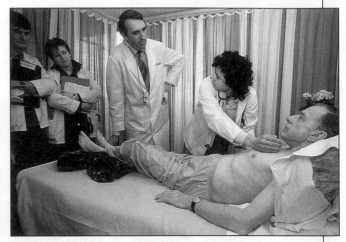

Medicine: seen as a respectable career for women.

During the 1980s many higher education institutions were forced to reduce their staff and facilities in order to operate within tighter funding limits. During the second half of the 1980s about 8,000 university posts were abolished or left vacant. A bitter debate arose about what universities were for. The government was determined that universities should serve the national interest, while many university educationists believed this denied the chance for self-expression, for them the true basis of all education. In fact, however, the cuts in funding hit the modern, often more technological, universities harder than the older more prestigious ones. As an example of the consequences, while France increased the number of mechanical engineering graduates by 50 per cent in the 1980s, Britain halved its output in only five years.

In 1988 the Education Reform Act established a new body, the Universities Funding Council, for disbursing government money to universities. This council may require universities to produce a certain number of graduates, or to produce a certain number of qualified people in specific fields, particularly in science and technology. Universities and polytechnics fear they may be competing for students under pressure for stricter accounting and performance-rating at a time when, for demographic reasons, the numbers entering higher education are going to fall.

Polytechnics and other larger colleges, which had previously been administered by local authorities, were made independent and funded in a similar way to universities. 'Polys' hope this will give them the opportunity to enjoy equality and equal standing with universities.

Both universities and polytechnics find themselves under financial pressure to seek supplementary funding from private sources. It is part of Conservative Party philosophy that the market should determine what is available. But it is less certain that commercial interests, or even undergraduate students, understand what the important long-term values of a university may be. Commercial companies are likely to encourage areas of study of immediate interest to them. Applied science and technology are likely to benefit but pure research, which often accounts for significant advances, will probably suffer.

Today many university science and technology departments, for example at Oxford, Cambridge, Manchester, Imperial College London, and Strathclyde, are among the best in Europe. The concern is whether they will continue to be so in the future. By the end of the 1980s academics' pay had fallen so far behind other professions and behind academic salaries elsewhere, that large numbers of the best brains were leaving for positions abroad. In 1988 alone over 200 professors and lecturers left. Adequate pay to keep the best in Britain remains a problem.

As with the schools system so also with higher education, there is a real problem about the exclusivity of Britain's two oldest universities. Yet Oxbridge is no longer the preserve of a social élite. In 1981, for the first time, Oxford took more entrants from state schools than from independent ones. Nevertheless, although now open to all according to intellectual ability, Oxbridge retains its exclusive, narrow and spell-binding culture. Together with the public school system, it creates a narrow social and intellectual channel from which the nation's leaders are almost exclusively drawn.

The evidence is surprising, even for most British. In 1989 very few people were in top jobs in government and administration, the armed forces, the law or finance, who had not been either to a public school or Oxbridge, and usually both:

1 Out of Prime Minister Margaret Thatcher's Cabinet of twenty-two in 1989, seventeen had been to Oxbridge, eighteen to independent schools and fifteen to both.
2 Out of ten Law Lords only two had not been to both independent school and Oxbridge.
3 Out of the nineteen most senior civil servants, only five had been to neither, while twelve had been to both. Since the war the average proportion of senior civil servants from Oxbridge has increased from two-thirds to three-quarters.
4 Seven out of eight of the Army's full generals had been to independent schools.
5 The chairmen of the four major high street banks had all been to both, while of those of the five lesser ones (including the new bank, Abbey National), only the chairmen of two Scottish banks had been to Glasgow University, rather than Oxbridge.
6 Out of the chairmen of eighteen major merchant banks, only two had not been to an independent school and only three had not been to Oxbridge. One of these three had served in the Guards and another had been to Harvard.

The problem is not the quality of education offered either in the independent schools or Oxbridge. The problem is cultural. Can the products of such exclusive establishments remain closely in touch with the remaining 95 per cent of the population? If the expectation is that Oxbridge, particularly, will dominate the controlling positions in the state and economy, is the country ignoring equal talent which does not have the Oxbridge label? As with the specialisation at the age of sixteen for A level, the danger is that Britain's governing élite is too narrow, both in the kind of education and where it was acquired.

Questions

Section analysis

1

a Name the three levels of school at which most children receive their education from the age of five to sixteen. How do they equate with the school system in your country?

b Name the two basic public examinations to assess English pupils at the age of sixteen and after another two voluntary years of schooling. Name the similar two for Scotland. How do they equate with the examination system in your country?

2 The story of British schools: After 1944 almost all children attended one of two kinds of school. What were they called? What was the difference between them? In the 1960s this system was changed. What kind of school was introduced? What effect did the change have?

3 Educational reforms in the 1980s: What changes took place in the 1980s? In your opinion which changes are likely to have good results? And which changes are likely to have bad results?

4 The private sector: Why does the author suggest that the public school system is socially divisive?

5 Higher education: Give the nicknames of two of the categories of university which reflect the different centuries in which they were established.

Chapter analysis and discussion

1 The number of students who qualified in 1987 in electrical engineering in three EC countries were as follows:

West Germany	134,000
France	98,000
Britain	30,000

Bearing in mind what you have just read, what characteristics do these statistics suggest about the British education system?

2 Do you accept the author's contention that élitism is a major problem in the British education system? Is there any textual evidence to suggest that state education can be as good as the private system?

3 Why do you think educational reforms are so controversial in Britain?

4 Compare what you believe to be the strengths and weaknesses of Britain's education system with your own. Make a comparative list of the respective strengths and weaknesses.

Visual interpretation

What do the following charts tell you about the comparative academic success of private and state education?

Most independent schools only accept children that meet their academic entrance requirements. State schools must accept everyone else (including, of course, those who don't even apply for a place at an independent school). Does this qualify the conclusions you draw from these charts?

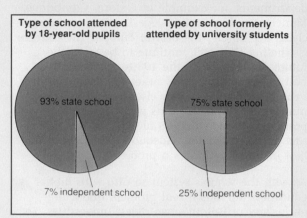

Type of school attended by 18-year-old pupils — 93% state school, 7% independent school

Type of school formerly attended by university students — 75% state school, 25% independent school

12 The media: press, radio and television

The press

Britain's first newspapers appeared over 300 years ago. Now, as then, newspapers receive no government subsidy, unlike in many other European countries today. Advertising has always been a vital source of income. As long ago as 1660, King Charles II advertised for his lost dog. Today, income from advertising is as crucial as income from sales.

Nevertheless, there are approximately 130 daily and Sunday papers, 1,800 weekly papers and over 7,000 periodical publications. More newspapers, proportionately, are sold in Britain than almost any other country. On average, two out of three persons over the age of fifteen read a national morning newspaper. Three out of four read a Sunday paper. National newspapers have a circulation of about 13.6 million on weekdays and 16.4 million on Sundays, but the readership is twice this figure. At first glance, therefore, the British press seems in good health.

The national newspapers, both on weekdays and on Sundays, fall into two broad categories: the 'popular' and 'quality' press. (See table overleaf.)

Ownership of the press, as can be seen, is in the hands of a few large press publishing groups. The most significant of these – both of which increased their hold during the 1980s – are News International, owned by the Australian-born press tycoon Rupert Murdoch, and the Mirror Group Newspapers, owned by the family of the late Robert Maxwell. Although the law provides safeguards against undue concentration of control in one company, the acquisitions of News International have caused concern. In particular, its purchase of *The Times* marked the beginning of a shift in that paper from an establishment view, politically slightly right of centre but independent, to a more right wing position, in line with the

right wing flavour of the Conservative governments in the 1980s. In 1989 News International entered the television market by launching a satellite TV network, Sky Television.

A newsstand on a Sunday.

National newspapers

Title	Owner	Political tendency	Circulation 1991 (000s)
National dailies			
Populars			
Daily Mirror	Mirror Group Newspapers	Lab	2,920
Daily Star	United Newspapers	Con	860
The Sun	News International	Con	3,700
Daily Sport	Sport Newspapers Ltd.	–	228
Today	News International	Con	470
Daily Express	United Newspapers	Con	1,560
Daily Mail	Associated Newspapers Ltd.	Con	1,700
Qualities			
Financial Times	The Pearson Group	Centre	180
The Daily Telegraph	The Daily Telegraph	Con	1,070
The Guardian	Guardian and Manchester Evening News	Lab	410
The Independent	Newspaper Publishing plc.	Centre	380
The Times	News International	Con	390
National Sundays			
Populars			
News of the World	News International	Con	4,800
Sunday Express	United Newspapers	Con	1,660
Sunday Mirror	Mirror Group Newspapers	Lab	2,760
Sunday Sport	Sport Newspapers Ltd.	–	360
The Mail On Sunday	Associated Newspapers	Con	1,910
Sunday People	Mirror Group Newspapers	Lab	2,270
Qualities			
The Sunday Telegraph	The Daily Telegraph	Con	580
The Observer	Lonrho International	Lab/Lib. Dem	550
The Sunday Times	News International	Con	1,100
The Independent on Sunday	Newspaper Publishing plc.	Centre	370

As the table above shows, private ownership affects the political viewpoint of most newspapers. Most proprietors, or owners, are more sympathetic to the Conservative Party than to Labour. Only the *Daily* and *Sunday Mirror*, and the *Sunday People*, express a view sympathetic to Labour, while among the quality papers, Labour's most sympathetic paper is *The Guardian*, which reflects a moderate left of centre view.

The table above categorises newspapers as either popular or quality. All the popular papers, with the exception of the *Sunday Express*, are 'tabloid' in format. The tabloids are essentially mass entertainment. They are smaller format than other papers, and are distinguished by large illustrations, bold captions and a sensational prose style. In the words of one ex-editor of *The Times*:

"The values of mass journalism are the traditional romantic values of energy, intuition, personality, sexuality, excitement and myth. The romantic element in the mass mind responds instinctively to the energy in the mass newspaper. Readers are presented with an exciting world of demons and temptresses, a flickering and exotic fairy tale. . . . By contrast the values of the serious press are those of analysis, rationality, truth, lucidity, balance, reality and, I would hope, compassion."

The result is that the tabloids' news content is minimal and their emphasis is on gossip, emotion and scandal. By contrast quality newspapers, known as 'broadsheets' on account of their larger, rather cumbersome format, emphasise news coverage, political and economic analysis and social and cultural issues.

Since 1971 there has been a massive desertion of 5 million readers from the middle market popular papers. Although there has been an increase of nearly 2 million for the tabloids and 700,000 for the quality papers, 2.3 million readers have been lost. A fundamental reason for the change lies with television becoming the main medium for news. Consequently all newspapers now give more attention to sports results, city finance and entertainment, but this has failed to halt the decline in readership.

Sunday readers have also declined. Since 1971 the number of papers read on a Sunday has dropped from 61 million to 44 million, largely in the tabloid market. Sunday quality papers have become fatter as the market competition increased during the 1980s. No Sunday quality paper can afford a circulation of less than about 400,000 without serious difficulty in attracting enough advertising. Although the *Sunday Times* is easily the market leader, the launch of *The Sunday Correspondent* (1989) and *The Independent on Sunday* (1990) led to fierce competition which drove *The Sunday Correspondent* out of business in 1990. In 1991 *The Independent on Sunday* was integrated with the daily *Independent* in order to reduce production costs.

During the 1980s virtually every paper was radically affected by new printing technology. Bitter conflicts were fought between management and the unions as the new technology was introduced. Hardly any newspaper was unaffected, but the most serious conflict was between News International and the typesetters and printers of *The Times* in Wapping in 1986. News International won and now has more than 500 computer terminals, one of the largest systems anywhere in the world.

The Wapping newspaper dispute, 1986.

Almost every newspaper left its historic home in Fleet Street, the centre of the British press for over a century. Some went to new sites in the London Docklands redevelopment, while others moved elsewhere. The arrival of the new technology increased the profitability of the press, and this in turn allowed the creation of new newspapers. Some of these flopped. The most important of the new papers was *The Independent*. Established in 1986, it rapidly seized the centre ground vacated by *The Times*, which had moved to the right following its purchase by Murdoch's News International in 1981. *The Independent*'s general outlook was politically independent, with a slightly right of centre economic outlook and a slightly left of centre social one. It attracted journalists of the highest calibre, including many abandoning *The Times*. By 1990 its circulation was only slightly behind its two main competitors, *The Times* and *The Guardian*, and it rivalled *The Times* as 'the newspaper of the establishment'.

The Observer's hi-tech offices in Battersea, south London.

Britain has a substantial number of regional newspapers also. Of these the two Scottish ones, *The Scotsman* and *The Glasgow Herald* are the most important. But others with a large circulation include the *Birmingham Evening Mail* (220,000), the Wolverhampton *Express and Star* (230,000), the Birmingham *Sunday Mercury* (150,000), and the Leeds *Yorkshire Post* (90,000).

Britain's ethnic minority communities also produce their own papers, both in English and in the vernacular languages. The oldest of these is the *Jewish Chronicle*, founded in 1841 and serving a community of 300,000 Jews. But there are Asian, Caribbean and even Arabic newspapers published in Britain.

Finally, there are over 900 free newspapers, popularly known as 'freebies', almost all of them weekly and financed entirely by advertising. They achieve a weekly circulation of over 40 million. They function as local noticeboards, where local events are advertised, and anyone can advertise in the 'for sale' or 'wanted' columns.

Among Britain's best selling periodicals, the favourites are the *Radio Times* and the *TV Times*, which provide detailed information concerning forthcoming programmes on BBC and independent television. Their popularity is evidence of the dominant place of television in national life (see below). Second to them in popularity are the women's magazines, *Woman's Weekly*, *Woman's Own*, *Woman*, *Woman's Realm*. The leading opinion journals are *The Economist*, a slightly right of centre political and economic weekly, the *New Statesman and Society*, a left of centre political and social weekly, the *Spectator*, a right of centre political weekly, and *Private Eye*, a satirical fortnightly with a reputation for devastating attacks on leading personalities, and some libel suits against it in the law courts.

With almost 900 correspondents in over 80 countries, no newspaper anywhere can compete with Britain's formidable news agency, Reuters. Across the world its name has become an assurance of objectivity, accuracy and reliability. Although run from London, Reuters deliberately avoids any image of being a British institution with English news values. As the day progresses, its world news file is edited from three different cities, switching time zones from Hong Kong to London to New York. Its reports are filed in French, German, Japanese, Arabic and Spanish, as well as English. It is read in the Kremlin, the White House and the Chancellery in Bonn.

Radio and television

In 1936 the government established the British Broadcasting Corporation (BBC) to provide a public service in radio. Since then the BBC has been most affected by the invention of television, which changed the entertainment habits of the nation, and the establishment of independent and commercial radio and television, which removed the BBC's broadcasting monopoly.

In spite of its much reduced evening audience, BBC radio still provides an important service. Its five radio stations provide (1) non-stop pop music; (2) light entertainment; (3) minority interests, e.g. classical music, arts programmes and academic material (some for Open University courses), cricket commentating in the summer months; (4) news and comment and discussion programmes; (5) sport and education. The BBC additionally runs thirty-seven local radio stations, providing material of local interest. There are also seventy independent local radio stations which provide news, information, music and other entertainment, coverage of local events, sports commentary, chat shows and 'phone-in' programmes. The latter provides an important counselling service to isolated, aggrieved or perplexed people.

An important but separate part of the BBC's work is its external services, essentially the BBC World Service and its broadcasts in thirty-five vernacular languages. These are funded separately from the rest of the BBC, by money from the Foreign Office. In other words, although the BBC has freedom in the content of what it broadcasts, the government decides in which foreign languages it

Behind the scenes at BBC Radio 2.

should broadcast, and the amount of funding it should receive. In this way the service is a promotional part of British foreign policy. In 1990 research showed that the BBC World Service enjoyed an audience of approximately 120 million listeners, who were predominantly young (aged between 25 and 35) and male. The strength of the BBC's external services has been the provision of relatively objective and impartial news and comment to listeners in countries where local censorship exists. With the steady ascendancy of television news in many countries and liberalisation in Eastern Europe, BBC world services face falling audiences. For this reason, in 1991 the BBC World Service commenced television services to Europe, on a subscription channel, and to Asia, as a channel of Star Television, Hong Kong. The World Service has also begun to market its programmes via national broadcasters. On account of its high reputation for quality news and comment, it has negotiated the provision of programmes to both Polish Radio and Japan Satellite TV. It has already supplied re-broadcast output to over 200 radio stations around the world free of charge since 1987.

Television is the single most popular form of entertainment in Britain. In the late 1980s the average adult spent twenty-five hours, and children eighteen hours, in front of the television set each week. They had four channels to choose from: BBC1 and BBC2, ITV (Independent Television) and Channel Four. Channel Four, which was established in 1982, specialises in minority interest programmes, but has proved highly successful. BBC television derives its income from the annual licence fee for television, while ITV and Channel Four are financed solely through advertising. *Coronation Street*, ITV's most watched show, attracts advertising worth ten times the cost of making the programme.

ITV has been governed through the Independent Television Authority, which was empowered to give regional franchises to a number of different companies. In 1990 there were fifteen such companies, providing high quality programmes many of which were sold or broadcast on other regional networks. Five major companies accounted for 85 per cent of evening network output – Granada, Thames, London Weekend Television (LWT), Central and Yorkshire. When ITV commenced in 1963 there had been fears that advertising would erode the high quality standards already set by the BBC. In fact ITV became fiercely competitive with the BBC in the production of high quality programmes which, like the BBC's, were sold profitably to many foreign networks.

Coronation Street itself.

The strength of British television lies in its high quality. "Go anywhere in the world," one leading political journalist has written, "and British television is an object of envy and admiration.... The foundation of Britain's excellence in the field of television is the tradition of public service broadcasting as upheld by the BBC." Many involved in television, including foreigners living in Britain, claim that British television is the best in the world. Its export record and high audience ratings certainly suggest it is among the best. The reason lies in the quality of its innovation and its willingness to experiment. For example, British television enthusiastically took the *Muppet Show*, when its creator, Jim Henson, had been rejected by the American networks. In the fields of TV documentary, comedy and satire, or drama, British television is a world leader.

Satellite television receivers.

In 1990 the government passed the Broadcasting Act, which promised to change the basis of television from 1992 onwards. This act was inspired by two factors: the Conservative government's free market ideology and the reality that satellite television would make it possible for viewers to receive programmes transmitted from outside Britain. This effectively destroys the regulatory controls previously applied by government. In order to prepare Britain's own commercial television for the 'white heat' of competing with satellite television for audiences, and thus for advertisers, the intention of the Act was to open British commercial television to genuine and open competition. In 1992, an Independent Television Commission (ITC) replaced the Independent Television Authority and auctioned television transmission licences. It had the authority to use its discretion in awarding franchises on the basis of high quality, not merely to the top financial bidders. It is a recognition that there cannot be a wholly free market in television. As a result of the auction two major networks, Thames Television and also the morning service, TV-am, both lost their franchises. The ITC also planned for a fifth television channel. But the danger remains that a larger number of channels will not, as is argued, provide greater choice. The greater the number of transmitting channels, the smaller the audiences will be for each individual channel. The smaller the audience, the less will be the advertising revenue possible, and if less advertising revenue is expected the production budget will be proportionately smaller. This is bound to hit hard a wide range of programmes, particularly minority ones.

It remains to be seen how this affects television in the 1990s. It will almost certainly be a turbulent period, in which unsuccessful rich bidders may seek to buy smaller, successful, high quality ones. It is also uncertain whether companies will still be willing to invest heavily in the origination of expensive new programmes unless they are assured they will enjoy a franchise long enough to recoup their investment. Television is still unquestionably something Britain does really well. It remains to be seen whether the Broadcasting Act supports Britain's leading position, or weakens it.

Considerable fear has been expressed concerning pornographic and violent programmes. The Broadcasting Act provides for increased censorship. Any policeman of superintendent rank or above may demand access to any untransmitted material under the obscenity or public order laws. In addition, the Broadcasting Standards Council, created in 1989, is empowered to veto transmission of any programme it considers indecent. It is also empowered to censor imported material, although this is made meaningless by the high number of joint ventures in which British television is now engaged. Many parents have expressed considerable concern at the amount of sex and violence portrayed on television, particularly before 9 p.m., the time when younger children are expected to have gone to bed. On the other hand many journalists are suspicious of the government's intentions and, in the words of one of them, "find it hard to separate zeal for market-led reform from a desire to destabilise a system capable of delivering tough and challenging programmes".

Government and the media

Writing in 1741, the philosopher and historian David Hume praised press freedom in Britain with the words: "Nothing is more apt to surprise a foreigner, than the extreme liberty which we enjoy in this country, of communicating whatever we please to the public, and of openly censuring every measure entered into by the King or his ministers." Is such a boast still justified? The relationship between government and the media is bound to be an uneasy one in any democracy. Governments are concerned with maintaining their own authority. The media must watch the exercise of that authority, and criticise when they feel it is wrongly used.

The British obsession with secrecy has already been discussed in Chapter 10. For over fifty years the government has had an arrangement for the protection of national security in the media. Its Defence, Press and Broadcasting Committee has agreed that in some circumstances the publication of certain information might endanger national security. In such cases a 'D (Defence) Notice' is issued. A D Notice does not quite have the force of law, but no newspaper editor would ignore a D Notice without incurring major penalties. Over the past twenty-five years there has been increasing criticism of the apparent abuse of the D Notice system in order to conceal, not matters of national security but, rather, potentially embarrassing facts.

During the 1980s the government frequently tried to prevent discussion of sensitive issues. Such attempts included acting against newspapers which revealed any of the contents of the book *Spycatcher*, and delaying the broadcast of controversial radio and television programmes concerning official secrecy or possible malpractice.

In 1989 the new Official Secrets Act greatly strengthened the government's ability to prevent disclosure of sensitive information. Any revelation of material obtained in any unauthorised way from a government source would make a journalist liable to prosecution. Not surprisingly, this provoked strong criticism from journalists. As the Deputy Director General of the BBC wrote:

"Only a threat to vital interests should prevent disclosure by journalists. Those interests include the safety of the realm: they do not include the sensitivities of foreign leaders or the avoidance of embarrassment to the United Kingdom government. A journalist who discovers – say from a confidential Foreign Office document – that a foreign government is using torture faces a dilemma. He or she will wish to publish. The journalist is aware that the regime concerned may respond by refusing contracts to British firms. The story would 'jeopardise' UK interests abroad; and the journalist would face criminal sanction. But at a trial he or she would not be able to argue that the benefit that may result from the revelation of torture outweighs the loss of business."

(John Birt, Deputy Director General of the BBC, *The Independent*, 7th March 1989.)

Nowhere is the issue of journalistic freedom more sensitive than in the case of the BBC, for it occupies a curious position. It is generally regarded as admirably independent of government. In the words of one Iraqi listener to the BBC Arabic Service: "The strength of the BBC is that it tells news against itself", in other words, news which may be embarrassing to the British government. This suggests that the BBC is an independent body. But is it? It is governed by a board of twelve governors appointed by the government. They are answerable to the government for all aspects of BBC broadcasting, and in the end the Home Secretary has the authority to replace them. In 1986 the governors came under intense pressure from the government on account of certain programmes which raised questions about government security, secrecy and its methods in Northern Ireland. One senior Cabinet minister publicly referred to the BBC as the "Bashing Britain Corporation". The BBC's Director General was sacked on account of two programmes, one which unfairly criticised two Conservative MPs, and another which revealed embarrassing facts about government expenditure on electronic and satellite surveillance. These events suggested that the BBC had less independence than many thought. The Independent Broadcasting Authority (IBA) was also a target for government pressure as a result of its coverage of potentially embarrassing security issues.

In 1988 the government prohibited live interviews with representatives of the IRA or its political wing, Sinn Fein, or with representatives of the Loyalist Ulster Defence Association. The government wished to deny terrorists "the oxygen of publicity". The media world, however, saw it differently. The Deputy Director General of the BBC wrote:

"Truth, they say, is the first casualty of war; British broadcast journalism is the latest victim of terrorism. After two decades of terrorism in Northern Ireland, our government has finally adopted a measure which may or may not counter terrorism but which inflicts certain damage on some of the most cherished elements of a democratic society – freedom of expression and the independence of the media."
(John Birt, *The Independent*, 21st November 1988.)

Nevertheless, the BBC is probably freer today than it was in the 1950s when its sense of national loyalty was defined in terms of loyalty to government rather than people. There has been a subtle change in vocabulary. Forty years ago, people would have asked of a controversial programme, "Was it in the *national* interest?" Today, people are more likely to ask whether it is "in the *public* interest".

There is another way in which the government exercises a hold on the media in order to reduce their true independence. This is through the 'Lobby', a system whereby government ministers and MPs may make disclosures to certain accredited journalists on the understanding that it is 'off the record.' The Lobby system began in 1884, and is thus over a century old. The advantage to journalists is that they learn many things officially still not admitted. The advantage to politicians is that they can make things public in an anonymous or deniable way. Officially such meetings between journalists and politicians 'never took place'. Typical newspaper reports begin, "Senior government sources are saying . . ." or, "Sources close to the Prime Minister . . .". Politicians use this method for various purposes,

very often to attack a colleague in a way they could not possibly do publicly. Prime Ministers, for example, have used this technique to undermine a minister's public standing before sacking him or her. Or it is a way of manipulating information before it becomes public, to ensure that the government version receives greatest coverage. It is often used to mislead, possibly to attract attention to one issue in order to avoid press attention on something else. On occasions it has been used simply to misinform.

One might suppose journalists would have nothing to do with such a system. But it is of mutual benefit. As one book by an expert on Westminster and Whitehall notes:

"Practically speaking, it is an information cartel. . . . Physical access is the prize: access to parts of the building that other journalists cannot reach. . . . There are as many as thirteen drinking places at Westminster and alcohol is an essential lubricant for the institutionalised intercourse between the Lobby-men and the politicians. But all these liaisons depend on the pretence that they never take place."

Several MPs disapprove of the system. Shortly after it began, in the 1880s, one MP remarked, ". . . 'I am enabled on undoubted authority to state' . . . 'I learn from a private but official source' . . . 'The government thinks' . . . All this sort of inventive trash, although disgusting to persons of good taste, has its effect with millions."

As a result of the increased use of the Lobby system in the 1980s for the disclosure of sensitive or damaging material, two newspapers, *The Guardian* and *The Independent* refused to accept anything from government ministers which they were not prepared to state 'on the record', and withdrew from the Lobby. On two occasions in the 1980s senior ministers found themselves having to deny reports in the press of what they had said 'off the record'. If the number of politicians and journalists who disapprove of the Lobby system continues to grow, it may well be abolished. But one should remember that as long as governments remain unashamed of the Lobby, there will always be some journalists willing to use it rather than investigate for themselves.

Privacy and self-regulation

It might seem that in the face of government secrecy, journalists must be allowed the fullest investigative powers. But how free should the press be? During the 1980s there was increasing popular disgust at the way in which some newspapers, most notably *The Sun*, attempted to investigate the private lives of well-known people. The prime targets were, of course, members of the Royal Family, who found it increasingly difficult to escape from the voyeurism of the popular press. But others had their careers ruined or damaged when their sexual activities were made public. A major reason for such revelations was a bitter struggle between the tabloids for a greater share of the market.

Many felt that the press had no right to publicise personal matters when they had no relevance to any public issue, and that the victims of inaccurate reporting were entitled to a right of reply. Several major libel cases took place during the 1980s in which large sums of money were awarded to the victims of inaccurate press reporting.

As a result of public anger, the editors of the national dailies made a joint declaration in December 1989, promising to respect privacy and provide an opportunity for reply. A few months later the newspapers published the names of the ombudsman each paper had appointed to deal with complaints. As one correspondent noted, however, "Most of the ombudsmen are from inside the papers that have appointed them. Not all are experienced in journalism. Almost the only thing they have in common is that they are [all] men." Time will tell how effective the ombudsman system will be.

Beyond each newspaper is a final court of appeal for outraged members of the public. This is the Press Complaints Commission established at the beginning of 1991. The Commission replaced the previous body, the Press Council, which progressively lost its authority since its own establishment in 1953. If the new Commission cannot convince the public that press self-regulation can be made to work, the government may bring in legislation to control the worst excesses of the press.

Questions

Section analysis

1 The press: Consider this list of the characteristics of British newspapers:

a Depend on advertising revenue

b Separate Sunday papers

c Format divided between quality broadsheets and popular tabloids

d Ownership in the hands of a few large publishing groups

e Variety of types of paper: national, regional, ethnic and local free ('freebie') papers

Now check this list against what you consider the essential characteristics of your own country's press. List the differences.

2 Radio and television: What were the two basic reasons why the Conservative government introduced a new Broadcasting Act in 1990, and what were the provisions of that Act?

3 Government and the media: In your opinion, should the media

a represent the national interest or the public interest?

b be permitted to reveal embarrassing facts about the government which might jeopardise commercial or political interests?

c publish information gained secretly from politicians?

4 Privacy and self-regulation: What is the essential dilemma faced by the press concerning the respect of privacy?

Chapter analysis and discussion

1 Is the British press predominantly left or right of centre on the political scale? Do you think this balance truly reflects the balance of political views among the British people?

2 Do you agree or disagree with the following statements?

a The BBC World Service broadcasts the views of the British government.

b The media in Britain has to defend its independence in the face of pressure from the government.

3 Make predictions about the future. Do you think

a that newspaper readership in Britain will increase or continue to decline?

b that British television will maintain its world reputation for excellence?

c that the British media will become more or less subject to government interference?

4 Make comparisons between the British media and the media in your country:

a Which newspapers are comparable to the main British tabloids and broadsheets?

b To what extent are newspapers, radio and television funded by advertising?

c Are there any limits to press freedom?

Textual interpretation

Consider the following statement:

"No doubt the confidentiality of the [lobby] system can be misused, but the existence of a group of specialist parliamentary journalists with behind-the-scenes contacts is probably desirable for MPs. Select committees, for example, are often able to cooperate with lobby journalists to the mutual advantage of both: the press receive information, the committee receives publicity. Backbenchers, too, are able to use the lobby to get their own ideas across, especially if those ideas are controversial."

(Paul Silk, *How Parliament Works* (Longman, 1987) page 99.)

In what ways does this statement agree or disagree with the opinions expressed by the author?

13 Religion in Britain

Only 17 per cent of the adult population of Britain belongs to one of the Christian churches, and this proportion continues to decline. Yet the regional variation is revealing. In England only 13 per cent of the adult population are members of a church. The further one travels from London, however, the greater the attendance: in Wales 23 per cent, in Scotland 37 per cent and in Northern Ireland no fewer than 80 per cent.

Today there is complete freedom of practice, regardless of religion or sect. But it was not always so. Until the mid nineteenth century, those who did not belong to the Church of England, the official 'established' or state Church, were barred from some public offices. The established Church still plays a powerful role in national life, in spite of the relatively small numbers of people who are active members of it.

The Church of England

There are two established or state Churches in Britain: the Church of England, or Anglican Church as it is sometimes called, and the Church of Scotland.

In 1533 the English king, Henry VIII, had broken away from Rome and declared himself head of the Church in England. His reason had been purely political: the Pope's refusal to allow him to divorce his wife, who had failed to produce a son. Apart from this administrative break, the Church at first remained more Catholic than Protestant. However, during the next two centuries when religion was a vital political issue in Europe, the Church of England became much more Protestant in belief as well as organisation.

Ever since 1534 the monarch has been Head of the Church of England. No one may take the throne who is not a member of the Church of England. For any Protestant this would be unlikely to be a problem, since the Chuch of England already includes a wide variety of Protestant belief. However, if the monarch or the next in line decided to marry a Roman Catholic it would cause a constitutional crisis. For the past 300 years that crisis has not arisen, but it has always been understood that if such a marriage went ahead, the monarch or heir would have to give up their claim to the throne. The monarch is crowned by the senior Anglican cleric, the Archbishop of Canterbury.

As Head of the Church of England, the monarch appoints the archbishops, bishops and deans of the Church, on the recommendation of the Prime Minister, who might well not be an Anglican. Prime Minister Thatcher, incidentally, became an Anglican, having been brought up as a Methodist. Many in England's ruling establishment still feel it appropriate to belong to the state Church. The Prime Minister makes a recommendation from two nominee candidates, put forward by a special Crown Appointments Commission (composed of bishops, clergy and lay members of the Church). All Anglican clergy must take an oath of allegiance to the Crown, a difficult proposition for any priest who is a republican at heart. Thus Church and Crown in England are closely entwined, with mutual bonds of responsibility.

The most senior spiritual leaders of the Church of England are the Archbishop of Canterbury, who is 'Primate of All England', and the Archbishop of York, who is 'Primate of England', a subtle distinction. They are head of the two ecclesiastical provinces of England, Canterbury and York. These two provinces are divided into forty-two dioceses, each under the charge of a bishop.

The senior bishops are those of London, Durham and Winchester, but there is no guarantee of promotion according to seniority. George Carey, for example, the present (103rd) Archbishop, was previously Bishop of Bath and Wells, no longer considered a senior bishopric. Because of the growth in population, some bishops are assisted by deputies assigned to a geographical part of the diocese. These are 'suffragan' bishops. Each

An Anglican church service.

George Carey, the Archbishop of Canterbury.

diocese is composed of parishes, the basic unit of the Church's ministry. Each parish has a vicar, or sometimes a team of vicars, if it includes more than one church.

The Archbishop of Canterbury is head of the Anglican 'Communion'. This Communion is composed of the various independent Churches which have grown out of the Church of England in various parts of the world. In fact England accounts for only two of the twenty-eight provinces of the Anglican Church. In theory, about 40 per cent of the English might say they were members of the Church of England. Far fewer actually ever attend church and only 1.2 million regularly attend, a small proportion of the 70 million active Anglicans worldwide. More Nigerians, for example, than English are regular attenders of the Anglican Church. Within the worldwide Anglican Communion are some famous people, for example Desmond Tutu, the

Archbishop of Capetown, and George Bush, who became President of the United States in 1989. Indeed, it is said that most of the 'ruling establishment' of Washington belong to the Episcopal Church, the Anglican Church of the United States. The Scottish Episcopal Church, the Church in Wales and the Church in Ireland are members of the Anglican Communion, but are not 'established' Churches and have small memberships of not more than about 100,000 each.

Once in every ten years the Archbishop of Canterbury invites all the bishops of the Anglican Communion to a conference at Lambeth in London to exchange views and debate issues of concern. Rather like the Commonwealth Conference, the Lambeth Conference provides an opportunity for the sister Churches from every continent to meet and share their different concerns and perspectives. The last conference was in 1988. Recently it has been suggested that either the Archbishop of Canterbury should represent one of the member Churches of the Anglican Communion which is larger than the Church of England, or that the present duties of the Archbishop of Canterbury should be divided into two separate posts, one to preside over the Anglican Communion worldwide, and the other to be concerned solely with the Church of England.

The Church of England is frequently considered to be a 'broad' church because it includes a wide variety of belief and practice. Traditionally there have been two poles in membership, the Evangelicals and the Anglo-Catholics. The Evangelicals give greater emphasis to basing all faith and practice on the Bible, and are sometimes criticised for being too literal in their interpretation of it. The Anglo-Catholics give greater weight to Church tradition and Catholic practices, and do not feel the same level of disagreement as many Evangelicals concerning the teaching and practices of the Roman Catholic Church. There is an uneasy relationship between the two wings of the Church, which sometimes breaks into open hostility.

Yet most Evangelicals and Anglo-Catholics are united in their dislike of the liberal theologians within the Church of England. These have challenged the literal validity of several beliefs of the Church, and have argued that reinterpretation must take place, partly as a result of biblical scholarship, but also because they believe that theological understanding changes as society itself changes and develops over the years. In that sense, one can divide the Church of England in a different way, into conservatives and modernists. It is estimated that 80 per cent of the Church of England are of evangelical persuasion, and the balance is divided almost equally between Anglo-Catholics and liberals. It should perhaps be borne in mind that a large number of churchgoers either feel no particular loyalty to any of these traditions, or feel more comfortable somewhere between them. Inevitably, since most bishops are theologians, the liberals are more strongly represented among the bishops than their numbers in church membership probably justifies.

The Church of England is above all things a church of compromise. It takes a long view, and distrusts zealous theological or ideological certainty. It prefers to live with disagreements of belief rather than apply authoritarian decisions. It fudges issues where it can, to keep its broad body of believers together. Most of its members are happy with the arrangement. In that sense the Church of England is profoundly typical of the English character. It distrusts the rigid logic of a particular tradition of theology and prefers the illogical but practical atmosphere of 'live and let live' within a broader church climate. Consequently there is always a concern to ensure that all wings of the Church are represented among the bishops, and that those appointed as archbishops shall be neither too controversial in their theology, nor too committed to one particular wing of the Church as to be unacceptable to others.

The Church is governed by its bishops. In that sense it is a hierarchical organisation. Nevertheless its regulating and legislative body is the General Synod, made up of three 'Houses', the House of Bishops (53 diocesan and suffragan bishops), the House of Clergy (259 representatives of the clergy) and the House of Laity (258 representatives of lay members of the Church). The General Synod meets twice yearly with two functions: (1) to consider matters concerning the Church of England, and to make provision in respect thereof; (2) to consider and express its opinion on any matters of religious or public interest. In order to reach agreement on any issue, General Synod requires a majority in each of its Houses. It is a cumbersome procedure, in the words of one religious affairs journalist, "a clumsy and largely ineffective cross between a parliament and a democracy. It is a typical Anglican compromise." (Andrew Brown, *The Independent*, 27th December 1988)

This has been particularly true in the area of greatest controversy within the Church in the 1980s, the hotly debated question of the ordination of women. Although women may be ordained priests in other Churches of the Anglican Communion, for example, in the American Episcopal Church, a sufficient number of priests and bishops in the Church of England feel so deeply hostile to the idea that its implementation has been repeatedly postponed.

A protest outside Lambeth Palace, in favour of women priests.

It is feared that too hasty a decision would split the Church. The conservatives point to the Bible to argue that women were not chosen as Christ's apostles and were subordinate to men. The modernists argue that this reflected the social conditions of Biblical times and that equality for all humankind is a fundamental principle of Christianity, and must qualify women as much as men for the priesthood. There is a tension, too, between two practical arguments. One states that the Church should recognise the functional equality which women are gaining in other spheres of life and affirm this equality within the Church. The other points out that women priests will cause fundamental doctrinal difficulties in relations with the Roman Catholic and Orthodox Churches. However, while great passion is aroused among some clergy and lay people on this issue, the large majority of church-goers do not feel strongly enough, either way, to force a decision.

Because of its historical position, the Church of England has been closely identified with the ruling establishment and with authority. As a result it used to be known as 'the Tory Party at prayer', a description which suddenly ceased to be appropriate from 1979 onwards when the Church became increasingly critical of the government's social policies (see below). The Church of England has been gradually distancing itself from the ruling establishment over the past twenty-five years or so, and may eventually disengage from the state. 'Disestablishment', as this is known, becomes a topic for discussion each time church and state clash over some issue.

Nevertheless, the Church of England remains overwhelmingly establishment in its social composition, having been mainly middle and upper class in character since the Industrial Revolution. Most working-class people in England and Wales belong to the nonconformist or 'Free' Churches, while others have joined the Catholic Church in the past 140 years.

Because of its position, the Anglican Church has inherited a great legacy of ancient cathedrals and parish churches. It is caught between the value of these magnificent buildings as places of worship, and the enormous cost of their upkeep. This is particularly acute in the case of cathedrals, for which repair bills often run into millions of pounds. Yet most visitors to England's forty-two cathedrals are tourists, not worshippers. In 1987, for example, 3.5 million people visited Westminster Abbey.

The other Christian Churches

The Free or nonconformist Churches are distinguished by having no bishops, or 'episcopacy', and they all admit both women and men to their ministry. The main ones today are: the Methodist Union (450,000 full adult members); the Baptists (170,000); the United Reformed Church (130,000) and the Salvation Army (56,000). These all tend towards strong evangelicalism. In the case of the Methodists and Baptists, there are also smaller splinter groups. In addition there are a considerable number of smaller sects.

Methodist simplicity.

In Scotland, the Kirk strongly rejects the idea of bishops, following a more Calvinist Protestant tradition. Its churches are plain. There is no altar, only a table, and the emphasis is on the pulpit, where the gospel is preached. The Church of

Scotland is also more democratic. Although each kirk is assigned a minister, it also elects its own 'elders'. The minister and one of these elders represent the kirk at the regional presbytery. Each of the forty-six presbyteries of Scotland elects two commissioners to represent it at the principal governing body of the Church, the General Assembly. Each year the commissioners meet in the General Assembly, and elect a Moderator to chair the General Assembly for that year. Unlike the Church of England, the Church of Scotland is subject neither to the Crown nor to Parliament, and takes pride in its independence from state authority, for which it fought in the sixteenth and seventeenth centuries. In keeping with its democratic nature, it admits women as well as men to the ministry. In 1988, for example, it admitted more women than men.

Among all these Protestant Churches, but particularly among the larger English ones, there has been a recent important development called the 'house church' movement. This grew in the 1970s and now has a membership of roughly 90,000, although attendance is far higher. This movement is a network of autonomous 'churches' of usually not more than 100 members in each. These churches meet, usually in groups of 15 or 20, in members' homes for worship and prayer meetings. Most of those joining such groups are in the twenty to forty-year-old age range and belong to the professional middle classes – solicitors, doctors and so forth, who have felt frustrated with the more ponderous style of the larger churches. They try to recapture what they imagine was the vitality of the early Church. But it is doubtful how long these house churches will last. If they are anything like some of the revivalist sects of the nineteenth century, they in their turn are likely to lose their vitality, and discontented members may return to the churches which their predecessors left.

The Protestant churches of Britain undoubtedly owe part of their revival to the vitality of the West Indian churches. West Indian immigrants in the 1950s and 1960s were not welcomed into Anglican churches, and many decided to form their own churches. Their music and informal joyfulness of worship spread quickly in evangelical circles. As Philip Mohabir, a West Indian, describes:

"Congregations that would have been cold, dull and boring, would now sing to guitar music, clap their hands, and even play tambourines. Those were things that only West Indian churches did. . . . Now people would raise their hands in the air and clap and even dance. English, white, evangelical Christians dancing and clapping their hands, praising God. That in itself is a miracle we West Indian Christians never thought would happen."

The Roman Catholic Church only returned to Britain in 1850. During the preceding 300 years the few Catholic families which refused to accept the new Church were popularly viewed as less than wholeheartedly English. The English Protestant prejudice that to be Catholic is to be *not quite* wholly English has only really disappeared in the past twenty-five years.

Since 1850 the Roman Catholic Church has grown rapidly with about 5.7 million members today, of whom 1.4 million are regular attenders. It is composed of four main social strands: immigrants from Ireland, working-class people in deprived areas among whom the Catholics concentrated much of their effort in the nineteenth century, a few upper-class families, of which the Howards – the hereditary Dukes of Norfolk – are the most famous, and finally middle-class converts, among whom the writers, GK Chesterton, Evelyn Waugh, and Graham Greene are perhaps the most famous. Its senior English cleric is the Archbishop of Westminster.

A Catholic Mass.

All in all, there can be little doubt that the formal Churches are in decline. Each time there is a census of church attendance and membership, the numbers in almost every Church have fallen slightly. In 1970 there were an estimated 8.6 million practising Christians. By 1985 the figure had fallen to 6.9 million. At Christmas, the major festival, perhaps five million will attend church, but on a normal Sunday it is no more than half this figure. One must conclude that numerical decline will probably continue in an age when people feel no apparent need for organised religion. Within the Church the debate is bound to continue between the modernists who wish to reinterpret religion according to the values of the age they live in, and conservatives who believe it is precisely the supernatural elements which attract people in the age of science.

On the national stage the Church has made its greatest mark in recent years in the area of social justice. In 1985 the Church of England produced a report, *Faith in the City: A Call for Action by Church and Nation*, which examined inner city deprivation and decline, and recommended measures both by church and state to reverse the trends. The Roman Catholic and Free Churches showed similar concern at increased social deprivation in the 1980s. In Liverpool, the Catholic archbishop, Derek Worlock, and the Anglican bishop, David Sheppard, formed a strong partnership on the city's social problems, to the embarrassment of some politicians but to the joy of many living in deprived areas. As a result of such work, for the first time, the Church was seen not as an integral part of the establishment but as possibly its most formidable critic.

Other religions

Apart from Christianity, there are at least five other religions with a substantial number of adherents in Britain. These are usually either immigrants or the descendants of immigrants.

The oldest is the Jewish community, which now numbers only about 300,000, of whom fewer than half ever attend synagogue and only 80,000 are actual synagogue members. Today the Jewish community in Britain is ageing and shrinking, on account of assimilation and a relatively low birth rate.

Jews returned to England in the seventeenth century, after their previous expulsion in the thirteenth century. At first those who returned were Sephardic, that is from Spain and Portugal, but during the last years of the nineteenth century and first half of the twentieth century a more substantial number of Ashkenazi (Germanic and East European) Jews, fleeing persecution, arrived.

As a result of these two separate origins, and as a result of the growth of Progressive Judaism, the

Reform and Liberal branches, the Jews are divided into different religious groups. The majority, approximately 200,000, are Orthodox and belong to the United Synagogues. They look to the Chief Rabbi of Great Britain for spiritual leadership. A much smaller number of Sephardic Orthodox still recognise a different leader, the Haham. The two Progressive groups, which roughly equate with the broad church and modernists of the Anglican Church, have no acknowledged single leader, but they do have a number of rabbis who command a loyal following who admire their wisdom. The Progressives account for barely 20 per cent of the entire Jewish community.

Jewish worship in a synagogue.

There is also a Board of Deputies of British Jews, the lay representation of Anglo-Jewry, to which 250 synagogues and organisations in Britain elect representatives. It speaks on behalf of British Jewry on a wide variety of matters, but its degree of genuine representation is qualified in two ways: fewer than half of Britain's Jews belong to the electing synagogues and organisations; and none of the community's more eminent members belongs to the Board. In fact many leading members of the community are often uneasy with the position the Board takes on issues.

As in the Christian Church, the fundamentalist part of Jewry seems to grow compared with other groups, and causes similar discomfort for those who do not share its certainties and legal observances. In the words of a *Jewish Chronicle* editorial in 1986, "There is undoubtedly a new and worrying streak of Jewish fundamentalism evident in our religious life, one which places the emphasis on the minutiae of performance and practice and has almost no time at all for the spirit of Judaism", a view with which these strict Orthodox Jews would almost certainly disagree.

There are also more recently established religious groups: Hindus, Sikhs, Buddhists and Muslims. There are about 1 million Hindus and 1.5 million Muslims. The most important of these, not only on account of its size, is the Muslim community. There are over 1,000 mosques and prayer centres, of which the most important (in all Western Europe) is the London Central Mosque at Regent's Park. There are probably 900,000 Muslims who regularly attend these mosques.

During the past quarter century, since large numbers of Muslims arrived in Britain, there has been a tension between those Muslims who sought an accommodation between Islam and Western secular society, one might call them modernists, and those who have wanted to uphold traditional Islamic values even when these directly conflicted with secular social values. The tension has been made a good deal worse by the racism all Asian Muslims feel in British society. Until 1989 it might be said that on the whole the former group prevailed, and that those Muslims who were relatively successful economically and socially were the prevailing example of how Muslims could live successfully in the West.

However, in 1988 many Muslims were deeply offended by the publication of Salman Rushdie's book *The Satanic Verses*, which they considered to be blasphemous. Early the following year the Iranian Ayatollah Khomeini announced that Muslims had a duty to execute Rushdie. The effect of this announcement was dramatic. Rushdie went into hiding with police protection, and within the Muslim community a small number of Muslims specifically supported the death call. Others distanced themselves from such an extreme measure, but called on the government to ban the book and charge Rushdie with blasphemy. Within the British Muslim community as a whole, which like Jewish and Christian communities, is divided into different sects and traditions, modernists rapidly lost influence to traditionalist Muslim leaders. Those who felt most alienated from mainstream British society, some highly educated Muslims, but mainly the poor, deprived or unemployed of economically depressed areas, responded to the traditonalist leadership. Mosque attendance increased, and religious observance became an outward symbol of Muslim assertion.

Muslims protest against Salman Rushdie's Satanic Verses.

Muslims were further offended by the reaction they saw from the rest of society and from government. They were unable to prosecute Rushdie for blasphemy for a technical reason. The blasphemy law, mainly on account of its age, only applied to Christianity. But perhaps what Muslims found most offensive was the patronising attitude of white liberals, who lectured them on the values of a democratic society in a way which was dismissive of Muslim identity and feeling. As Ishtiaq Ahmed, spokesman of the Bradford Council of Mosques, remarked, "It is not just about a writer. It is about whether we can live as a religious community without fear of indignity and abuse. That is fundamental." Furthermore, Muslims suddenly found themselves in conflict with those who had previously been perceived as their friends, those who had championed immigrant rights and most strongly opposed racism. In the words of Ishtiaq Ahmed, "The problem is that the anti-racist movement is secular and led from the left. There is no place in it for understanding that religion can be the core of someone's identity."

Only the Church seemed able to respond to the complaints of Muslim communities with understanding. This is partly because the Church has been increasingly concerned with racism and Britain's immigration laws. But it mainly results from the Church's close understanding of life in deprived inner city areas, where many Muslim communities are forced to live. The Church has maintained contact with these communities over many years.

The Rushdie episode proved deeply damaging to race relations. It demonstrated how quickly and easily a religious issue for an ethnic minority could turn into a racial matter. White racists began to vandalise mosques and to taunt Asians no longer as 'Pakis' (Pakistanis), the previous term of abuse, but as 'Muslims' which now acquired among racists its own abusive meaning.

The government has also failed to soothe Muslim frustration and anger. Furthermore it has resisted other demands. Some Muslims want Muslim family law to be recognised within British law, a measure which would allow Muslim communities in Britain to follow an entirely separate lifestyle governed by their own laws. Others demand state-supported Muslim schools, where children, particularly girls, may receive a specifically Muslim education in a stricter moral atmosphere than exists in secular state schools. The state already provides such funding for Anglican, Catholic and Jewish schools within the state system. As with the law of blasphemy, there is a case either for applying the same ruling to include Muslims, or abandoning it altogether for all religions. Muslims believe they have good reason to feel discriminated against. Although they have traditionally supported the Labour Party, many Muslims feel disappointed by it and some founded an Islamic Party in 1989 as, in the words of Ishtiaq Ahmed, "a mark of the failure of other political parties to take on board the very specific needs of the Muslim community". This may threaten Labour in certain constituencies in future elections. But just as Labour does not want black sections within the party, so it does not wish to reinforce religious divides within society.

Although mainstream society takes the view that religion is essentially a matter of private belief, the particular status of the Church of England suggests that religion is also a public matter. For Muslims religion is certainly still a public matter, and a number of Muslims, who were anxious to avoid further damage, decided in 1991 to imitate the Jewish Board of Deputies by creating a recognised representative body for Muslims.

The London Central Mosque in Regent's Park.

Questions

Section analysis

1 The Church of England: In what way does the author believe that the Church of England is "profoundly typical of the English character"?

2 The Church of England: What remains, from the 1980s, the most controversial issue in the Church of England?

3 The other Christian churches: What are the essential differences between the Church of England and the Church of Scotland, the two 'established Churches' of Britain?

4 The other Christian Churches: What is the 'house church' movement?

5 Other religions: What are the main religious and secular institutions of the Jewish community in Britain?

6 Other religions: List the ways in which Muslims have felt alienated within British society in recent years.

Chapter analysis and discussion

1 Read the following:

"Why not bow to the inevitable of falling rolls and consign the Church, with its privileged status, its links through the monarch – its head – with the Prime Minister, and its 26 seats in the House of Lords, to the dustbin of history . . . ?"

Do you agree or disagree with this statement? Give your reasons.

2 Read the following: "Politicians, national or local, don't rate at all in Toxteth [the scene of inner city riots]; the clergy do." Why do you think this person believes that the clergy are more important than politicians in the inner city area of Toxteth?

3 Do you think that religious pluralism offers different communities a way to make sense of the world they inhabit? Or does it lead to nothing but intercommunal conflict? Which do you think is true of Britain? Which is true of your own country?

Visual interpretation

Study this graph. What does it tell you about the nature of declining religious observance in Britain?

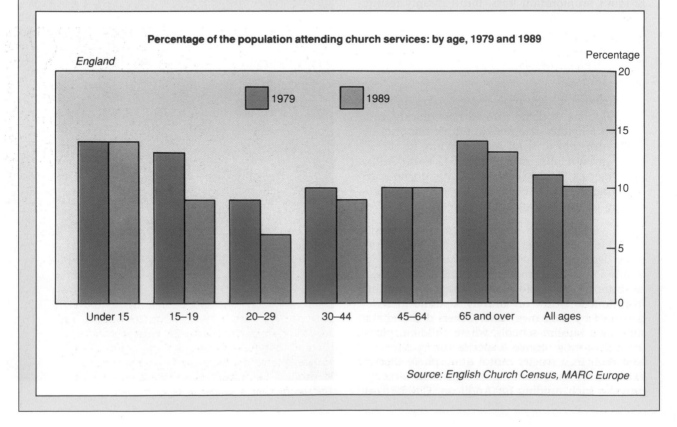

Percentage of the population attending church services: by age, 1979 and 1989

England

Percentage

1979   1989

Under 15   15–19   20–29   30–44   45–64   65 and over   All ages

Source: English Church Census, MARC Europe

14 Transport:
the threat of paralysis

"Major improvements in the movement of passengers and freight have resulted from the construction of a network of motorways, the extension of fast inter-city rail services (such as those operated by high-speed trains), the modernisation of many ports, the use by airlines of more efficient and quieter aircraft, and expansion schemes at many airports."

This is the comfortable claim made in the official government handbook *Britain 1990*. In fact Britain faces a growing crisis as its roads, rail and air services fall further and further behind demand.

Rail

In the case of rail, the system operated by the national carrier, British Rail (BR), is still essentially a nineteenth-century one. It is slow, dirty and often unreliable, except on the main Inter-City routes, and it compares poorly with the systems of its neighbours, Germany, the Netherlands, Belgium and France. By 1990 it was entering its most serious period of crisis since railways were first built, 160 years previously.

The failure to modernise the rail system is partly a failure to recognise its environmental advantages, and also a failure to invest adequately. A particularly serious aspect is its shrinking freight business. By 1990 British Rail carried only 13 per cent of the country's freight, the remainder adding to the congestion on the road system.

During the 1980s it was part of the government's free market policy that the rail service should operate on increasingly commercial lines, rather than as a public service. As a result the government subsidy to British Rail was cut by 51 per cent during the years 1984–89, and a further cut of 25 per cent on the remaining subsidy was planned for the years 1990–93. By 1989 BR was

the least subsidised rail system in Western Europe, receiving £605 million compared with £4.8 billion received by the West German system.

In order to survive this stringent policy, BR was forced to reduce its services and to increase fares substantially. This coincided with the biggest single increase in rail travel since the nineteenth century. Between 1984 and 1989 an exta 100,000 commuters started travelling into London by train, because of road congestion. As a result, travel on British Rail was not only less reliable and more crowded, but it was also twice as expensive per mile as, for example, in Belgium and a third more expensive than Germany, France and the Netherlands.

Strike action by British Rail staff.

Without sufficient investment to respond to increased demand, BR introduced longer coaches so that the average train in the crowded south east sector carried 1,400 rather than 1,000 passengers. In spite of higher fares, the increase in capacity drew yet more commuters back to rail transport from the roads. BR is now unable to increase the load further without remodelling station platforms to allow for longer trains. Without substantial investment in the whole system further expansion is unrealistic.

The need for infrastructure

In 1989 the Confederation of British Industry produced a report *Trade Routes to the Future* which, in its own words, "recognised that the nation's transport infrastructure is hopelessly inadequate. It is already costing £15 billion a year, or in excess of £10 per week for every household." The problem is not, of course, merely a matter of inconvenience or of added expense. Britain is already disadvantaged within the European Community because of the additional transport costs of an offshore island. If it fails to offer investors standards of transport communications at least comparable to the European mainland, it will simply lose foreign and British business investment. In the words of the Director General of the CBI, "We will force business to emigrate, especially to northern France where land is cheap, skills are available, and interest rates are lower; and where there is an excellent infrastructure into the rest of Europe."

In order to avoid a flight of investment in the 1990s the CBI called for the investment of £21 billion in improving road, rail and air networks. A major concern with both the road and rail system is its inadequate service to the country's peripheral regions. If the more distant parts of Britain are not to wither economically, it is vital that they are properly linked to the south east.

There is also concern that Britain's air system is failing to meet the rapidly growing demands placed upon it. There are 15 million international business trips each year from British airports. Although there are regional airports at Manchester, Glasgow, Birmingham, Belfast, Edinburgh, Aberdeen, Newcastle and in the East Midlands, the heaviest concentration is in the London area, at Heathrow, Gatwick, Stansted and Luton. Heathrow remains the largest international airport but there is pressure to expand it with a fifth terminal, to enlarge Gatwick with a second runway and to enlarge Stansted also. In 1988 a small new airport, City Airport, was opened in the heart of London's Docklands for short-haul business travel to Paris, Brussels, Frankfurt and other close continental locations. By 1990 there was growing pressure for the runway to be extended in order to take larger carriers. While those living close to these airports oppose their expansion and the increased noise and pollution this would bring, the danger is that a failure to expand will lead to a loss of business opportunities.

Congestion on a motorway.

Roads

The state of Britain's road system is hardly happier. During the 1970s the new motorway system was quickly filled by the new cars, as these became affordable to an increasing proportion of the population. Although the rate of car ownership is well below French or German levels, there are more cars than the road system of Britain can handle. In 1989 there were 23 million cars and lorries on 217,000 miles of road. If every vehicle was driven at the same moment, there would be less than 20 metres of road-space per vehicle. It is estimated that the number of cars will increase by 30 per cent during the 1990s, and may double by 2020. Yet only modest expansion in Britain's road system has been planned for the 1990s.

Congestion at Heathrow Airport.

A conjunction of failure in road, rail and air systems is a nightmare prospect. Yet this was the picture described by *The Sunday Times* on 28th August 1988:

"The really serious breakdown will come when the deficiencies of one sector, such as roads, start to interact with the inadequacies of another, such as rail, to magnify the already intractable problems of a third, such as air.

This is already happening on a not insubstantial scale, as anyone who regularly uses the main London airport at Heathrow can testify. Because there is still no effective rail link from central London, and the only recently available Underground line is not always convenient, more travellers are going there by car.

Because the main approach roads – the M1, the M40, the M4, the M3 and the M25 – are among the most notoriously clogged arteries in Europe, these motorists need to allow more and more time for their journey.

Because the longer-term car parks are so crowded and so distant from the four existing terminals, it can now take up to an hour to find a space and reach the check-in desk, which in turn is increasingly pressed to deal with the weight of last minute arrivals. A fifth terminal, which was supposed to relieve some of this pressure, may have to be shelved because the M25 cannot cope with the extra traffic it would attract."

While this was possibly an exaggeration of the difficulties in 1988, it was an accurate description of the situation that would occur without the development of an integrated transport infrastructure.

Greater London

Nothing illustrates Britain's acute transport dilemma more sharply than the construction of London's three-lane orbital motorway, the M25. It was opened in 1986 and within two years was experiencing serious traffic jams almost daily. The obvious argument was that the M25 was simply inadequate for the amount of traffic, and steps were taken to provide a fourth lane in particularly heavily used sections. However, another argument was that bigger and better roads would merely draw more cars onto the roads and lead to worse jams.

Greater London and its outlying commuter areas place a very high demand on transport services, and it is the failure of one system that leads to the heavy use of another. While the resident population of London has declined, each year more commuters enter the capital. In 1988 there was a 2 per cent increase on the previous year. More than 1.5 million vehicles enter or leave central London every working day. As a result, the critics of plans to enlarge the M25 argue that the real way to reduce traffic congestion throughout the Greater London area is not to build new roads or enlarge old ones, but to improve the speed, capacity, and regularity of mainline and underground trains.

In fact 85 per cent of commuters already travel on public transport. British Rail carries almost 48 per cent of the 1 million commuters who work in central London. In 1984 it carried 386,000, and by 1989 this had increased to 470,000. Yet anyone who was using the system at the end of the 1980s found it exasperating, heavily overcrowded and with frequent cancellations of services because BR's wage levels did not attract a sufficient number of reliable employees.

The reason many people do not choose to drive to work is simple. By 1990 the average speed of traffic in London had fallen to 16km per hour, equivalent to the speed of horse-drawn transport in the captial a century earlier. During the 1970s and early 1980s there was a progressive increase in the use of cars in London: a 25 per cent increase in daily peak travel hours between 1975 and 1985. Outside peak travel times there was a 37 per cent increase in traffic. The growth of road traffic slowed down as the roads reached saturation point and as people became fed up with the stress of traffic jams and crowded roads.

By 1989 the level of traffic reached a critical point where a major traffic holdup in Wandsworth, south of the Thames, could trigger a series of traffic jams right across central London. In fact that year there were six major 'gridlocks' or total jams in London. Yet, in spite of the acute crowding, the number of cars in the capital is set to increase from the 1989 level of 2.2 million to 2.8 million by 2001.

An increasing number of those who live in Greater London use the third main transport facility, the Underground, or 'Tube', train service, which was built from the mid nineteenth century onwards. Between the years 1948 and 1982 the number of passengers slowly fell, from 700 to 500 million annually, as more people used cars. Since then the numbers crowding onto these trains have increased dramatically, by 60 per cent in the period 1982–88. The number of users continues to climb, and this added pressure requires replacement and expansion of infrastructure. Yet in the years 1987–88 the government cut its subsidy to the Underground by 20 per cent. The stress placed upon the system is well illustrated by one of its busiest stations, Victoria. Eighty million people pass through Victoria

Underground station each year. At peak hours over 300 enter it each minute, and at critical moments the entry barriers are closed to prevent the crush of users resulting in people being pushed off the platforms below.

In the absence of a coherent overall plan, local solutions must be sought. In London BR faces an increase in passenger load of about 35 per cent during the 1990s. It would like to lay two new cross-city tunnels under London, and upgrade a third. But these require heavy investment, and by 1990 it was unclear where the necessary funds would come from. By the end of the century congestion on the Underground will also become chronic without much greater efficiency at the main interchanges of the system, and without new lines being tunnelled through the capital.

There is a further problem concerning Greater London's transport system. The capital acts as a major obstacle to traffic wishing to pass through the area but not wishing to enter it. This has major implications for increased traffic with continental Europe. Systems need to be devised not only to facilitate movement within the region but also across or around it.

The abolition of the Greater London Council in 1986 removed the obvious strategic transport planning body for the capital. The policy of building more roads to relieve congestion merely makes the road system more crowded unless it is part of a broader scheme. As *The Independent* argued at the end of 1988, "Only a master plan laying down a timetable for coordinated, coherent investment can give the capital the public transport system it requires. Without such an approach, and some judicious discouragement of the private motorist, London will surely choke to death."

Outside London ten cities, Birmingham (the largest city in Europe without a rapid transport system), Bristol, Sheffield, Cardiff, Edinburgh, Leeds, Portsmouth, Nottingham, Gloucester and Chester plan the introduction of a rapid light railway system during the 1990s as an economic and environmentally sensitive solution to congestion problems. Newcastle and Glasgow already have one. As in London, such local solutions are unlikely to solve fundamental problems unless they are part of much wider planning. Without an integrated national plan it is difficult to see how a national transport system in a modern economy can respond effectively and efficiently to the different demands placed upon it. In Britain

Congestion on the London Underground.

the provision and implementation of such a plan has, for too long, been sacrificed to doctrinal arguments over free market and nationalised services.

The Channel Tunnel

The construction of the Channel Tunnel, due for completion in 1993, raises fresh and difficult questions. It had been assumed by Eurotunnel, the Anglo-French consortium promoting the tunnel, that a high-speed rail link would be in operation from 1998 onwards. It had reckoned that by 2003 the tunnel would be carrying over 17 million passengers and 800,000 tonnes of freight.

However, after much hesitation, the government in 1990 dismissed the idea of a high-speed railway from Dover to London, even though the Channel link will be served by high-speed rail on the French side. It had already dismissed the idea of high-speed rail from Dover *beyond* London, which would have ensured that the Midlands, Wales, the north and Scotland could benefit from the new Channel Tunnel link, despite the fact that between 17 and 30 per cent of trade with Europe (other than oil shipments) will in due course pass through the tunnel.

Quite apart from the question of high-speed rail links, some transport experts argue that there is a fundamental need to convert the rail system to

The Channel Tunnel under construction.

the continental Berne gauge, in order to enable the free flow of continental freight. There is also anxiety that British Rail's estimate of 13.4 million passenger journeys yearly through the Tunnel from 1993 to 1998 may be too low and too close to the extra 15 million passenger maximum capacity on existing lines. It must be borne in mind that the existing capacity is already heavily loaded with commuter traffic to London.

By 1990 no effective plan had been made to ensure freight and passenger traffic could pass through London without delay. The warning of the Director General of the CBI, that business will emigrate to the other side of the Channel, may well be fulfilled unless a future government is willing to spend the money necessary to make Britain competitive in its communications.

Questions

Section analysis

1 Rail: Why did the Conservative government cut the subsidy to British Rail so severely in the 1980s?

2 Roads: Why is a 30 per cent increase in cars during the 1990s likely to be a major problem?

3 The need for infrastructure: What are the penalties to Britain's economy if an effective transport infrastructure is not created?

4 The need for infrastructure: How does an inadequate infrastructure affect Heathrow Airport?

5 Greater London: List the basic problems of commuting into central London by a) car; b) rail; c) tube.

6 Greater London: Based on the information avilable, what measures would you recommend to improve commuters' journeys?

7 The Channel Tunnel: Why is the potential of the Channel Tunnel unlikely to be realised for some years after it opens?

Chapter analysis and discussion

1 What do you think is the most serious problem with Britain's transport system?

a Failure to modernise the railways

b An inadequate network of roads

c An unwillingness to subsidize public transport

d A lack of overall planning, especially in London

e Inadequate integration with the European transport networks as part of the Channel Tunnel development

2 "There is still an island mentality at large in this country which is preventing us from seeing the tremendous implications of high-speed trains for Europe."

Do you agree with this statement about Britain?

3 How does Britain's transport system compare with the system in your own country? Discuss the following points:

a Provision of railways, roads and airports

b Level of government subsidy

c Future planning to meet growing demand

d   Solutions to traffic congestion in major cities

Visual interpretation

What are the implications of this graph? What measures do you think are necessary in response to this information?

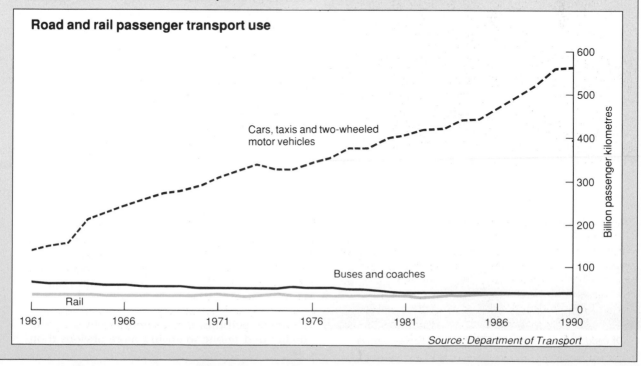

Road and rail passenger transport use

Cars, taxis and two-wheeled motor vehicles

Buses and coaches

Rail

Billion passenger kilometres

Source: Department of Transport

15 The environment

Environment and pollution

As in other countries, at the end of the 1980s Britain became much more conscious of the way in which it degraded the environment. Two relatively minor incidents in 1988 triggered a major shift in attitudes. One was the death of hundreds of seals in the North Sea as a result of a pollution-related virus. The other was a scandal concerning the intended dumping of a shipment of toxic waste in Britain.

A dead seal, the victim of pollution on Britain's coastline.

Suddenly the public were aware that Britain was rapidly turning into a wasteland. In October 1988 Prime Minister Margaret Thatcher, who had previously been hostile to interference by environmentalists made a historic speech concerning the threat of pollution. All political parties suddenly began talking about the environment, as well they might. In the European elections in 1989 the Green Party attracted over 10 per cent of the national vote. Green politics had arrived.

National concern about the environment has occurred not a moment too soon. With its high population density Britain is more susceptible than most to environmental degradation. As a result it requires close governmental control and planning in order to protect and regulate all aspects of environment use. Strategic planning is primarily the responsibility of county (or Scottish regional) councils, while district councils undertake local plans and development control. Nevertheless, central government retains overall authority, and overturns county council decisions when it wishes to do so. Inevitably this is an area of tension between national and regional concerns, particularly where ideological matters are concerned.

The Conservative government of the 1980s believed strongly in the privatisation of many local authority services, most notably the provision of water and the disposal of publicly owned housing. While such changes may have been economic, it was inevitable that a change in motivation from the provision of public service to profitability caused deep disquiet in local government. For example, with the sale of regional water authorities to private enterprise, large tracts of land of outstanding natural beauty became private property. There was considerable anxiety concerning the future use of this land, and its protection in the public interest. The need for profitability was likely to be in direct conflict with public wellbeing.

Nowhere, perhaps, is the conflict between profitability and public wellbeing more obvious than

2005. In order to reduce the emission of pollutants, flue gas desulphurisation (FGD) equipment must be installed, costing in 1990 £350 million per power station. The coal industry is likely to suffer, because British coal has a high sulphur content. Allowing newly privatised electricity companies to break with the old promise to buy British coal is bound to have damaging consequences for the coal industry. During the 1990s and well into the next century the British will discover that a cleaner environment will be costly.

Country and town planning

One major area of environmental concern has been the protection of the countryside from urbanisation. During the 1980s the Conservative government found itself caught between its own philosophy of encouraging the development of green-field sites in the countryside, particularly around London, and the fury of the people who lived in these areas who were the backbone of Conservative support. In particular there was a high level of concern to protect the Green Belt, the area of countryside around London designated for absolute protection from urbanisation. One of the strongest indicators of community mobilisation in Britain is the way in which protesters organise and effectively lobby against many road or housing development plans. In the 1980s such protesters were frequently derided with a brand new word, 'nimby', an acronym meaning 'not in my back yard'.

The pressure for more homes in the south east continues to grow, and there can be no doubt that green-field sites are more attractive both to developers and to those who wish to live there. In the end, of course, development destroys the very qualities which make these areas so attractive. Meanwhile, by 1990 it was estimated that in all Britain the number of derelict urban sites was equivalent to the area of Greater London.

The revitalisation of Britain's cities depends upon people wishing to live in them, for it is only a resident community which provides the urban environment with culture and colour. In some cases local people are acting to rescue derelict areas. In 1989 in Finsbury Park in north London, for example, local residents helped set up a development company to redevelop an area of old railway sidings, 36,000 square metres, which had been derelict for twenty years. The project, by 1990 involving £30 million, aims at creating

Replacing masonry damaged by acid rain, Westminster Abbey.

in the question of pollution. The excessive use of nitrates in Britain's intensive agriculture, and the emission of carbon dioxide by industry and transport, pose a dilemma for any government between environmental loss and economic gain. In 1989 an investigative team from *The Sunday Times* showed that the level of river pollution was rising to dangerous levels, with 10 per cent of Britain's rivers no longer able to support fish. Among the leading pollutants were major companies which were seldom prosecuted. In any case penalties for pouring toxic waste into rivers were usually substantially less than the profits such companies could make by ignoring legislation, and less than the cost of finding safe means of toxic waste-disposal.

There was also a belated recognition of the polluting propensity of fossil fuels, causing acid rain and global heating (the 'greenhouse effect'). In 1990 the government committed itself to a 30 per cent reduction in carbon dioxide emissions by a housing estate which will provide attractive but low cost housing. Elsewhere there are many cases of corporate owners or councils refusing to attend to their neglected land. However, the idea of community intervention – usually initiated by a handful of angry local people – has started a growing movement of popular action to reclaim such sites.

Urban reclamation is an important issue in Britain if its cities are not to follow in the footsteps of North American ones, where the core of the city dies, and people live and work around the periphery. It is too important to be left to unsupported local community action. The need is for government intervention to provide attractive urban amenities and a highly efficient transport system. This means reducing the number of vehicles in urban areas by making it quicker and cheaper to travel by public transport, and planning those arterial routes which are necessary in a way which does not destroy local life. It also means reversing the trend towards shopping by car at superstores, and reinvigorating the shopping parade, the traditional focus for each local community.

Alarmed partly by the urban riots in the first half of the 1980s the government started a number of urban revival programmes, to improve inner city prospects. City Action Teams were created in 1985 for certain particularly poor areas, for example in London, Liverpool, Manchester, Newcastle and Birmingham, and in 1986 a series of inner city initiatives were launched, to bring together central and local government, the local community and private business, in an attempt to regenerate these areas.

In addition successive governments have established entirely new urban areas over the past fifty years. Thirty-two new towns have been built since 1946, housing 2 million people. In the 1980s the most dramatic development was the reconstruction of London's old docklands. Many old wharves, or warehouses, by the river were refurbished as luxury flats, in an attempt to revive the local community with a wealthier stratum and also to draw more economic activity into the area. The most famous and controversial part of the plan involves Canary Wharf on the Isle of Dogs. This site, almost 300,000 square metres, is the biggest ever business development in Europe. Twenty-six buildings under construction will provide over 1 million square metres of office space for up to 60,000 workers. At the centre of Canary Wharf stands a tower 244 metres high

Local people protest over the route of the Channel Tunnel rail link.

Canary Wharf, London Docklands.

which, in the words of its architect, Cesar Pelli, "addresses itself to that proposition – that Britain has a future". But it is not only the contractors who are excited with the project. Sir Roy Strong, former director of the Victoria and Albert Museum, believes, "Canary Wharf is a return to the Grand Tradition. I can't think of anything that has given such a sense of spectacle for a very long time . . . since London can't go west any more and can only go east, it will change the centre of gravity. In 25 years it will have changed the face of London." In fact, the project went bankrupt in 1992.

Developments of this kind require enormous confidence as well as finance. In 1990 London Docklands was in crisis with falling land prices and 42 per cent of office space vacant. Although part of the loss of confidence resulted from the general economic situation, it was also the result of the inadequate public transport system for the area. Adequate transport may not be in place until the late 1990s. By then more firms will have moved out of London, rather than face the congestion at its heart.

Outside London the new towns have had uneven success. In general the closer these have been to the south east, the more successful they have been. Peterborough is a good example of what is possible. In 1960 Peterborough was a dismal and dirty city in decline. Thirty years later it is a bustling cathedral city, with an added 50,000 inhabitants, and an added 30,000 jobs. It is the centre of modern automated engineering with a broad based service economy. It is also, perhaps less healthily, a commuter town for London. According to the planners who revived Peterborough's fortunes, there were three vital ideas running through the city's redevelopment: an eighteenth-century English idea of bringing the countryside right into the heart of the city (as Regent's Park and Hyde Park do for London); a nineteenth-century industrial utopianism that produced model factories and worker housing; and finally a determination to create a coherent new town within clear confines rather than a sprawling area of random development.

Even in new towns, however, there can be unexpected problems. Milton Keynes, in Buckinghamshire, was established in 1971 and today has about 150,000 inhabitants. They live, for the most part, in leafy estate villages. Unlike the organic growth of traditional communities, Milton Keynes has been carefully planned on a grid road system. Roads are numbered according to their vertical (V)

Milton Keynes.

or horizontal (H) position on the grid. The town hospital, for example, lies at the junction of V8 and H8.

Milton Keynes boasts a semi-rural life for those who go to live in it. Its population is generally young, prosperous and energetic. Yet its health service has found a remarkably high level of sickness and depression within the community. Partly it is explained by the fact that its population has left family and friends in other places in order to become part of the new society. But there is also growing unease that Milton Keynes' grid layout has been overplanned, to leave the town with predictability but without spontaneity. 'New town blues' is the description a doctor has given to the widespread state of depression he has found.

Housing

Britain has an unusually high proportion of owner-occupied dwellings. This is a late twentieth-century phenomenon. In 1914 less than 10 per cent of the population lived in their own homes. Ninety per cent of dwellings then were privately rented. The real change took place after 1945. Today over 63 per cent of dwellings are owner-occupied, a considerable increase from 44 per cent in 1960. For a highly urbanised country, Britain is also distinctive because of its 22 million dwellings

Everyone likes to live in their own house.

only just over 4 million are flats, or apartments. The rest are houses.

During the 1980s it was naturally part of Conservative government philosophy to encourage home-ownership. This philosophy was particularly critical of state-owned housing, as failing to cultivate local pride and responsibility for property by all classes. The provision of public housing had become important after 1918, and became even more so with the establishment of the welfare state after 1945. The Conservative government decided to encourage the occupiers to purchase their homes. During the 1980s many were sold. Local authorities were also encouraged to hand over the management of the rest of their houses to private housing trusts which, the government believed, would maintain them more efficiently on a commercial basis. As in other

issues there was popular fear that commercial considerations would undermine the idea of public service.

Some councils resisted the wholesale discarding of their housing stock. Whether they held onto them or not, central government applied budgetary pressures to ensure that rents were increased, becoming closer to commercial ones in the private sector.

Also in line with its belief in free-market forces, the government abandoned almost entirely the practice of its predecessors of constructing public housing. In the 1970s approximately 100,000 publicly funded homes were built each year. By 1987 the annual figure had fallen to 15,000, and by 1990 it had fallen below 10,000. The government looked to the private sector to build new homes. As a result the number of homes built fell dramatically. But private builders naturally built the type of home they believed would be most profitable, for upwardly mobile professional people.

By the end of the 1980s there was a severe shortage of suitable low-cost housing. Almost 4 million new dwellings will be required nationally by 2001 to meet the growing demand. A substantial number of these must be low cost, and directed to single people. In 1987 22 per cent of dwellings were occupied by single people. By 2001 this proportion will be over 30 per cent.

The rural sector was particularly badly affected. Because of a steep increase in house prices caused by the purchase of country cottages by commuters and city dwellers wanting second homes, it was estimated in 1990 that on average twelve low cost homes would have to be built in each village by 1995 in order to keep pace with the estimated need. This was six times greater than the planned housing increase.

A major reason for housing difficulties has been the vagaries of the market. When demand outstrips supply, as it did during most of the 1980s, prices are forced upwards, making it particularly difficult for young, first-time buyers. Although this may make things harder for everyone, it is the lower-income groups which suffer most. During the past thirty years almost everyone has borrowed money in order to buy their home. The usual source for a mortgage loan is a building society, formed to help house purchase by the provision of low interest loans. Building societies are normally willing to provide a mortgage loan up to three times a purchaser's salary, in order to help in a purchase. As a result, the greater the salary, the greater the possible mortgage. Furthermore, while the government gives no help to those who rent accommodation, it provides tax relief on mortgages. In other words, the government subsidises the purchase of private property and, except for the more expensive homes, the subsidy increases with the size of mortgage. Those who cannot afford the cheapest home enjoy none of this financial help. From 1989, however, growing recession changed the tendency towards home ownership. House prices ceased rising and began to fall, a trend which brought about a major slump in the housing market and the construction industry. Rising interest rates meant that an increasing number of those who had purchased property in the 1980s could no longer keep up with their mortgage repayments. By 1992 this had reached crisis proportions with over

100,000 homes repossessed, casting doubt on Conservative enthusiasm for property ownership and reviving the idea that public and private rented accommodation were an important component of housing policy.

Alongside this problem the Conservative housing policies contributed to the rising number of homeless people which doubled during the 1980s, probably exceeding 350,000 people. In theory each local authority is obliged by law to provide accommodation for the homeless of the borough or district. But the 1977 law was modified in 1983 to disqualify those who have intentionally left homes "where it would have been reasonable" for them to stay, giving local authorities considerable freedom to refuse to accommodate people. In 1987, according to Shelter, the voluntary organisation which campaigns on behalf of homeless people in Britain, a quarter of a million people who applied were refused homeless status by local authorities. That year in Bedfordshire only 15 out of 600 people on its accommodation waiting list were housed, a rate at which it would take forty years to house those already on the list. In Birmingham, on the other hand, only 3 out of 7,000 applicants for homeless status were deemed intentionally homeless and therefore refused help. Of the remaining cases, Birmingham even managed to house half of those considered non-priority.

The vast majority of homeless people flock to London, where they hope to find some way of earning a living. The majority are young school-leavers who may have been thrown out of home

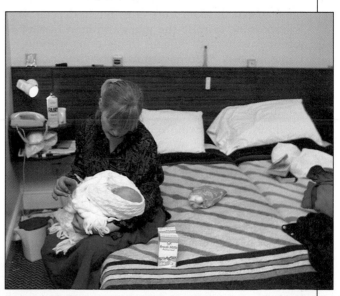

Bed and Breakfast accommodation for the homeless.

'Cardboard City'.

or been the victims of domestic violence or sexual abuse. In London they find a new difficulty. In order to rent a room they must pay a deposit. It is impossible to raise the money without having a job. It is extremely difficult to get a job without a home address. Even government job training is refused to people without an address.

As a result of government policy to return as many psychiatric patients as possible to the community, a growing number of mentally ill people have ended up on the streets. By 1990 there were probably about 130,000 homeless people in London, of whom about half were living in 'squats' or empty houses, or in badly equipped hotels or hostels.

In 1988 it was estimated that 27,000 local authority dwellings in London were empty and derelict, while 7,300 families were housed in bed and breakfast hotels. The reason for this strange situation is simple. Local authorities either have inadequate housing stock or have insufficient funds to refurbish derelict accommodation, but they can obtain central government funding for temporary accommodation. In 1988 this cost on average about £11,000 yearly per family, while a suitable permanent family dwelling would have cost £50,000 to build. The financial waste and human suffering involved is a product of a belief that the state should reduce the provision of state-owned housing in order to make people more self-reliant. It has not worked.

In addition to those living in hostels or hotels, there are about 2,000 people who sleep rough each night in London. Many are mentally ill. They are known as 'dossers', embarrassingly visible evidence of the underclass. The largest single concentration is highly visible to the wealthier citizens of London. 'Cardboard City' is to be found under the National Theatre and in other parts of the South Bank complex, a sharp reminder to the rich, as they leave the theatre or concert hall, of the proximity of human pain and misery.

Questions

Section analysis

1 Environment and pollution: What are the major causes of pollution in Britain?

2 Country and town planning: What is meant by urban reclamation? Why is it important? How can it be achieved?

3 Country and town planning: What are the advantages and disadvantages of life in the new towns?

4 Housing: During the 1980s, a free market approach to housing brought about major changes. What problems have those changes caused? Who has benefitted from them? Who has suffered?

5 Housing: What proportion of people in Britain own their own homes? How does this compare with your country? How many dwellings in Britain are flats, and how many are houses? How does this compare with your country?

Chapter analysis and discussion

1 Has government action
a helped to protect the environment?
b succeeded in controlling pollution?
c promoted successful town planning?

2 Compare Britain's environmental problems with those of your country under the following headings:
a River pollution
b Acid rain and the production of 'greenhouse' gases
c Preservation of the countryside
d Urban reclamation

3 Discuss the impact on the environment of the following:
a Out of town shopping centres
b Privatisation of water authorities
c Intensive agriculture
d An efficient urban transport system
e The purchase by town dwellers of weekend country cottages

Visual interpretation

Consider the relationship between these four graphs. What conclusions would you draw about the provision of mortgages, the state of the economy, and the strong encouragement given to purchasing property during the 1980s?

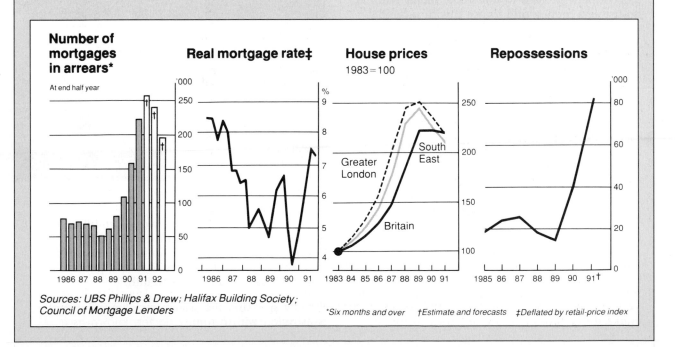

Number of mortgages in arrears*

At end half year

'000

1986 87 88 89 90 91 92

Real mortgage rate‡

1986 87 88 89 90 91

House prices

1983=100

Greater London

South East

Britain

1983 84 85 86 87 88 89 90 91

Repossessions

'000

1985 86 87 88 89 90 91†

Sources: UBS Phillips & Drew; Halifax Building Society; Council of Mortgage Lenders

*Six months and over   †Estimate and forecasts   ‡Deflated by retail-price index

16 A nation's health and wellbeing

Ever since 1945 the state has recognised it has a fundamental responsibility to ensure that nobody should be without the basic necessities of life as a result of poverty, unemployment, old age or sickness. In order to fulfil this responsibility the state created health and welfare services which have been the core of the welfare state. The system has grown over the years, funded mainly by tax, but also through National Insurance contributions, compulsory payments made by all earners and their employers. These contributions guarantee a small pension on retirement (normally at the age of sixty-five for men, sixty for women), a period of income support after becoming unemployed, and a pension if unable to work because of sickness.

By the end of the 1970s it was clear that these services were becoming increasingly costly and bureaucratic. During the 1980s the Conservative government decided to undertake major reforms, to use less money and to use it with more discrimination. Reforming the welfare system, however, has proved more complex than expected. The system still suffers from serious problems, and some critics would argue that new problems have arisen from the attempts at reform.

The National Health Service

Britain's National Health Service (NHS) is Europe's largest employer. It has over 1 million staff. It is hardly surprising that so large a structure has all the problems of any large bureaucracy. At the end of the 1980s the Conservative government decided to restructure the basis on which the NHS operates. It was, depending upon one's viewpoint, a courageous or foolhardy decision. To reform such a complex system, as health economists all over the world are painfully aware, is as likely to make things worse as to make them better.

A busy NHS hospital.

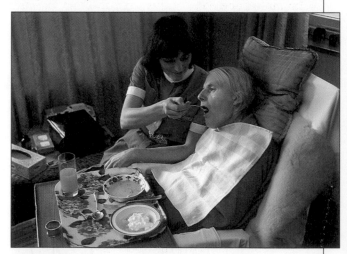

A health visitor assists an old woman.

The National Health Service was established in 1948 to provide free medical treatment both in hospital and outside. Its fundamental principle from the beginning was the idea of equitable access for all, regardless of wealth.

Broadly speaking the system rests on individual registration with a family doctor, known as a general practitioner, or GP. Today most GPs operate within a group practice of three or four GPs. People may register with any GP they choose, as long as the GP is willing to register them. A GP with a full register might refuse extra patients. Beyond the group practice lies the whole arrangement of hospitals and community health services, for example health visitors who monitor the health of vulnerable categories of people, such as those with newborn babies, or the old and infirm.

Except in the case of an emergency, it is normally the GP who refers a patient to hospital for more specialist care or for an operation. It is also usually the GP who alerts the health visitor to the need to keep a closer eye on a particular patient. On average each GP has about 2,000 people on his or her register. Many of those on the register will hardly ever visit the GP. Others, the old, the very young, the infirm and the depressed, may be regular callers at the doctor's surgery. On a normal day a GP might see about 35 patients in surgery, and make perhaps up to ten home visits to those who feel too ill to attend surgery. The strength of the system lies in a good working knowledge of the families and individuals in the catchment area, their housing, lifestyle and employment conditions. Good GPs build up an intimate knowledge of their 'parish', and take into account not merely the specific complaint of a patient but also the patient's general conditions of life.

The NHS is the responsibility of the Secretary of State for Health. England is divided into 14 Regional Health Authorities, usually based upon a university medical school. Each regional authority is subdivided into between 10 and 15 districts, each based on a large hospital, but also covering other hospitals.

The entire system is free, with the exception of prescribed drugs, dental treatment and spectacles, for which there are standard charges, except for old age pensioners and children under 16 and some other categories for whom some of these items are free. Anyone entering hospital for surgery will receive all their treatment while in hospital, including drugs, free of charge. Over 80 per cent of the costs of the NHS are funded out of the income tax system. The balance is paid for out of National Insurance contributions and from the prescription charges mentioned above.

On the whole the system has worked extremely well. It has been the envy of many countries with less satisfactory systems. Foreign health economists tend to admire the NHS for its family doctor system; its tight cost control; its treatment for all, regardless of the ability to pay; a tax-based funding relating the service to income rather than to need; finally, they admire its relative efficiency – a characteristic that would probably surprise the patients in most British hospital waiting rooms. Such foreign experts also criticise the lack of consumer choice, and believe that British doctors should delegate more tasks to nurses, and nurses more tasks to orderlies.

The cost of providing the service has always been enormous. By the late 1980s, the health budget reached one fifth of all public spending. Sixty-six per cent of this budget provides hospital and community services, while 30 per cent funds family practitioner services, the GPs, dentists and pharmacists. There has always been little flexibility for reformers, since over 70 per cent of the budget goes on staff costs.

During the 1980s the government applied tight financial measures to improve NHS efficiency. Hospitals were persuaded to discharge patients from hospital earlier than had been the case. The average stay in hospital dropped from 9.4 days in 1979 to 7.3 days in 1986, a reduction of 20 per cent. As a result the hospital service could boast a 26 per cent increase in the number of 'in' and 'day' patients it treated in the decade 1978–88.

For the NHS such stringency was extremely uncomfortable, for as leading health professionals point out, Britain spends proportionately less on its health service than any of the 20 industrialised members of the Organisation for Economic Cooperation and Development (OECD), with the exception of New Zealand, Greece, Portugal and Spain. The sense of pride and frustration of many NHS professionals is summed up in the assessment of an American professor of medicine at Harvard University: "I don't know of any country where there's greater value for the investment. But given that the investment has been held down so low it is not surprising that there should be the deficiencies which are so often ascribed to the NHS itself rather than the fact that it's been underfunded."

Since the mid 1980s the annual demand on the NHS has been growing by 2 per cent, a seemingly innocent shortfall. The most important factor affecting the growing workload of the NHS is the ageing population, accounting for an annual 1 per cent increase in NHS costs. Every person over the age of seventy-five costs the NHS seven times more than one of working age. In addition, the NHS is a victim of medical advances, since these add about one half per cent onto NHS costs. Finally, the emphasis on greater community care has increased short-term costs, although in theory an effective preventive service should reduce the long-term demands on hospitals.

In the winter of 1987–88 the NHS moved into a state of open crisis with the sudden closure of 4,000 beds all over the country, and the Presidents of the three Royal Colleges, of surgeons, physicians, and obstetricians and gynaecologists warned that the NHS had "almost reached breaking point". The difficulty was compounded by the loss of health personnel to the growing private sector, which was able to pay more. The crisis persuaded the government to embark upon the most fundamental reforms of the NHS since its

A demonstration in support of the NHS.

foundation 40 years earlier. In 1990 the government, after much discussion and opposition from the health profession, announced its proposals for radically changing the system, in the National Health Service and Community Care Act. Its fundamental plan, in keeping with its free-market philosophy, was to make the system 'demand-led'.

In order to achieve this goal, and to put further pressure on the medical services to achieve greater efficiency, hospitals now operate on contracts, with some of them being allowed to opt out of control by the district health authority, to become self-governing 'NHS trusts'. In 1990 the first fifty-six hospitals and units were given this status. Health authorities are funded for their size of population rather than for the services they provide. Their responsibility switches from providing hospitals and services, to "purchasing these services for the population in their area from the hospitals of their choice".

General practitioners are paid not, as hitherto, according to the number of patients on their register, but according to health screening targets to ensure that all their patients are regularly checked for early detection of such things as heart disease and cancer. In order to relieve the load on hospitals GPs are expected to perform minor surgery, something in the past referred to hospitals. Finally, GPs are given budgets for hospital referrals, thus giving GPs the freedom to choose which hospital to send a patient to.

Will such reforms help or hinder the work of the NHS? The hospitals are caught between two 'purchasing' customers, the health authorities and the GPs. During the 1990s the implications of the new system will become clear. In the past the health authorities have funded their hospitals on a regular basis. Since 70 per cent of the budget goes on staff costs, any attempt by health authorities to purchase particular services from one hospital one year and from another in the next would create serious staffing dislocations. At the same time, the provision of budgets to GPs, to increase their choice of hospital for their patients, is liable to undermine the overall planning powers of the health authorities. During the 1990s government may have to decide whether regional health authorities exist to plan, or whether an unplanned free-market health service is better.

With the health authorities established as purchasers of care, it may be possible for planners to give higher priority to the wider social conditions which put such a strain on the formal health services: an ageing population (there will be half a million people over ninety by the year 2001), smoking, alcohol and drug abuse, poor nutrition, industrial pollution and other aspects of public health. Take smoking, which accounts for 100,000 premature deaths and 30 million lost working days each year, and costs the NHS £500 million annually in treatment. The level of adult smoking currently is about 33 per cent, lower than it was fifteen years ago. Although young people are smoking less today than ten years ago, teenage girls are twice as likely as boys to smoke, and women have found it harder than men to give up the habit and this may damage the health of any babies they may bear. Britain still allows cigarette manufacturers to advertise and to sponsor sporting events, subliminally associating youthful physical ability with smoking.

Although Britain has a lower alcohol consumption per capita than over twenty other industrialised countries, alcohol abuse is a serious social ill because it is concentrated among a minority which drinks to excess. There are similarities with smoking. Consumption overall is falling slightly, with a decline among men, but an increase among women, by 15 per cent in the 1980s. It is

a symptom of the growing part played by women outside the home and the greater stress this implies. One million people have a serious drink problem, but the disturbing feature is that it has become a *young* addiction. Twenty is the peak age for alcoholic consumption, in contrast with half a century ago when few young men drank. Yet even among the young, as with smoking, alcohol consumption, after rising in the 1970s and early 1980s, again seems to be in decline. In 1984 almost half a million young people went to pubs almost daily. By 1989 this figure had fallen to 300,000. In 1979 14 per cent of adults were teetotal, drinking no alcohol at all. Ten years later this proportion had risen to 18 per cent.

Yet Britain still has a drink problem. Unlike other cultures where drink often sends people to sleep, in Britain drink often makes people aggressive and abusive, and accounts to a considerable degree for hooliganism and football violence. Alcohol remains a substantially more serious social problem than either drug abuse, or AIDS (Acquired Immune Deficiency Syndrome). In fact in 1990 Britain had an AIDS rate of 41.7 compared with a European Community average of 66.7 per million.

A government poster to discourage smoking.

197

Social security and services

By the end of the 1980s the provision of social security cost twice as much as the NHS, in fact 35 per cent of all public spending. This was because of the increase in unemployed and elderly people, and the substantial increase in those considered poor. It is a pattern which is likely to continue during the 1990s, unless some unforeseen economic recovery results in almost full employment.

Social security is provided by central government, but social services are almost entirely the responsibility of local government. These local authorities are responsible for services to the elderly, for example institutional accommodation (only about 5 per cent of those over sixty-five live in institutional accommodation) and support services to encourage them to continue to live at home. Such support includes the home delivery of hot meals ('meals on wheels'), domestic help, laundry services and adaptations in the home, for example fixing handrails in the bathroom. Most of these services are either free or heavily subsidised. Many of the 6.5 million who are physically and mentally disabled enjoy similar support, and also counselling on the personal and social problems arising from their disability. Residential accommodation is available for the severely disabled, and for the mentally ill. A fundamental principle, however, has been to encourage, wherever possible, the handicapped or ill to stay within the community, rather than enter institutions. Although this sounds self-evidently sensible, in practice it has proved controversial.

For example, during the 1980s a large number of less severely mentally ill and handicapped patients were discharged into the community. It was supposed that these people would do better in normal circumstances than in an institution. In 1989, however, the Westminster Association for Social Health discovered that 28 per cent of those discharged in the previous five or so years were homeless, living on the streets or in temporary hostels. One charity which provides shelter for homeless workers and vagrants, the St Mungo's Trust, reported that half those seeking a bed were mentally ill, a fivefold increase since 1983.

The local authority also has social welfare responsibilities for those with particular problems, such as single parents and children at risk of injury, neglect or abuse at home. During the 1980s, for example, local authorities became much more aware of the sexual abuse of children, something which had previously been thought of as a rarity. It began to be recognised that possibly 8 per cent

The need for community support: food and shelter provided by a temporary hostel.

of children suffer some kind of sexual abuse, and that physical violence to children and sexual abuse were related. In certain cases the local authority is empowered to remove children from home if they are considered to be at risk. Local authorities are also required to provide child day-care facilities.

The local authorities could not possibly carry out these responsibilities without the help of voluntary social services. In fact, over 65,000 registered voluntary organisations exist to provide particular forms of help. A few are known nationally, serving, for example, the blind, or those with cerebral palsy and other specific problems. The vast majority, however, operate on a local level, supported by volunteers.

In the London Borough of Richmond, for example, the Vineyard Project provides a day centre in a church basement, with activities for a wide range of people who require community support. Some have had mental illness, others are homeless or feel alienated in some way. They have somewhere to go where they are welcome. Nearby the Single Persons' Emergency Accommodation in Richmond (SPEAR), provides accommodation for up to three weeks for those stranded without a home. It can accommodate 12 people, providing them with a base from which to seek a job and to seek somewhere to rent. Its wardens assist in the search for long-term accommodation. Such is its success, that many of those who pass through SPEAR continue to use it afterwards as a social centre in the evenings. Voluntary support on a daily basis is provided by the churches of the locality. Both the Vineyard Project, and its daughter project, SPEAR, only began as a result of the concern and determination of local people. Each year they must find the money and the volunteers to keep them going. This is the kind of thing being done all over Britain by many of these 65,000 voluntary organisations.

Such voluntary efforts, however, came under greatly increased pressure during the 1980s. The government believed the community, i.e. the churches and voluntary organisations, should shoulder more of the welfare burden. But its social security policy (see below) also resulted in increased homelessness and poverty for certain categories. Organisations like SPEAR came into being to respond to a growing need.

Because of the steep rise in the cost of unemployed people in the early 1980s, the government also decided to reform the social security system. It wished to reduce expenditure, which by 1985 was costing about half Britain's oil revenue. The Social Security Act of 1986, which came into force in 1988, sought to reduce the burden on government, and to target assistance more effectively. It encouraged people to move away from the State Earnings-Related Pension Scheme (SERPS) into private pension schemes. This was because with the progressive increase in the proportion of elderly people, the government feared the state would be unable to honour its commitments.

The Vineyard Project: community help provided by local volunteers.

The Social Security Act also tried to slim down its system of help to particular categories of people. The young unemployed were particularly hard hit. The new Act refused to recognise those under twenty-five as homeless, since it argued that people under this age were still the responsibility of their parents. This contradicted the government argument that people should be willing to leave home in order to find work. It also ignored the fact that a substantial number of young homeless

were fleeing family conflict, or had been brought up in council care. Sixteen-year-old school-leavers have been particularly vulnerable since they are not eligible for unemployment benefit until they are eighteen. A growing number have ended up sleeping rough. The result of government policy, in the view of one critic, "has been, at best confusion and at worst it means children at risk on the streets – discarded youngsters sleeping in disposable boxes". What will happen to today's homeless youngsters between now and the year 2000? What damage will be done to them? Will it be possible to rehabilitate them? No one knows the answers, yet few can be optimistic unless energetic steps are taken to bring them back into society.

The reduction of income and housing support undoubtedly put pressure on some to seek employment more actively, as the government intended. Indeed, the legislation was supposed to end forever the old idea that some people could be better off without a job than they would be going to work. Family credit, which sought to 'top up' low pay, was meant to fulfil this intention, but fails to rescue many people from the 'poverty trap'. This poverty trap is well described by one opponent of family credit: "Family credit is bad news, I'm afraid. . . . Many families will be getting more benefit, but you will be trapping them in poverty because each time they earn an extra pound in net income they will lose 70p in family credit and, taking housing benefit into account, they will lose up to 97p in the pound."

It is easy to be critical of the attempt to reform complex social systems. Inevitably the 1986 Act is full of anomalies, and has provoked bitter arguments about who gains and who loses under the new scheme. The most controversial part of the new system is the Social Fund. Previously the government had made single cash grants for the purchase of essential items – for example, for the purchase of clothing or a heater. Under the Social Fund, most money is loaned, and the borrower must demonstrate the ability to repay the money. The central characteristic of the poor, however, is the absence of financial prospects.

Although the Labour Party has traditionally attached more importance to the provision of effective social security, a future Labour government is likely to find reforming the system as difficult as the Conservatives have found it. It is extremely difficult to create a simple but fair system which effectively helps people become self-reliant and economically independent. The solutions remain as elusive as ever, and further attempts to produce a better system are likely in the 1990s.

One of the government measures welcomed by all political parties, and by local authorities and charities, was the community care part of the otherwise controversial 1990 National Health Service and Community Care Act. In the past central government provided the money for institutional care for the old and the handicapped. It had provided no real help for those who were cared for by their families at home. Because of inadequate institutional provision many families were unable to place an invalid in an institution, yet endured great difficulty keeping the invalid at home. Yet because of inadequate accommodation, the authorities have naturally tried to persuade families of their 'responsibility'. In the words of Polly Toynbee, a well known journalist on social affairs:

"They [the authorities] lean as hard as they can on family, friends, or anyone who has an arm to twist. They squeeze every ounce of guilt out of carers, especially spouses and children, sometimes nephews and nieces, even neighbours. They warn that the sufferer will degenerate faster in an institution. They do everything they can to keep the patient 'in the community'. But it has nothing whatever to do with the community – it often means people . . . on their own."

The new policy was to place responsibility on local authorities to assess the needs of these categories and to provide appropriate assistance in a flexible way. The intention is to use money more flexibly to provide substantial support for those caring for relatives at home. The theory is that this is better for the invalid, better for the carer (many of whom in the past suffered great stress), and better for government, since it should lead to a long-term saving on institutional care. It is worth noting that the number of people in Britain over the age of 85 will have doubled in the 20-year period up to 1996. In the short term, however, it requires increased local government expenditure. Because of the electoral unpopularity of this, the government postponed implementation until 1993, to the natural dismay of the 1 million or so carers who receive no real support.

As the demand for social services grows inexorably, there is bound to be disappointment that the welfare state is one or more steps behind the real needs.

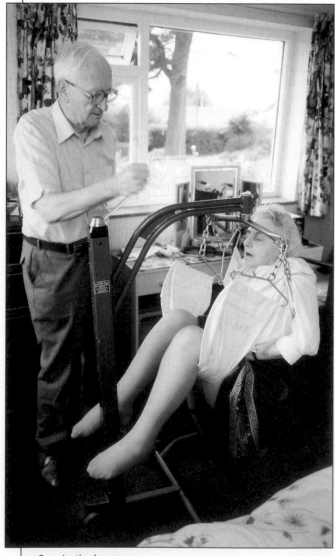

Care in the home.

Questions

Section analysis

1 The National Health Service: What is the strength of the GP system?

2 The National Health Service: What are the main reasons for the steep rise in the cost of the NHS?

3 The National Health Service: What reforms did the Conservative government introduce for hospitals, GPs and regional health authorities from 1990?

4 Social security and services: The handicapped and mentally ill are now encouraged to stay 'within the community' rather than stay in hospitals and institutions. Why is this policy controversial?

5 Social security and services: In what ways did the 1986 Social Security Act try to reduce help provided for young people? What problems resulted?

6 Social security and services: What aspect of the 1990 National Health Service and Community Care Act was particularly welcome to all political parties?

Chapter analysis and discussion

1 Policies on health care and social security have changed since the 1970s. In what ways have the following developments affected these changes?

a The huge increase in the number of elderly people

b The growing number of unemployed people

c The desire of government to spend less on health and social security

2 The 65,000 voluntary organisations in Britain provide many forms of help. Do you think that voluntary organisations

a allow the government to avoid its responsibilities?

b put pressure on the government to meet its responsibilities?

c should provide more free help for those in need?

3 Compare the situation in Britain with that in your own country under the following headings:

a Availability of free medical treatment

b Incidence of alcoholism

c Provision of residential accommodation for the elderly, disabled and mentally ill

Visual interpretation

Consider this graph. The following are all conclusions some people have made about the NHS compared with the health service in comparable countries:

a The British probably get best value for money

b Britain is underfunding its health service

c Britain's health system is unsophisticated and old-fashioned

What is your opinion? Find evidence in the text to support your view.

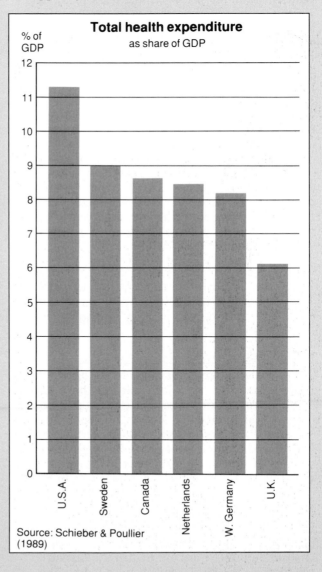

Total health expenditure
as share of GDP

% of GDP

Source: Schieber & Poullier (1989)

17 Time for a drink: the British pub

It is appropriate that any book on Britain should end where many British people relax at the end of the working day, in that most popular of places for relaxation, the pub. The British pub exercises a special fascination for foreigners. In fact it is so popular that many imitations exist around the world, some relatively successful, others less so.

Public houses date back to the inns and taverns of the Middle Ages, places where local people met and where travellers stayed. They have always been characterised by conviviality, intimacy and an egalitarian atmosphere. They have always been immensely popular, as Dr Samuel Johnson, the eighteenth-century writer, remarked: "No, Sir, there is nothing which has yet been contrived by man, by which so much happiness is produced, as by a good tavern or inn."

For many British that feeling persists, but standards vary considerably. They still like to walk into their 'local' and be sure they will meet someone they know. "In a good pub," according to *The Good Beer Guide*,

"the greatest attention is given to the drink, and in particular to the beer. Sociability, on both sides of the bar, comes a close second. A good pub encourages social intercourse, and is not dominated by cliques. . . . In a good pub, whatever further services are offered, there is always one bar (and preferably two) to accommodate those people who simply want to drink and chat without distraction or inhibition induced by overbearing décor, noisy entertainment, or intrusive dining."

This succinct verdict sums up characteristics that should be present but are frequently missing in some of the 80,000 British pubs today. The reasons are manifold, but are largely to do with

A typical country pub.

the integration and growing homogeneity of British society. During the 1960s half a dozen major beer breweries began to buy both small local breweries and local pubs. By the 1980s only a handful of small breweries and barely a quarter of all pubs remained independent. The big breweries bought the pubs in order to market their own beer as effectively as possible.

Traditional English ale or beer rapidly disappeared from most pubs during the 1960s and 1970s. This 'real ale' required special care, for it remained alive and continued to ferment in its wooden cask in the pub cellar, beneath the bar. It was made from barley, hops and pure water and required storage at a constant cool temperature. It was not refrigerated and contained no carbon dioxide gas. To those used to drinking refrigerated lager, real ale can taste flat, warm and weak. To many British, it is the only beer with real taste. The big breweries found it easier to produce 'keg' beer, a pasteurised brew, containing carbon dioxide, that required no special care. It was stored in metal barrels under pressure. It was easier for the manufacturer and for the publican who served the beer to the customer. But it did not compare with the real thing.

The big breweries, in fierce competition with each other, each tried to create their own 'house' style by ripping out the interiors of old pubs and re-furbishing them according to what they believed would attract most customers. In so doing they destroyed an essential appeal of many pubs, their individuality. They also endeavoured to improve efficiency and reduce the number of staff required to serve drinks. Most pubs had at least two different rooms for drinking, the public bar and a smarter and slightly more expensive 'saloon bar'.

It was only to saloon bars that women were taken until the greater social liberalisation of the 1960s. Pubs, it should be noted, are still essentially male preserves. Although the days are long past when a woman entering a pub alone was disapproved of, there are still a few pubs particularly in socially conservative areas where women are not welcome, and it is still true that men use pubs far more than do women. A survey in 1983, for example, revealed that 64 per cent of men visit a pub at least once a month, compared with only 46 per cent of women. It should be added that almost all these women said they had been accompanying men.

The impact of big brewery control, therefore, was primarily twofold. The quality of the beer went down, and the large open rooms which replaced two or three less efficient but cosy rooms destroyed the intimacy which made pubs attractive. The pubs owned by big breweries also began to concentrate on a particular clientele. In particular they tried to appeal to younger people in their twenties. This was not a new development. Many pubs were known for their special character. For example in socially mixed parts of town one pub might be proudly working class and another might attract middle-class people. In Kilburn in London where a large Irish community exists a number of pubs have a strong Irish character. Some pubs have also become favoured by particular sub-cultures: motorbikers, punks, and so forth. But the increased 'specialisation' of pubs has undermined an essential feature of pubs as local community centres where young and old, men and women may meet to relax. In particular, the absence of older men and also of women in many 'specialist' pubs, and the creation of large open rooms in place of more intimate nooks removes some of the restraining influences which discourage young men from drinking too much and misbehaving.

During the 1980s there was a revolt against the power of the big breweries. The Campaign for Real Ale (CAMRA) gained much popular support and a growing number of pubs began to stock real old-fashioned beer as well as keg beer. The big breweries began to allow their tenant publicans to develop the character of their pub as they chose, and to stock a wider variety of beer than merely one brand. In part this was because the big breweries found that pubs were now more profitable than the drink they produced, and that diversification in pubs was desirable.

Today an increasing number of pubs serve food, and coffee or tea as well as alcoholic drinks. Food, which accounted for only 10 per cent of profits in 1980 now accounts for more like 30 per cent. Providing good cheap food is now an important source of profit. The best pubs produce excellent home-made fare and welcome families. The best also, even if they attract people from far and wide, still rely on a reliable local clientele who give the pub its basic atmosphere. The worst pubs remain impersonal and only serve mass-produced food, which is often more expensive and less tasty than homemade fare.

In 1988 the government relaxed the previously strict opening hours, to allow pubs to remain open all day. Fewer than expected have used the opportunity, except to stay open on Saturday afternoons or to remain open for an extra hour on Sunday afternoons.

Pubs will continue to vary greatly, between the delightful and the ghastly. But in some ways they reflect more accurately than anything else the strengths and weaknesses of British society – strong community feeling in one pub, for example, and the bland tasteless homogeneity of modern society in another. It is also in the pub that people are usually unafraid to express their views, whether these conform to traditional British characteristics of understatement and moderation or whether they reflect a new stridency in the British nation. For anyone interested in understanding Britain better, the pub is not a bad place to start.

Glossary

Compiled with the help of the *Longman Dictionary of Contemporary English* and the *Longman Dictionary of the English Language*

after-glow a pleasant feeling that remains after a happy experience

appeal a formal request to a higher law court to change the decision of a lower court

arena an area of great activity, especially of competition or fighting

audit an official examination of the accounts of a business

baby boom a period of high birth rate

backbone the part of a group that provides the main support

bagpipes a musical instrument played especially in Scotland

ballot (v) to find out the views of a group by holding a vote

bed and breakfast (hotel) a small hotel that provides a place to sleep for the night and breakfast the next morning

black economy business activity that is carried on unofficially, especially to avoid taxation

bobby on the beat a policeman on duty walking his regular route

boo to express disapproval of, especially by shouting 'boo'

boom town a town where wealth and population are growing very fast

buck to oppose in a direct manner

buzz a very pleasant stimulation

by-election a special election held between regular elections

cadre an inner group of highly trained people in society or an organisation

caste a group of people set apart from the rest of society on the basis of differences in wealth/rank/profession

caution a spoken warning given by a police officer, when the person has broken the law but when the crime is not serious

charter a signed statement from a government, giving rights, freedoms, etc. to the people

chat show a radio/television show on which well-known people talk to each other and are asked questions

claptrap nonsense – talk or writing

clique a closely united (small) group of people who do not allow others to join their group easily

clubland the world of nightclubs

code, criminal/civil/of practice a collection of laws/rules

conurbation a group of towns that have spread and joined together to form an area of high population

cream-off to remove the best

Cup Final, football the last match to decide the winning team in the football league competition

custom-built made especially for a group of people

dayglo of a bright colour, such as orange, green or pink that seems to give out light in the daytime

dodge to avoid responsibility in some dishonest way

electoral roll the official list of people who have the right to vote

establishment (adj) supportive of the established order of society

estate, country a (large) piece of land in the country, usually with one large house on it and one owner

estate, housing a piece of land on which houses have all been built together in a planned way

flagship the finest product in a set of things made by a company/industry

flashy unpleasantly big, bright, decorated, etc., ostentatious

freeze to fix prices or income officially at a particular level

harness to use something to produce power

high street the most important shopping/business street of a town

hinterland an area far from urban centres

hipster a person who has a keen awareness of or interest in the newest (cultural) developments

house style the style adopted by a particular company

hub the centre of activity/importance

hung of a parliament: evenly divided between opposing parties, so that decisions cannot be made

lobby a group of people who his/her for or against a planned action, in an attempt to persuade those in power to change their minds

local (n) a pub near where one lives, where one often drinks

market forces the free operation of business/trade without any controls by government

national park an area of natural interest kept by the government for people to visit

nerve centre a place from which a system is controlled

off the record given/made unofficially and not to be publicly reported

old boy a former pupil of a school

peer a member of any five noble ranks: Baron, Viscount, Earl, Marquis, Duke

peer, life a peer who cannot pass on his/her rank to a son/daughter after death

pin-striped of dark suit/cloth with thin white vertical lines to form a pattern

plant to hide something on someone, so it will be found and the person will seem guilty

power-house a place which produces things with great forcefulness

revamp to give a new and better form to something

rosy giving hope, especially without good reason

rough-and-ready simple

rubber stamp something which acts only to make official the decisions already made by another

run-down in bad condition

seat a place as a member of (parliament)

seat, marginal a seat which may be lost or won by a small number of votes

seat, safe a seat which is certain to be won in an election by the present holder

self-made having gained success and wealth by one's own efforts alone

shadow (v) to watch closely

shopping arcade a covered passageway or avenue between shops

shopping parade a row of shops

sleep rough to sleep without proper lodging

stalemate a situation in which neither side in a quarrel can get an advantage

stand to compete for an office in an election

stir excitement

test (match, cricket) any of a series of international sports matches, especially cricket matches

tightly knit closely united by social/political/religious beliefs/activities

twist someone's arm to persuade someone forcefully to do what one wants

upwardly mobile able to move into a higher social class and become wealthier

wanted column a column of advertisements in a newspaper placed by people wanting things

white heat a state of intense activity

Index